STRONG MEASURES

CONTEMPORARY AMERICAN POETRY IN TRADITIONAL FORMS

EDITED BY
PHILIP DACEY AND DAVID JAUSS

Foreword by
Richard Wilbur

1817

HARPER & ROW, PUBLISHERS, New York
Cambridge, Philadelphia, San Francisco, Washington,
London, Mexico City, São Paulo, Singapore, Sydney

Sponsoring Editor: Phillip Leininger
Project Editor: Susan Goldfarb
Text Design Adaptation: Suzanne Bennett & Associates/Graphic Design
Cover Design: Suzanne Bennett & Associates/Graphic Design
Production: Jeanie Berke
Compositor: ComCom Division of Haddon Craftsmen, Inc.
Printer and Binder: The Murray Printing Company

Strong Measures: Contemporary American Poetry in Traditional Forms

Copyright © 1986 by Harper & Row, Publishers, Inc.

Acknowledgments begin on page 467.

Library of Congress Cataloging in Publication Data

Main entry under title:

Strong measures.

  1. American poetry—20th century.   I. Dacey,
Philip. II. Jauss, David.
PS613.S86   1986   811'.54'08   85-8592
ISBN 0-06-015484-5   86 87 88 89 90 MPC 10 9 8 7 6 5 4 3 2 1
ISBN 0-06-041471-5 (pbk.)   90 MPC 10 9 8 7 6

Contents

CONTENTS

Foreword

Some of the crudity with which we discuss matters of artistic form has to do with politics; and there have, in fact, been moments of history in which an artist's choice of form was a clear political statement. The "picturesque" mode of landscape gardening was, as the writings of its advocates show, antiauthoritarian in its simulation of wild and "untamed" nature; it was opposed to the geometric constraints of, let us say, Versailles. Stendhal reflects this politicization of gardening in the second chapter of *The Red and The Black,* where we learn from an indignant Liberal that M. de Rênal, the mayor of Verrières and the embodiment of "despostic" repression, annually causes the plane-trees of the town to be trimmed and pollarded. In 1831, Stendhal and his reader knew precisely the social overtones, *for them,* of formal regularity in horticulture; but in the present century, such explicit significance has faded from park and garden, or become at most a matter of individual response. Forms, in other words, survive their moments of social or other bearing and become mere available instruments of expression.

It does not seem to me that, at the present moment, the assignment of definite meaning or effect to poetic forms can be very persuasive. To be sure, there are people who associate meter and rhyme with order and good sense, or denounce them as affected and reactionary; there are those who regard free verse as sincere and forward-looking, and those who dismiss it as squalidly prosaic. But not much of that blather holds up if we look at what has actually been written in this century, and at what is being written now. Was populism more at home in the jaunty measures of Vachel Lindsay, or in the loose chants of Carl Sandburg? One could readily think of twenty similar questions about modern and contemporary verse, questions which would destroy themselves in the asking. The fact is that no form belongs inevitably with any theme or attitude; no form is good or appropriate in itself, but any form can be *made* good by able hands.

If a number of poets are now turning toward meter and stanza and the like, it may be a near-sufficient explanation to recall Yeats' notion that in art, as in all things, impulses exhaust themselves and give way to counter-impulses. That is, a number of contemporary poets may simply be tired of what they and others have been doing, and in their assault upon sameness they may be finding challenge and refreshment in neglected technical resources. The attraction is not merely to formal means, I should guess, but toward some new scope and style. Both attractions and rejections, in art, have always involved more than form. I think, for example, of certain poets who, a few decades back, made war upon "the sonnet." These militants were not, actually, objecting to a fourteen-line paradigm having a number of possible rhyme-schemes. Their true objection was to how that form (and others) was being used by a group of accomplished and well-known lyricists, who dealt perhaps too exclusively in passionate love, natural beauty, and a vocabulary of breathless words like "riant." The issue was not merely form but also, and far more importantly, vision and lexicon. The sonnet survives all attacks and misuses, of course; it does so as a possible arrangement of materials, and as such may say, "before poetry was, I am." It also survives because in many ages—the twenties and eighties included—it has proven a valid instrument for an extraordinary diversity of poets.

Mr. Barry Goldensohn, addressing the question of why "revolutions" in English-language poetry always take the form of a supposèd return to "the language of ordinary men," finds the cause in Shakespeare: the influence of our greatest poet has, he thinks, repeatedly moved us to repudiate any too-elaborate style and move in the direction of a dramatic poetry based upon "real speech." That is probably right. If so, I should describe the last two decades as a time of widespread "revolution" in which, despite lively individual achievements, the prevalent styles have been mistakenly closer to flat declarative talk than to dramatic poetry, a mode in which "real speech" is always honed, charged, and heightened by artifice. I hope that a persistence or resurgence of metrical writing, and of artifice in general, will now restore some lost force and expressive capability to American poetry.

If that happens, many poets will learn by experience that good rhyme is not ornament but emphasis, ligature, and significant sound; that a good poet is not coerced by any technical means, however demanding they may be; that one does not set out to write a quatrain, but rather finds that one is doing so. And so on. Without being contentious—without denying the merits of Whitman, say, or Williams—I send my particularly good wishes to poets who think this a time for strong measures.

RICHARD WILBUR

Introduction

The revolution is over. The war has been won. As Stanley Kunitz has said, "Non-metrical verse has swept the field." A casual survey of our country's leading journals, prize-winning collections of poetry, and the annual *Pushcart Prize* selections will reveal how overwhelmingly successful the free verse revolution has been. In fact, free verse is now so dominant that a half dozen recent anthologies—most notably, Stephen Berg and Robert Mezey's excellent *Naked Poetry* and its companion *New Naked Poetry*—are devoted to poems in "open forms." And all other recent anthologies contain so few examples of traditional verse that they are virtually indistinguishable from the anthologies devoted to free verse. Free verse was once revolutionary, but it has long since become the fashion. Given this fact, it is easy to understand why the young poet Barton Sutter has said, "The most radical poem a poet can write today is a sonnet."

Radical or not, sonnets—and virtually every other kind of formal poem—have been written, and written well, throughout the contemporary period. Free verse may have "swept the field," but many poets have continued to write in traditional forms. By doing so, they have kept vital a way of writing that has had value for centuries but has met with misunderstanding and hostility in this century. It is the purpose of this anthology to demonstrate that poetry in fixed forms continues to have value and relevance. Rhyme, meter, and pattern have lost their hegemony—and that is good—but they have not lost their effectiveness. Indeed, it would be unaccountable if these devices, which have enriched poetry for hundreds of years, had suddenly lost their value.

It is not the purpose of this anthology, however, to suggest that formal verse is superior to free verse. There is no need to claim for formal verse more than is its due. Nor is there any need to deny or diminish the great achievement and continued promise of free verse. To do so would be to ignore much of our century's finest poetry. Despite their proponents' battle-rhetoric, traditional and free forms are not the two scales of a balance, the ascension of one depending upon the decline of the other. The strongest poetry can be written, we believe, when all options, formal and free, are open to the poet. When one option is discredited, as free verse was earlier in this century and as formal verse is now, poetry runs the risk of becoming limited and narrow. American poets were right to rebel against "the tyranny of the iamb." But "freedom" can tyrannize as much as the iamb, and therefore our principal aim in compiling this anthology is to help foster a more balanced view of poetry, one that recognizes that both traditional and open forms are indispensable resources for contemporary poets. We hope to accomplish this aim by doing for contemporary traditional verse what Donald Allen's *New American Poetry* and Berg and Mezey's *Naked Poetry* and *New Naked Poetry* did for contemporary free verse: provide a showcase for its practitioners' finest work. By doing so, we hope to encourage future anthologists to present a more balanced picture of this period's poetry, one which would highlight the finest achievements in both free and formal verse. And we also hope that the anthology will help instruct poets, and students of poetry, in the techniques of formal verse, so that the beauty and power of traditional forms will not be lost to future generations.

As W. S. Merwin has said, "the only possible justification of any form," the only "answer to 'why that form?'," is the poem itself. We believe that the poems anthologized here give ample testimony to the value of traditional forms. Further testimony comes in the form of statements contemporary poets have made as apologists for formal verse (which is not to say as opponents of free verse) in interviews, essays, and books. These statements tend to deal with the four principal issues of the formal verse–free verse debate: freedom, originality, artificiality, and relevance. We'd like to examine each briefly.

At the heart of the debate about traditional forms is the issue of freedom. As Donald Hall has noted,

> An implied politics confuses prosodical argument, and we need to dismiss the analogy before we can be serious. I wish we had called free verse something else, because the form has nothing to do with liberty. It seems clear that for many American poets the idea of freedom is confused into the definition of free verse, or the activity we undertake when we write it. . . . Well, Keats's iambic pentameter—Wordsworth's, Shakespeare's, Frost's, Wal-

lace Stevens's—was not a slavemaster or a tyrant or an imperialist-Fascist. Meter is neither hierarchical nor elitist in itself, and the political analogy corrupts thought. In the term "free verse," we use "free" as when we say the water is free from contamination—which is not to speak of democratic or egalitarian water. Free verse is free of meter as Sanka is free of caffein.

But many poets are unwilling to dismiss the political analogy. In language more appropriate to the criticism of totalitarian governments, they accuse traditional forms of "restricting freedom of speech," even "freedom of thought," and of "making the trains run on time—with black boots and whips." But other poets have responded by praising the limitations imposed by traditional forms as paradoxically freeing, just as a dancer might praise the limitation of gravity for making dance possible in the first place. Howard Nemerov put it negatively and comically when he said that "Having to fill up traditional poetic forms is marvelous; it keeps you from being stupider than the law allows." Others, like Maxine Kumin, put it more positively: "The poems that are the hardest for me to write are the ones I work most passionately at getting into matching stanzaic patterns and rhyme schemes, because in a paradoxical way that liberates me to say the hardest truths." Richard Hugo also suggests that the restrictions of traditional verse can free, rather than hinder, expression. He says that rhyming—arbitrarily deciding to write "immaculate" within seven syllables after writing "chocolate" is his example—"gives you a chance to surprise yourself on the page, to create things to say, maybe, or to find ways to say things you never expected to say. Often, what you never expected to say is really what you've always wanted to say. You increase your chances that way." Richard Wilbur makes the same point about traditional forms generally: "they can liberate you from whatever narrow track your own mind is running on, and prompt it to be loose and inventive, to entertain possibilities it hadn't foreseen."
To complain, then, that traditional forms "won't let you say what you want" is naive; that they at times won't is precisely their strength. Their restrictions simultaneously help keep poets from "being stupider than the law allows" and free them to discover "the hard truths" they may never have expected to say but always, deep down, wanted to express. As this suggests, traditional forms don't prevent originality of expression: they stimulate it. And even though

the forms themselves are "unoriginal"—indeed, *because* they are
unoriginal—they provide a context in which originality can become
possible, perhaps even inevitable. Alfred Corn seems to address this
paradox in his poem "Afternoon" when he writes: "though the bike
always / Takes me for the same ride, for staying the same, / It
changes all the more." Robert Hass also believes that traditional
form and originality are not only compatible but inseparable. "We
speak of the sonnet as 'a form'," he says, "when no two sonnets,
however similar their structures, have the same form." As Hass's
comment suggests, it is misleading to think of a form as something
singular and repeatable, to associate "form" only with the abstract
structural requirements and to ignore the influence of sound, diction, sentence structure, and even content on form. To write a poem
with such a narrow view of form, X. J. Kennedy suggests, would be
like "trying to fall in love with whoever conformed to a certain chest
measurement." It just doesn't work. Poets can only "fall in love"
with their poems, and write originally, when they are in love with
more than the poems' measurements. As we will see later in this
Introduction, when we discuss contemporary experiments with
traditional forms, our poets have been less in love with measurements—with "structure"—than with "form," and as a result have
written with exceptional originality.

Although formal verse is like free verse in that it encourages
freedom and originality of expression, it differs in that its forms, or
at least what Hass would call its "structures," are usually chosen, not
invented. Because of this fact, traditional forms have been criticized
as "inorganic," "unnatural," and "artificial," all terms of oppro-
brium in these Romantic times. As J. V. Cunningham has disapprov-
ingly noted, "The measured, the formal, the contrived, the artificial
are, we feel, insincere; they are perversions of the central value of
our life, genuineness of feeling." But artifice can be considered the
ultimate test of sincerity: if poets sincerely respect their medium,
vision, and audience, they will develop their techniques of expression to the utmost. This sort of sincerity marks the best poetry, be
it formal or free, and is surely different in kind, not just in degree,
from the sincerity of an adolescent would-be poet under the influence of love and Hallmark greeting cards. In short, "genuineness of
feeling" isn't enough; artifice is required if the poet wants to communicate genuine feelings. And all sincere poets, whether they write in
traditional or open forms, do use artifice, and constantly. Just as the

traditional poet manipulates meter, rhyme, and pattern, so the free verse poet modulates rhythm, sound, line length, and sentence structure to achieve certain formal ends. In short, both traditional and free verse can be called, with honor, "artificial," and neither can be fairly accused of being "insincere." The only insincere poetry is that which ignores artifice—which is to say, ignores *form*.

Just as both formal and free verse are "artificial," so too are they both "natural," though not of course in the same way. Free verse stakes its claim to naturalness largely on the basis of its "organic" method of development; formal verse, on its origins in human physiology and its similarities to structures found in nature. "Basically," John Frederick Nims has said, the iamb, the most common rhythm in speech and poetry, "is the *lub-dúbb* of the heartbeat, perhaps the first sensation that we, months before our birth, are aware of. Nothing unnatural about that as a rhythm." And he goes on to speculate about why so much of our poetry is not only iambic but measured into ten-syllable lines: "Why, by the way, *penta*meter? Could it have anything to do with the physiological fact that our heart pulses five times, on the average, for every time we breathe?" Not only does meter correspond to human heart and breath patterns, but rhyme represents the natural pattern of human perception. As Denise Levertov, a champion of organic form, has observed, rhyme and other methods of "reiteration" such as "chime" and "echo" not only serve "to knit the elements of an experience" but often are "the very means, the sole means, by which . . . the returning or circling of perception can be translated into language, apperceived."

The similarities between traditional forms and the forms of nature are perhaps even more striking. As Donald Justice has pointed out, natural objects such as leaves are, like traditional forms, characterized by "marks reflecting similitude and kind, marks such as symmetry, repetitive and predictive numerical features or patterns." John Frederick Nims has even demonstrated that proportions based on the "golden numbers" of the Fibonacci sequence (in which each number is the sum of the two preceding ones: 1, 1, 2, 3, 5, 8, 13, and so forth) recur again and again in nature—"in the way rabbits breed, in the generation of bees, in the number and pattern of leaves or petals on certain plants, in the spirals of the sunflower . . . in the curling horns of mountain goats, in the tusks of elephants, in the claws of a cat, the beak of a parrot"—even in the symmetry of the human body itself. And, importantly, also in some poetic forms.

Nims concludes: "Nature . . . far outdoes our artists with her own use of mathematical symmetry." Joseph Langland echoes this sentiment, saying, "I hear the cry, 'Be natural!' and then I walk out and examine rocks, leaves, grass, birds, animals, people, the flow of wind and fire and water. They all cry out, 'Form!' . . . The absence of form is unnatural." Of course, free verse has its form too: we do not wish to deny that fact, merely to point out that the elaborate symmetry and mathematical precision of traditional forms are, in their own way, as "natural" as the organic form of free verse. If a form seems artificial, it is no more so than any other form found in nature.

Because traditional forms are so elaborately ordered, many poets have rejected them as inappropriate to our times, as "irrelevant." The social shatterings of the twentieth century have convinced these poets that the ordered nature of a fixed-form poem cannot possibly represent the chaos of modern life. Certainly the verse experiments of modern times have been a response to events in the public world, events having their correspondence in individual souls. And certainly as well we are past the time when a poet could write with confidence of "heavenly harmony," as Dryden did, reflecting his vision of the world in the chiming music of his verse. But poets who argue that one can't express disorder in an ordered form are guilty of what Yvor Winters called "the fallacy of imitative form." This fallacy holds that form should imitate content; hence, if the subject is chaos, the poem should be chaotic. Winters calls this belief a fallacy because art is, if anything, the triumph of order over chaos. Furthermore, there are countless examples of formal poems that accommodate a profound sense of disorder and meaninglessness, and arguably not only accommodate it but provide the means whereby it is, at least in certain cases, most fully grasped. This century alone provides the example of William Butler Yeats, whose belief that "Things fall apart; the centre cannot hold" only strengthened his faith that "Measurement began our might." And the example of Robert Frost, who could confront perfectly modern desert places without needing to abandon conventional structures. And Wallace Stevens, the poet of Nothingness, who faced it, more often than not, through the lens of blank verse. The list could go on. As Lucien Stryk has said, "How can anyone aware of the tugs and thrusts of modern verse *condemn* the forms that carry the achievement of Yeats, Eliot, Crane, Frost, Thomas and Stevens, and that may have been responsible for the tensions distinguishing them? . . . Arbitrary and fussy as such structures may appear to some, to such writers they were essential—which is the one point worth making. Such were the wrestles with *their* chaos. Let others, as important, wrestle in ways more natural to them, but need it be necessary to claim that theirs is a way more modern or American?" We submit that contemporary formal poets have not been ignoring the social and moral dilemmas of our century by using forms associated with more "ordered" times; rather, they are doing what good poets of all times have done: coming to terms with the chaos of self and world through the crucible of traditional forms.

But contemporary poets have not just repeated the forms of the past. They have adapted the old forms to current attitudes about poetry, language, life, and order. As a result, perhaps the most obvious and pervasive characteristic of contemporary formal poetry is that it experiments with traditional forms. Almost every poem experiments with form in some substantial way. No doubt readers will enjoy discovering the many different ways contemporary poets experiment with traditional forms, but lest they be perplexed by some of the anthology's untraditional-looking traditional poems, we would like to define nine of the principal methods of experimentation. They are:

1. DISGUISING FORMS

The first, and perhaps least revolutionary, way contemporary poets experiment with traditional forms is by disguising a poem's form. Some poets disguise their forms, and thereby make rhyme and repetition less obtrusive, through unconventional stanza divisions. In "Why God Permits Evil," for example, Miller Williams delays and mutes the rhymes of his *abcb* quatrains by dividing them into couplets. Similarly, William Logan and Alberto Rios divide their sestinas unconventionally in order to hide that form's tendency toward insistent repetition. Sestinas are traditionally printed as six sestets plus one three-line envoi, but Logan's "Tatiana Kalatschova" is divided into quatrains and Rios's "Nani" is divided into only three stanzas—two of eighteen lines and one, the envoi, of three.

Another, more common method of disguise is slant rhyme. Slant rhymes are not peculiar to the contemporary period, of course, but they are used almost to the exclusion of full rhymes by most poets. In their almost obsessive avoidance of full rhymes, contemporary poets have clearly differentiated their use of forms from that of their predecessors. There are probably many reasons for their desire to mute the effects of rhyme, but no doubt the most important is the influence of free verse. Slant rhyme is a sort of halfway house between the conventions of free and formal verse, and many poets have taken up residence there. William Stafford's "Traveling Through the Dark," which rhymes "killing" and "belly," "waiting" and "hesitated," "swerving" and "river," is a good example of the contemporary use of slant rhyme. Other poems use what we might call "slant refrain." A refrain is, of course, an extended "rhyme," or echo. Almost all contemporary villanelles, rondels, rondeaus, triolets, and the like use slant refrains to disguise their forms' repetitions. In Marilyn Hacker's "Villanelle," for example, the initial refrain "Every day our bodies separate" is "repeated" in the last stanza as "our bodies. Every day we separate." And in his pantoum "In the Attic," Donald Justice takes the principle of slant refrain to its extreme. Instead of repeating verbatim the second and fourth lines of each quatrain as the first and third lines of the following quatrain, as the form "requires," Justice repeats only the last word of each "refrain" line.

Usually slant rhyme and slant refrain simply serve to disguise a poem's form, but sometimes the disguise is so elaborate and complete that, in effect, the form is redefined. Such is the case with James Merrill's "Mirror." In this poem, Merrill disguises the fact that he's writing couplets by making the last syllable of each couplet's second line rhyme with the second- or third-to-last syllable of its first line. The rhymes are full rhymes, but because one of the rhyming syllables is "buried," the rhymes are in effect slant. By disguising his form in this manner, Merrill manages to avoid the "heavy" rhymes that are the couplet's special peril.

2. GRAFTING FREE VERSE ONTO TRADITIONAL FORMS

Perhaps the most obvious way contemporary poets experiment with traditional forms is by grafting the variable rhythms and line lengths of free verse onto those forms. This technique is almost the rule rather than the exception. Whereas a typical poem will adhere strictly to its form's rhyme scheme, refrain requirements, and so forth, it will depart from the form's "required" meter. Clearly, many of our most important formal poets have rejected "the tyranny of the iamb" as much as our free verse poets have. They, too, have taken to heart the third of Pound's famous tenets of Imagism: "As regarding rhythm: to compose in the sequence of the musical phrase, not in sequence of a metronome." Pound's tenet derives not so much from a sense that the iamb limited the music of poetry as from an almost mystical belief in "organic" rhythms. "I believe," he wrote, "that every emotion and every phase of emotion has some toneless phrase, some rhythm-phrase to express it." As he noted, "This belief leads to *vers libre. . . .*" It has also led many contemporary poets to use organic rhythms in otherwise formal poems. By doing so, these poets have produced the contemporary equivalent of what Gerard Manley Hopkins, one of their forebears, called "sprung rhythm." While some critics argue that nonmetrical rhythms prevent a poem from being truly formal, we believe that they merely redefine a form according to the rhythmic values of a time. In our opinion, the structure of a poem as a whole (i.e., the pattern of its stanzas, rhyme scheme, and so forth) is a more important factor in determining whether or not a poem is formal than the structure of a line (i.e., the pattern of its rhythm). Apparently, contemporary poets agree, for the marriage of free verse rhythms and traditional structures is a common characteristic of the formal verse of our period.

Two examples of poems that graft free verse rhythms and line lengths onto fixed forms are William Heyen's "Arrows" and Jane Miller's "Time; or, How the Line About Chagall's *Lovers* Disappears." Both poems employ the conventional *abba* rhyme scheme of the envelope quatrain, but they do not use the regular metrics or line lengths we associate with such quatrains. The lines range in length from three to nine syllables in Heyen's poem and from two to seventeen syllables in Miller's, and few of the lines in either poem can be scanned in any consistent meter. Because the poets use different rhythms and line lengths, their quatrains bear little resemblance to each other. As this fact suggests, grafting free verse onto traditional forms can increase the variety of effects possible. In the past, it was chiefly content and diction that distinguished one poet's envelope quatrain from another's, but now that poets have incorporated the variable rhythms and line lengths of free verse into their forms, we find even more marked differences among poems employing similar forms.

3. ALTERNATING BETWEEN FORMAL AND FREE VERSE

For decades, many poets have alternated between the writing of formal verse and the writing of free verse. But in recent years, some poets have begun to bridge the gap between formal and free verse by alternating between them within a single poem. Marvin Bell's "Obsessive" is one of the most effective examples of this technique. In it, two couplet sestets frame a free verse sestet. The free verse sestet provides a sad, adult commentary on the loss of childhood and innocence, and the couplet sestets ironically invoke the rhythms and rhymes of "Mother Goose" to convey a child's first encounter with death. The bitter contrast between childhood innocence and adult angst is reflected in the tension between the poem's formal and free techniques. Joseph Langland's "Conversations from Childhood: The Victrola" is an even more elaborate example of contemporary poets' interest in alternating between free and traditional verse in a single poem. It is designed so that it is *simultaneously* in formal and free verse: if it is read from left to right, it is in couplets; if the left column is read before the right, it is (with the exception of one stanza in each column) in free verse.

4. SHIFTING STANZAIC PATTERNS

One more way that contemporary poets have expanded the range of formal possibilities is by using more than one stanzaic form within a single poem. Poets past and present have recognized the value of metrical substitutions. But today's poets are also employing what could be called *stanzaic* substitutions. Just as past poets would substitute one metrical foot for another for the sake of metrical variety, so contemporary poets substitute one stanzaic form for another for the sake of *structural* variety and complexity. This principle is hardly new, of course. Even the eighteenth-century poets, fond as they were of the heroic couplet, found it necessary to use an occasional triplet to avoid monotony. But contemporary poets shift stanzaic forms within a poem far more frequently and dramatically. Among the many examples of this technique are Anne Sexton's "The Abortion," which alternates between enclosed tercets and couplets; Judith Moffett's "Now or Never," which consists of envelope, hybrid, and nonce sonnets; and Barry Sternlieb's "Valley Blood," which employs Sicilian, Italian, and couplet quatrains as well as a nonce quintet.

5. CREATING HYBRID FORMS

So far, all of the modes of experimentation we have mentioned involve modification of the forms in question. In some cases, however, poets have not just modified forms, they have created "new" ones. For these poets, Pound's injunction to "make it new" did not mean to "start over"—to invent new forms—but to make the old forms "new." One way poets have done this is by combining two existing forms to create a third, "hybrid," form. This technique is especially common in the writing of sonnets. Perhaps because the sonnet bore the brunt of early attacks on traditional form (witness William Carlos Williams's famous charge that "the sonnet is a fascist form"), many contemporary poets have avoided traditional sonnet patterns. Some poets have created nonce sonnets with entirely new rhyme patterns (John Berryman's "The Poet's Final Instructions" and Denis Johnson's "Passengers" are examples) but most have combined elements of the English and Italian sonnet patterns to create hybrid forms. One type of hybrid sonnet consists of the opening two quatrains of an English sonnet followed by the concluding sestet of an Italian sonnet. Among the numerous examples are Marilyn Hacker's "Sonnet Ending with a Film Subtitle," Muriel Rukeyser's "On the Death of Her Mother," and James Wright's "Saint Judas." Another type of hybrid sonnet is composed by replacing the Sicilian quatrains of an English sonnet with Italian quatrains, as in William Hathaway's "Why That's Bob Hope" and in the third section of Judith Moffett's "Now or Never."

Other poets have combined more dissimilar forms. For example, Adrienne Rich, Gregory Corso, Albert Goldbarth, and others have combined the couplet and sonnet forms to create "couplet sonnets." And Michael Heffernan has combined two even more dissimilar forms: the sonnet and the sestina. In "A Colloquy of Silences," he follows the general form of an English sonnet, but instead of rhyming, he repeats terminal words as in a sestina. There are four terminal words, instead of the sestina's six, and they are repeated over the course of three quatrains instead of six sestets, but as in a sestina, they appear in an elaborately varied order. Furthermore, the concluding couplet of the poem follows the pattern of the sestina's envoi in that each of the terminal words appears either within or at the end of a line.

6. INVERTING FORMS

Contemporary poets have also redefined traditional forms by inverting them. An example of this technique is W. D. Snodgrass's "A Visitation," a poem about Adolf Eichmann. In this poem, Snodgrass inverts the terza rima form—the form of *The Divine Comedy*—to correspond with both his conviction that life is a Secular Tragedy and his paradoxical inversion of "traditional" attitudes toward Eichmann. In terza rima, the second line of each tercet rhymes with the first and third lines of the following stanza, but in Snodgrass's poem, it rhymes with the first and third lines of the *previous* stanza. As "A Visitation" suggests, writing in free verse is not the only way poets can imply that the "old order" no longer obtains; indeed, inverting a past form may make the same point even more forcefully.

7. TRUNCATING FORMS

Still another way that contemporary poets have redefined traditional forms is by truncating them. This technique is especially prevalent in two French forms that require considerable repetition: the sestina and the villanelle. Many poets have truncated the sestina form by eliminating its final stanza, the envoi, so that the poem consists of thirty-six instead of thirty-nine lines, but others have truncated the form in more dramatic ways. George Starbuck, for example, has shortened the form from thirty-nine to twenty-one lines by using three repeated end-words instead of six in his "Double Semi-Sestina." Similarly, Donald Justice's "Women in Love" shortens the nineteen-line villanelle form to thirteen lines by eliminating two stanzas (and, therefore, two repetitions of refrain lines).

8. EXTENDING FORMS

Contemporary poets not only shorten forms, they also on occasion lengthen them. Like carpenters building an addition to an old house,

they generally try to extend a form in a manner that is in keeping
with its architecture. Sonnets, for example, frequently end with couplets, so it is only natural that when William Stafford extended his
Italian sonnet, "Friend Who Never Came," he did so by adding a
line that created a concluding couplet. However, sometimes a form
is not just extended by the addition of a few lines; sometimes it is
extended through *multiplication*. In "Double Sonnet," for example,
Anthony Hecht extends the Italian sonnet form by doubling its
requirements: instead of an octave rhyming *abbaabba*, Hecht creates
a sixteen-line stanza that rhymes *abbaabbaabbaabba*, and instead of a
sestet rhyming *cdecde*, he invents a twelve-line stanza rhyming *cdecdecdecde*.

9. INVENTING NONCE FORMS

Perhaps the ultimate way contemporary American poets "make it
new" is by using traditional techniques such as rhyme, meter, and
the repetition of terminal words in patterns invented "for the
nonce," that is, for the occasion. In a sense, these nonce poems are
"new traditional" forms: just as poets of the past invented stanza and
poem patterns that have become our traditions, so contemporary
poets have invented patterns that may become the future's traditional forms. Some examples of such nonce forms are Louise Glück's
"Phenomenal Survivals of Death in Nantucket," Maxine Kumin's
"January 25th," and James Tate's "The Book of Lies." As one might
guess, some of these nonce forms combine existing forms in new
combinations. But they do not stop there, as the hybrid forms do.
In "Mr. Edwards and the Spider," for example, Robert Lowell
combines an envelope quatrain, a triplet, and a couplet into a "new"
stanza pattern. But he makes the stanza more than a hybrid by
imposing several additional requirements on it: the first, second,
sixth, seventh, and eighth lines of each stanza must be written in
iambic pentameter measures; the third and fourth in iambic tetrameter; the fifth in iambic trimeter; and the ninth in iambic hexameter.
As Lowell's poem suggests, many of the nonce forms invented by
contemporary poets are as rigorous and complex as any that past
poets devised. In "To Christ Our Lord," for example, Galway Kinnell invents a quintet pattern that at first appears to rhyme *abbcc*.
However, the form also requires that the last syllable of each quin-

tet's first line—the rhyme that appears to "dangle"—rhyme with the penultimate syllable of the fourth line.

As this brief survey of contemporary experiments with traditional forms should suggest, many of the poems included in this anthology depart in some significant way from the classical definitions of their forms. As a result, classifying these poems is not always a simple matter of scanning lines and noting rhyme patterns. The difficulty of classifying some contemporary formal poems according to the terminology of the past is like the difficulty grammarians find in defining modern English in terms of ancient Latin: there are correlations, but they are incomplete, or inexact. But as much as these poems at times depart from their classical definitions, they do not abandon them.

In selecting the poems that comprise this anthology, we kept several criteria in mind. First, and most important, we chose only poems that we judged to be of considerable merit. As we've said, we believe that the best argument for the validity of traditional forms is the best poetry, and so we selected poems which demonstrate mastery of craft without seeming artificial in the worst sense of the word and which offer a depth of vision and emotion that would make them valuable whether they were formal or free.

Second, we selected poems without concern for the author's reputation or poetic "politics." Most anthologies of the contemporary period contain representative works by a relatively small number of leading poets; ours contains the best formal poems we could find, regardless of who wrote them or how representative they are of the author's work as a whole. As a result, we have included poems by such relative newcomers as James Bertram, Ron Block, Barry Steinlieb, and Daniel Wolff. We have also included poems by poets who have seldom written formal verse (Allen Ginsberg and Denise Levertov, for example) or who have renounced their early work in forms for free verse (Galway Kinnell, W. S. Merwin, and Adrienne Rich, among others). As we said earlier, we consider formal verse only one option available to contemporary poets. *Strong Measures* contains work by poets who have taken that option, be it once or a thousand times.

Third, we tried to represent as many forms as possible. However, if the only examples of a form available to us had little to recommend them except the fact of their form, we chose not to represent that form. Fortunately, the quality of contemporary formal verse is so high that we were unable to represent only a handful of the major traditional forms—the terzanelle and the Spenserian sonnet, for example.

Fourth, we restricted our selections to poems that use fixed, identifiable, and repeatable patterns. Many poems use rhyme, meter, and other traditional devices sporadically, without creating a pattern, and as much as we would have liked to include such poems, we believe it is the presence of a repeatable pattern that chiefly distinguishes formal from free verse.

Fifth, we attempted to represent as many poets as the criterion of excellence allowed in order to demonstrate that the practice of traditional form is widespread if, in a sense, underground. So often we have heard people say, "No one uses rhyme and meter anymore." Those people simply have not been looking in the right places. We hope to help move the "underground" above ground.

Finally, we tried to present the entire spectrum of traditional verse from the beginning of the contemporary period (the end of World War II) to the present. Hence the poets represented here range from the older established masters (Roethke, Warren, Lowell, and so forth) to the younger writers who will soon become their counterparts. While we have included many selections from the masters, we have stressed the work of younger writers and more recent years to indicate American poets' persistent—even expanding—interest in traditional forms.

Stéphane Mallarmé once said that a poem is never finished, only abandoned. The same could be said about an anthology. Doubtless there are many other poems that rightly belong in this collection. Because of space limitations, we have had to exclude at least another anthology-worth of excellent poems. Also, there are surely many fine poems that, for one reason or another, have managed to escape our notice. And even as this anthology goes to press, splendid formal poems are no doubt being written. We would like to be able to include all of these deserving poems, but that is impossible. It is our hope that our anthology calls attention not only to the formal poems we have selected, but also to the many "strong measures" that we have not been able to include.

To aid the reader's appreciation of the poems which follow, we have added four appendixes. Appendix A discusses the basic elements of meter and scansion. Appendix B provides definitions of the forms and identifies the poems written in each form. (We are indebted to Lewis Turco and his excellent handbook, *The Book of*

Forms, for many of the definitions included in this appendix.) Appendix C lists each author's poems and identifies the forms they employ. And Appendix D contains a list of recommended books and articles about traditional forms and prosody for further study.

PHILIP DACEY
DAVID JAUSS

Jon Anderson

Jon Anderson was born in Somerville, Massachusetts, in 1940 and is a graduate of Northeastern University and the University of Iowa. His five books include In Sepia *(1974),* Cypresses *(1981), and* The Milky Way: Poems 1967–1982 *(1982). He has been awarded fellowships from the Guggenheim Foundation and the National Endowment for the Arts, and in 1982 he received the Shelley Memorial Award. He teaches at the University of Arizona.*

THE BLUE ANIMALS

When I awoke this morning
they were there, just as blue
as the morning, as calm
as the long green lawn

they grazed upon, turning
their delicate heads. You
would have said: No harm
shall befall us. But you were gone.

So these two opened my morning
gracefully wide and blue   10
as the morning sky. Their calm
mouths moved over the lawn,

and as I was turning
to call out again for you,
I saw there was no harm
at all, though you were gone.

John Ashbery

Born in Rochester, New York, in 1927, John Ashbery is perhaps the most prominent of the New York Poets. He studied at Harvard, Columbia, and New York University and traveled widely in Europe. The author of art criticism for the New York Herald Tribune, Art International, *and* Newsweek *and a former editor of* Art News, *he has said that in his poems he attempts "to use words abstractly, as an abstract painter uses paint." In 1975 his* Self-Portrait in a Convex Mirror *received the Pulitzer Prize, the National Book Award, and the National Book Critics Circle Award. His other books include* Some Trees *(1956),* The Tennis Court Oath *(1962),* Three Poems *(1972),* Shadow Train *(1981), and* A Wave *(1984). A co-recipient of the 1985 Bollingen Prize, he lives in New York City.*

SOME TREES

These are amazing: each
Joining a neighbour, as though speech
Were a still performance.
Arranging by chance

To meet as far this morning
From the world as agreeing
With it, you and I
Are suddenly what the trees try

To tell us we are:
That their merely being there   10
Means something; that soon
We may touch, love, explain.

And glad not to have invented
Such comeliness, we are surrounded:
A silence already filled with noises,
A canvas on which emerges

A chorus of smiles, a winter morning.
Placed in a puzzling light, and moving,
Our days put on such reticence
These accents seem their own defence.   20

PANTOUM

Eyes shining without mystery,
Footprints eager for the past
Through the vague snow of many clay pipes,
And what is in store?

Footprints eager for the past,
The usual obtuse blanket.
And what is in store
For those dearest to the king?

The usual obtuse blanket
Of legless regrets and amplifications   10
For those dearest to the king.
Yes, sirs, connoisseurs of oblivion,

Of legless regrets and amplifications,
That is why a watchdog is shy.
Yes, sirs, connoisseurs of oblivion,
These days are short, brittle; there is only one night.

That is why a watchdog is shy,
Why the court, trapped in a silver storm, is dying.
These days are short, brittle; there is only one night
And that soon gotten over.   20

Why, the court, trapped in a silver storm, is dying!
Some blunt pretense to safety we have
And that soon gotten over
For they must have motion.

Some blunt pretense to safety we have:
Eyes shining without mystery
For they must have motion
Through the vague snow of many clay pipes.

FARM IMPLEMENTS AND RUTABAGAS IN A LANDSCAPE

The first of the undecoded messages read: "Popeye sits in
    thunder,
Unthought of. From that shoebox of an apartment,
From livid curtain's hue, a tangram emerges: a country."
Meanwhile the Sea Hag was relaxing on a green couch:
    "How pleasant
To spend one's vacation *en la casa de Popeye*," she scratched
Her cleft chin's solitary hair. She remembered spinach

And was going to ask Wimpy if he had bought any
    spinach.
"M'love," he intercepted, "the plains are decked out in
    thunder
Today, and it shall be as you wish." He scratched
The part of his head under his hat. The apartment   10
Seemed to grow smaller. "But what if no pleasant
Inspiration plunge us now to the stars? *For this is my
    country.*"

Suddenly they remembered how it was cheaper in the
    country.
Wimpy was thoughtfully cutting open a number 2 can of
    spinach
When the door opened and Swee'pea crept in. "How
    pleasant!"
But Swee'pea looked morose. A note was pinned to his
    bib. "Thunder
And tears are unavailing," it read. "Henceforth shall
    Popeye's apartment

Be but remembered space, toxic or salubrious, whole or
    scratched."

Olive came hurtling through the window; its geraniums
    scratched
Her long thigh. "I have news!" she gasped. "Popeye,
    forced as you know to flee the country   20
One musty gusty evening, by the schemes of his wizened,
    duplicate father, jealous of the apartment
And all that it contains, myself and spinach
In particular, heaves bolts of loving thunder
At his own astonished becoming, rupturing the pleasant

Arpeggio of our years. No more shall pleasant
Rays of the sun refresh your sense of growing old, nor the
    scratched
Tree-trunks and mossy foliage, only immaculate darkness
    and thunder."
She grabbed Swee'pea. "I'm taking the brat to the
    country."
"But you can't do that—he hasn't even finished his
    spinach,"
Urged the Sea Hag, looking fearfully around at the
    apartment.   30

But Olive was already out of earshot. Now the apartment
Succumbed to a strange new hush. "Actually it's quite
    pleasant
Here," thought the Sea Hag. "If this is all we need fear
    from spinach
Then I don't mind so much. Perhaps we could invite Alice
    the Goon over"—she scratched
One dug pensively—"but Wimpy is such a country
Bumpkin, always burping like that." Minute at first, the
    thunder

Soon filled the apartment. It was domestic thunder,
The color of spinach. Popeye chuckled and scratched
His balls: it sure was pleasant to spend a day in the
    country.

David Baker

David Baker was born in Bangor, Maine, in 1954 and holds B.S.E. and M.A. degrees from Central Missouri State University and a Ph.D. from the University of Utah. He has served on the editorial staffs of Quarterly West *and* Kenyon Review. *An accomplished musician, he has played the guitar and other instruments with several jazz, rock, and country bands. Currently an assistant professor of English at Denison University, he is the author of three books:* Laws of the Land *(1981),* Summer Sleep *(1984), and* Haunts *(1985).*

ICE RIVER

Only after a couple of months of hard
cold, by mid-January usually,
no sooner, is the river ready, shards
of ice dropping to it from the white trees.
Before this, even in the early snow,
a frost-crust on mud and weed, it runs slowly

on, and on past wherever I might stand
to watch it, finally, freeze. Now it has.
I walk out toward that blue light at the bend
in its banks, the cold end of day, out past   10
the shore and skid of frozen mud to where
the snow lies flat as a road: the river

itself. I have waited this long to be
alone and small. Here the only sound is that
dull chewing, boots on snow. Even the trees
along the banks loom close, bent, the wet

rock-face bearded with long ice. I have come
back as to some trackless past, and I'm numb

with cold. Nothing moves, or appears to. Yet
under this sheet—snow on ice, thin inches   20
of support—the river runs black and fast.
As I walk I feel its deep pulse in the clenched
sagging of my weight. Even now, the ice
cracks a little, and small shoots pass

from my steps, to the river-edge, like roots.
In a few months I may return to fish
or walk long on the green land. Still, this mute
day is ending now, no sun, only this:
wind pulling in the heavy trees, the faint
light of snow, the blood stopped cold in my feet.   30

Marvin Bell

---

*Born in 1937 in New York City and raised on Long Island, Marvin Bell
attended Alfred University, Syracuse University, the University of Chicago,
and the University of Iowa, where he has taught since 1965. A long-distance
runner, for many years he wrote a popular column in* American Poetry
Review *entitled "Homage to the Runner." His books include* A Probable
Volume of Dreams *(1969), which won the Lamont Prize,* Residue of
Song *(1974),* Stars Which See, Stars Which Do Not See *(1977),*
These Green-Going-to-Yellow *(1981), and* Drawn by Stones, by
Earth, by Things that Have Been in the Fire *(1984).*

From THE ESCAPE INTO YOU

OBSESSIVE

It could be a clip, it could be a comb;
it could be your mother, coming home.
It could be a rooster; perhaps it's a comb;
it could be your father, coming home.
It could be a paper; it could be a pin.
It could be your childhood, sinking in.

The toys give off the nervousness of age.
It's useless pretending they aren't finished:
faces faded, unable to stand,
buttons lost down the drain during baths.   10
Those were the days we loved down there,
the soap disappearing as the water spoke,

saying, it could be a wheel, maybe a pipe;
it could be your father, taking his nap.
Legs propped straight, the head tilted back;
the end was near when he could keep track.
It could be the first one; it could be the second;
the father of a friend just sickened and sickened.

Bruce Bennett

Bruce Bennett was born in Philadelphia in 1940. A graduate of Harvard's doctoral program, he co-founded and served as editor of Field *and* Plough-shares. *He has taught at Harvard, Oberlin, and Wellesley, and currently teaches English and creative writing at Wells College in Aurora, New York. His books are* Coyote Pays a Call *(1980),* The Strange Animal *(1981), and* Straw Into Gold *(1984).*

THE TRUE STORY OF SNOW WHITE

Almost before the princess had grown cold
Upon the floor beside the bitten fruit,
The Queen gave orders to her men to shoot
The dwarfs, and thereby clinched her iron hold
Upon the state. Her mirror learned to lie,
And no one dared speak ill of her for fear
She might through her devices overhear.
So, in this manner, many years passed by,
And now today not even children weep
When someone whispers how, for her beauty's sake,   10
A child was harried once into a grove
And doomed, because her heart was full of love,
To lie forever in unlovely sleep
Which not a prince on earth has power to break.

John Berryman

John Berryman was born in McAlester, Oklahoma, in 1914 and educated at Columbia and Cambridge. According to the Times Literary Supplement, *he created "one of the few unmistakable dictions in modern poetry." During his career, he received the Pulitzer Prize, the National Book Award, the Bollingen Prize, and numerous other awards. His books include* Homage to Mistress Bradstreet *(1956),* Berryman's Sonnets *(1967),* The Dream Songs *(1969), and* Love & Fame *(1972), as well as collections of fiction, essays, and a biography of Stephen Crane. Haunted by his own father's suicide, Berryman leapt to his death from a bridge in Minneapolis in 1972.*

From THE DREAM SONGS

29

There sat down, once, a thing on Henry's heart
só heavy, if he had a hundred years
& more, & weeping, sleepless, in all them time
Henry could not make good.
Starts again always in Henry's ears
the little cough somewhere, an odour, a chime.

And there is another thing he has in mind
like a grave Sienese face a thousand years
would fail to blur the still profiled reproach of. Ghastly,
with open eyes, he attends, blind.   10
All the bells say: too late. This is not for tears;
thinking.

But never did Henry, as he thought he did,
end anyone and hacks her body up
and hide the pieces, where they may be found.
He knows: he went over everyone, & nobody's missing.
Often he reckons, in the dawn, them up.
Nobody is ever missing.

HE RESIGNS

Age, and the deaths, and the ghosts.
Her having gone away
in spirit from me. Hosts
of regrets come & find me empty.

I don't feel this will change.
I don't want any thing
or person, familiar or strange.
I don't think I will sing

any more just now;
or ever. I must start   10
to sit with a blind brow
above an empty heart.

THE POET'S FINAL INSTRUCTIONS

Dog-tired, suisired, will now my body down
near Cedar Avenue in Minneap,
when my crime comes. I am blazing with hope.
Do me glory, come the whole way across town.

I couldn't rest from hell just anywhere,
in commonplaces. Choiring & strange my pall!
I might not lie still in the waste of St Paul
or buy DAD's root beer; good signs I forgive.

Drop here, with honour due, my trunk & brain
among the passioning of my countrymen   10
unable to read, rich, proud of their tags
and proud of me. Assemble all my bags!
Bury me in a hole, and give a cheer,
near Cedar on Lake Street, where the used cars live.

James Bertram

A native of Texas, James Bertram has been a newspaper reporter and a graduate student at the University of Southern Mississippi. "Is It Well-Lighted, Papa?", his first published poem, appeared in a special issue of Mississippi Review *devoted to freedom and form in contemporary poetry.*

IS IT WELL-LIGHTED, PAPA?

Is it well-lighted, Papa—this place
where you have gone to escape and erase
dreams gone dry and bare-teethed critics' remarks
that tormented you like the old man's sharks?
Do we dare term your suicide disgrace?

Clean, like your prose, the bell tolled and the chase
no longer, you knew, was "El Campion's" race.
A' final shotgun sentence rings truly stark.
        Is it well-lighted, Papa?

Weak man or strong man? Why can't we embrace   10
the truth: a fawn with a grizzly bear face.
For despite your indelible machismo mark,
you always told us how you feared the dark.
        Is it well-lighted, Papa?

this poem alludes to E. Hemingway.

Elizabeth Bishop

Elizabeth Bishop was born in Worcester, Massachusetts, in 1911, raised in New England and Nova Scotia, and educated at Vassar. She lived much of her life in Brazil, leading Philip Booth to call her "our most valuable export" to that country. Her many awards include the Pulitzer Prize, the National Book Award, and the Shelley Memorial Award. She was also the first American—and the first woman—to win the Books Abroad/Neustadt International Prize for Literature. She is the author of The Complete Poems *(1969) and* Geography III *(1976), among other works, and the translator of* The Diary of Helena Morley *(1957). She died in 1979.*

SESTINA

September rain falls on the house.
In the failing light, the old grandmother
sits in the kitchen with the child
beside the Little Marvel Stove,
reading the jokes from the almanac,
laughing and talking to hide her tears.

She thinks that her equinoctial tears
and the rain that beats on the roof of the house
were both foretold by the almanac,
but only known to a grandmother.   10
The iron kettle sings on the stove.
She cuts some bread and says to the child,

It's time for tea now; but the child
is watching the teakettle's small hard tears
dance like mad on the hot black stove,
the way the rain must dance on the house.
Tidying up, the old grandmother
hangs up the clever almanac

on its string. Birdlike, the almanac
hovers half open above the child,   20
hovers above the old grandmother
and her teacup full of dark brown tears.
She shivers and says she thinks the house
feels chilly, and puts more wood in the stove.

It was to be, says the Marvel Stove.
I know what I know, says the almanac.
With crayons the child draws a rigid house
and a winding pathway. Then the child
puts in a man with buttons like tears
and shows it proudly to the grandmother.   30

But secretly, while the grandmother
busies herself about the stove,
the little moons fall down like tears
from between the pages of the almanac

into the flower bed the child
has carefully placed in the front of the house.

Time to plant tears, says the almanac.
The grandmother sings to the marvellous stove
and the child draws another inscrutable house.

THE ARMADILLO

For Robert Lowell

This is the time of year
when almost every night
the frail, illegal fire balloons appear.
Climbing the mountain height,

rising toward a saint
still honored in these parts,
the paper chambers flush and fill with light
that comes and goes, like hearts.

Once up against the sky it's hard
to tell them from the stars—   10
planets, that is—the tinted ones:
Venus going down, or Mars,

or the pale green one. With a wind,
they flare and falter, wobble and toss;
but if it's still they steer between
the kite sticks of the Southern Cross,

receding, dwindling, solemnly
and steadily forsaking us,
or, in the downdraft from a peak,
suddenly turning dangerous.   20

Last night another big one fell.
It splattered like an egg of fire
against the cliff behind the house.
The flame ran down. We saw the pair

of owls who nest there flying up
and up, their whirling black-and-white
stained bright pink underneath, until
they shrieked up out of sight.

The ancient owls' nest must have burned.
Hastily, all alone,   30
a glistening armadillo left the scene,
rose-flecked, head down, tail down,

and then a baby rabbit jumped out,
*short-*eared, to our surprise.
So soft!—a handful of intangible ash
with fixed, ignited eyes.

Too pretty, dreamlike mimicry!
O falling fire and piercing cry
and panic, and a weak mailed fist
clenched ignorant against the sky!   40

ONE ART

The art of losing isn't hard to master;
so many things seem filled with the intent
to be lost that their loss is no disaster.

Lose something every day. Accept the fluster
of lost door keys, the hour badly spent.
The art of losing isn't hard to master.

Then practice losing farther, losing faster:
places, and names, and where it was you meant
to travel. None of these will bring disaster.

I lost my mother's watch. And look! my last, or   10
next-to-last, of three loved houses went.
The art of losing isn't hard to master.

I lost two cities, lovely ones. And, vaster,
some realms I owned, two rivers, a continent.
I miss them, but it wasn't a disaster.

—Even losing you (the joking voice, a gesture
I love) I shan't have lied. It's evident
the art of losing's not too hard to master
though it may look like (*Write* it!) like disaster.

Ron Block

*Ron Block was born in 1955 in Gothenburg, Nebraska. He earned a B.A.
in English and linguistics from the University of Nebraska, an M.A. in
creative writing from Syracuse University, where he won the Delmore
Schwartz Award for Poetry, and an M.S. in telecommunications and film
from the S. I. Newhouse School at Syracuse University. His poems have
appeared in* The Iowa Review, Prairie Schooner, Epoch, New Letters, *and other journals. He currently teaches English at North Dakota
State University.*

BALLADE OF THE BACK ROAD

My father's in business, takes it a day at a time,
just keeping ahead of the wolves, he says, and goes
from Gothenburg, looking for a way to find
a deal on irrigation pipes. He knows
the man will give him credit, and he also knows
the farmer he'll deliver it to won't think
it too forward to ask for a check. "That's how it goes,"
my father says. "No problem. Everything touches
    everything

if you take it by steps. If I get to the bank on time,"
he says, "I'll be able to cover the checks I wrote   10
to sell this pipe, buy lunch, drive back, not counting the
        dime
I'll use to call this man who maybe owes
me some. Tomorrow I'll pay off what I owe
this other guy, but maybe I'll sell something
before then, or maybe I'll take out another note,"
he says. "No problem. Everything touches everything.

Now if you'll just help me load this load there's time
for maybe another delivery for the cash flow
to start tomorrow with." He drives me out to find
this farmer's farm, and soon we're lost, driving along rows   20
and rows of corn, and my father says, "I suppose
it wouldn't hurt to get to this first thing in the morning.
Let's start driving back before the gas stations close."
He says, "No problem. Everything touches everything.

If you leave out the middle you'll never come close
to what you're trying to get at, which in this case is
        gasoline.
Seems I can't remember where this road goes,"
he says. "No problem. Everything touches everything."

Philip Booth

Philip Booth was born in Hanover, New Hampshire, in 1925 and grew up on the Maine coast. After undergraduate study at Dartmouth, he earned an A.M. from Columbia. The recipient of the Lamont Prize and the American Academy of Poets Fellowship, he has published a number of books, including Letter from a Distant Land *(1957),* Margins *(1971),* Available Light *(1976), and* Before Sleep *(1980). He teaches at Syracuse University and lives in Castine, Maine.*

FIRST LESSON

Lie back, daughter, let your head
be tipped back in the cup of my hand.
Gently, and I will hold you. Spread
your arms wide, lie out on the stream
and look high at the gulls. A dead-
man's float is face down. You will dive
and swim soon enough where this tidewater
ebbs to the sea. Daughter, believe
me, when you tire on the long thrash
to your island, lie up, and survive.   10
As you float now, where I held you
and let go, remember when fear
cramps your heart what I told you:
lie gently and wide to the light-year
stars, lie back, and the sea will hold you.

John Bricuth

John Bricuth was born in Houston in 1940. He served in the U.S. Navy, worked at the NASA Manned Spacecraft Center in Houston, received his doctorate from Rice Univerity in 1970, and taught school. He now lives in seclusion. In 1970 he won the Emily Clark Balch Prize from Virginia Quarterly Review *for his long poem, "The Musical Emblem." His first*

volume of poems, The Heisenberg Variations, *was published in 1976,
and he is currently at work on a second volume entitled* People Who
Vanish.

SONG OF THE DARKNESS

For Zelda Fitzgerald

Beneath a striped umbrella
Whose brown sunlight is rain,
My colors melt and run.
There's an old ache in my brain.

Set your face in a smile—
Rough grains within a glass
Will char the fragile neck.
The sick never get well.

What was the tune I laughed?
Just once I knew myself   10
Falls before the leaf
Broke the sun in half.

Darling, why don't you come?
We could waltz, and whirling, you
Would forget words they say,
Loving the steps I do.

Strands of the musical stave,
Twisted with spikes of time,
Score the white throat.
My wires catch and sting.   20

Who said it was ill
To love by giving pain?
If time cures the sick,
The sick never get well.

Van K. Brock

Van K. Brock was born in Boston, Georgia, in 1932. After doing under-
graduate work at Emory University, he took M.A., M.F.A., and Ph.D.
degrees at the University of Iowa. The poetry editor of National Forum *and*
founder of Anhinga Press and Sun Dog, *he has published several books,*
among them Final Belief *(1972),* Spelunking *(1977),* The Hard Essential Landscape *(1980), and* The Window *(1981), and he has re-*
cently completed a book-length sequence entitled Unspeakable Strangers.
He lives in Tallahassee, where he co-directs the writing program at Florida
State University.

LYING ON A BRIDGE

We saw anchored worlds in a shallow stream.
The current tugged at clouds, the sun, our faces.
And while we stared, as though into a dream,
The stream moved on; the anchors kept their places.
Even the white rose thorned into your hair
Stayed there, though its refracted, scattered aura
Circled your abstract face, like snow in air;
Then the rose fell onto that gentle water,
Shattering our faces with their mirror. But sun
And clouds, and all their height and depth of light,   10
Could not feel so involved, nor watch when one
Bloom touched that current and waltzed it out of sight.
Though rising, we saw how all things float in space:
The stars and clouds, ourselves, each other's face.

THE SEA BIRDS

No light except the stars, but from the cliff
I saw in motion, out on the rolling waves,
The white sea birds that swim beyond the surf.

Their movements made a pattern on the mauve,
Contorted stretch of cold, corrosive water,
Where even the images of stars dissolve.

When I had thought the birds were fixed in order,
I saw the swimming rim of their starlit ring
Minutely swerve and spiral toward the center:

The birds that had been swimming in between   10
Were shuttled outward on a wheel of light,
Reflecting, like the sea, the star's design.

I paused, and looked, and saw a star burn out
And sink back into space as through a fissure.
It was an ancient word without a thought.

Perhaps birds move in pattern for the measure
It imposes on the ruptured waves at night;
Perhaps they spiral purely for their pleasure.

While I was trying to untie this knot,
A motion in the motion of the weather   20
Turned, and the birds turned too and tore the net

I knitted for them (a star had torn another
I had knitted for stars). I saw them climb the gale
That drove small arrows in through every feather—

One by one they spread their flapping sails.
I think the stars are moving in a school
With restless birds above a freezing pool,
And no one shall put salt on their bright tails.

Gwendolyn Brooks

Gwendolyn Brooks, who "loved poetry very early and began to put rhymes together at about seven," was born in Topeka, Kansas, in 1917 and grew up and attended Wilson Junior College in Chicago, where she still lives. In 1950 she became the first black writer to receive the Pulitzer Prize (for Annie Allen*). Her other collections of verse include* Selected Poems *(1963),* In the Mecca *(1968),* Aloneness *(1972), and* To Disembark *(1981). She has also published a novel,* Maud Martha *(1953), and her autobiography,* Report from Part One *(1973). In 1969 she was appointed poet laureate of Illinois, succeeding Carl Sandburg.*

WE REAL COOL

The Pool Players.
Seven at the Golden Shovel.

We real cool. We
Left school. We

Lurk late. We
Strike straight. We

Sing sin. We
Thin gin. We

Jazz June. We
Die soon.

THE RITES FOR COUSIN VIT

Carried her unprotesting out the door.
Kicked back the casket-stand. But it can't hold her,
That stuff and satin aiming to enfold her,
The lid's contrition nor the bolts before.
Oh oh. Too much. Too much. Even now, surmise,
She rises in the sunshine. There she goes,
Back to the bars she knew and the repose
In love-rooms and the things in people's eyes.
Too vital and too squeaking. Must emerge.
Even now she does the snake-hips with a hiss,   10
Slops the bad wine across her shantung, talks
Of pregnancy, guitars and bridgework, walks
In parks or alleys, comes haply on the verge
Of happiness, haply hysterics. Is.

Michael Dennis Browne

*Born in Walton-on-Thames, England, in 1940, Michael Dennis Browne
attended Hull University and Oxford. In 1965 he came to the United States
on a Fulbright scholarship to study at the University of Iowa. Among his
published collections are* The Wife of Winter *(1970),* Fox *(1975),* The
Sun Fetcher *(1978), and* Smoke from the Fires *(1984). A successful
librettist, he lives in Minneapolis, where he is a professor of English at the
University of Minnesota.*

THE WIFE OF WINTER'S TALE

She lies by the man her husband
in the high white bed,
their breathing through the dry dark farm,
his head near her head.

But far from the farm in the hills,
under the moon's strange stare,
the wolves in hardest December
cry out through the frozen air.

The farm sleeps dark on its slope,
the woman lies by the man,   10
but she is not with him there,
not under his breath or his hand

but out in the far clear cold
hills where he may not go,
where she and her glistening lover race
over a murderous snow.

Henry Carlile

Henry Carlile was born in San Francisco in 1934 and studied at Grays Harbor College and the University of Washington. His first book, The Rough-Hewn Table, *was the Devins Award winner in 1971.* Running Lights, *his second book, appeared in 1981. Since 1967 he has taught at Portland State University.*

HAVANA BLUES

Tonight I thought of you as I smoked a cigar
Smuggled in from your birthplace by a senator

Who gave it to a friend who gave it to me.
Why speak as though to someone I could see?

I try to know why fathers leave their sons.
Why it is easy to forget—it must be, when

You've never written me to say you're well—
If you're alive—and that you wish me well,

Would like to visit when you have a chance.
Were you too proud or grieved? The evidence   10

Suggests you were, and so I understand
And must forgive. If you would only send

A card to say Hello again! Your Father.
But I'm talking to myself. Why bother?

You might be dead for all I know or care.
I care, and yet I must confess my fear

Is finding you, not knowing what to say.
I'm talking to myself, a game I play

With words, your face the paper that I press,
Blank father, ghost! And if I miss   20

You now I miss for both for us. At two,
A small imperfect replica of you.

Hayden Carruth

A poet whose work reveals the influence of jazz and the blues, Hayden Carruth was born in 1921 in Waterbury, Connecticut. He studied at the University of North Carolina and the University of Chicago and served in Italy in World War II. He is the author of twenty-two books of fiction, criticism, and poetry, including From Snow and Rock, From Chaos *(1973),* Brothers, I Loved You All *(1978),* The Sleeping Beauty *(1982),* If You Call This Cry a Song *(1983), and* Asphalt Georgics

(1985). His anthology, The Voice That Is Great Within Us *(1970),
is the largest-selling anthology of twentieth-century American poetry. He
teaches at Syracuse University.*

LONELINESS

AN OUTBURST OF HEXASYLLABLES

Stillness and moonlight, with
thick newfallen snow. I
go to the hollow field
beneath the little ridge
of spruces. The snow lies
on the trees, drapery
white and unmoving. I
cannot see any light
from here, no farmhouse, no
car moving through darkness.   10
A bird makes a sleepy
sound somewhere, probably
a pine grosbeak in the
trees. Often I visit
this place, here where no lights
show, only the cold moon
and the stars, for I have
so long a loneliness
(I think of all my time
compounded with all time)   20
that often it might cry
if it saw a lighted
window in the night. Now
a little breath of cold
air in the stillness sways
the white trees with a sigh.

                    *

Between two snow-heavy
boughs, a bright star; perhaps

many stars combined in
one sparkling, perhaps a   30
galaxy. I look up
to incalculable
space, on which my two boughs
almost close. Somewhere there
a world like this exists,
as beautiful as this,
snow in moonlight gleaming,
yet with no mind. Nothing
on that world knows what is
beauty or loneliness.   40
Only the snow-draped trees.

                    *

Moonlight is "reflected
light reflected again
on snow." It seems—no, it
actually is from
everywhere. It casts no
shadow. It is pale and
what is called, with justice,
ethereal; and yet
its brightness is enough   50
to show up everything,
"as bright as day." But this
is not daylight; it is
the visible aspect
of stillness: the two are
one. See how the spruces
stand in moonlight as in
the silence, unmoving
and soundless, held like that
to be reflectors of   60
loneliness, the arras
hung in this empty room.
These spruces belong to
Marshall Washer, my friend

and neighbor, whose light I
can never see from here.

*

Cursed, cursed from childhood with
incapacity, with
the vision of the void.

*

Everyone now has thought   70
how it may be when soon
universal death comes
down the mountainsides, creeps
up from the seas, appears
out of the air like snow,
and how one might escape
in all the multitude
and survive alone. This
is the archetypal dream
or daydream of our years.   80
That one will be alone,
alone, more alone than
anyone ever was;
no look, no voice, no touch,
no mind in all the world.
It might be me. It might
be now, this moment, here.

*

The snow sculpts this object,
a snow-tree, and does it
neither by carving nor   90
by molding, for there is
a third way nature knows
and a few men besides
(who will not give themselves
to the controversies
of theorists). Rather
this sculpture is made by
the whole of motioning,

all in a concert, which
condenses out of air—   100
out of universal
substance—the exact form
this tree must take. Never
a flake too many or
too few: it is exact.
All growth is a kind of
condensation, like these
intense words gathering
here. Its exactness is
all that we understand   110
of perfection. Yet it
cannot last. That dream was
a folly, for the sun's
first minutest degree
of heat at dawn, the wind's
least pressure, will change it
irretrievably. This
snowy spruce is good for
these few hours only, in
a quiet winter's night.   120

                        *

This is being alone,
this learning with the years
how exactness fails, how
it must fail always, how
the momentary fit
of mood and circumstance
must necessarily
decay. One consciousness
in the night can never
find another to share   130
or even know this, this
particular felt hour.
O God, I know you don't
exist, or certainly
you would blast us or lift
us backward into that

simplicity they knew
long ago when people
had someone to talk to.

                    *

But if it were only   140
the problem of a new
metaphysics! One could
invent something, almost
anything. Think what schemes
and dreams have served. But I
am here in this real life
that I was given, my life
of a withered tongue. I
brush through the trees, and snow
spills down on me, a chill   150
colder than the cold. Mad,
maddened, turning around,
I beat the tree with my
arms; unweighted branches
spring upward and snow flies,
a silent fury. Then
I fall back, winded, wet,
snow melting in my shirt;
I stumble in ruckled
snow, all exactness gone,   160
only the stillness left
in its indifferent
perfection on my ruin;
and I am limp, frightened
of myself, yet saddened
by such futility.
I go away, slogging
in my own tracks that make
an erratic passage
like a wounded bear's, scuffed   170
over the lovely snow.

                    *

At home the fire has died,
the stove is cold. I touch

the estranging metal.
I pour tea, cold and dark,
in a cup. The clock strikes,
but I forget, until
too late, to count the hours.
I sit by the cold stove
in a stillness broken   180
by the clock ticking there
in the other room, by
clapboards creaking, and I
begin to shiver, cold,
at home in my own house.

                    *

Down in the duckpen they
are moving around in
the moonlight and they are
affected by it, they
gabble, and from time to   190
time—now—the hen ducks break
into quacking, raucous
in the still nighttime. I
cannot decide if it
is laughter. I cannot
decide if this laughter
is derisive or just
maniacal and sad.

                    *

I do my work, all night
until the dawn comes, late   200
in this week of solstice.
Then pink, as I look up,
is the snow out in the
garden, pink is the snow
on the spruces, pink the
immense snowy mountain
across the valley. I
lean on the cold window.
A jay slips down and lights

on the birch, dislodging   210
drops of snow from his bough.
The moon is a pallid
disk on the horizon,
as if it had been washed
with snow. The world has turned
from night to day, and this
event is still touching
deep sources in me, though
I do not know what they
are. The cold weight of my   220
body pulls downward and
I feel it as if my
years were heavy, and I
feel a drop of moisture
sliding down my nose, cold
and weighted, until it
meets the glass. I know that
I am a fool and all
men are fools. I know it
and I know I know it.   230
What good is it to know?

18–19 December 1974

From THE ASYLUM

II

Winds; words of the wind; rumor of great walls pierced
Like these, windward, but bomb-pierced. I know. Sun
Burnished the gape, spilled through, dispersed,
Quenched in the murk. Someone
Removed his helmet. Sorrow-stunned at first
Stood we, even we, dunced at such grave bomb-burst;
But then groped forward through the nave.
Wind in a ruined choir. None save
A pigeon to meet us, bird fabulously white
That rose as we came near,   10

Climbing and fluttering up the cascade of sunlight,
Quick wing-clamor in cumbrous air,
And vanished, left us there in that wrecked church.
Silence then; only the old world's wind to hear.
But we, with rifles poised, kept on our search.

LATE SONNET

For that the sonnet no doubt was my own true
singing and suchlike other song, for that
I gave it up half-coldheartedly to set
my lines in a fashion that proclaimed its virtue
original in young arrogant artificers who
had not my geniality nor voice, and yet
their fashionableness was persuasive to me,—what
shame and sorrow I pay!
              And that I knew
that beautiful hot old man Sidney Bechet
and heard his music often but not what he   10
was saying, that tone, phrasing, and free play
of feeling mean more than originality,
these being the actual qualities of song.
Nor is it essential to be young.

Turner Cassity

Self-described as "by investment, temperament, and conviction a burgher,"
Turner Cassity was born in Jackson, Mississippi, in 1929 and educated at
Millsaps College, Stanford, and Columbia. His books include Watchboy,
What of the Night? *(1966),* Yellow for Peril, Black for Beautiful

(1975), The Defense of the Sugar Islands *(1979), and* Keys to
Mayerling *(1983). He lives in Atlanta, where he is Collection Development
Librarian at Emory University.*

LINKS

My young grandfather, for the me of four
Blew smoke rings. I, these long years more,

Without much gift, can, nonetheless,
Redeem my breath from utter shapelessness.

I have no grandsons, having had no sons.
Still, it is good to know that as he once

Made fire his speech and bridged a clinging void,
However differently employed,

I sometimes smoke a little too,
And might bring off the tricks he used to do.   10

Fred Chappell

*Fred Chappell was born in Canton, North Carolina, in 1936 and educated
at Duke University. His publications include five novels, one volume of short
stories, and ten books of poetry, including* The World Between the Eyes
(1971), Awakening to Music *(1979),* Midquest *(1982), one of the
most ambitious long poems written in English in recent years, and* Source
*(1985). A co-recipient of the 1985 Bollingen Prize, he is a professor of
English at the University of North Carolina at Greensboro.*

RIMBAUD FIRE LETTER
TO JIM APPLEWHITE

That decade with Rimbaud I don't regret.
But could not live again. Man, that was *hard.*
Nursing the artificial fevers, wet
With Falstaff beer, I walked the railyard,
Stumbled the moon-streaked tracks, reciting line
After burning line I couldn't understand.
In the long twilight I waited for a sign
The world its symbols would mount at my command.

My folks thought I was crazy, maybe I was.
Drinking behind the garbage back of Maxine's Grill,   10
I formulated esoteric laws
That nothing ever obeyed, or ever will.
"Les brasiers, pleuvant aux rafales de givre.—Douceurs!"
I must have dreamed those words a hundred times,
But what they meant, or even what they *were,*
I never knew. They glowed in my head like flames.

Four things I knew: Rimbaud was genius pure;
The colors of the vowels and verb tenses;
That civilization was going up in fire;
And how to derange every last one of my senses: 20
Kind of a handbook on how to be weird and silly.
It might have helped if I had known some French,
But like any other Haywood County hillbilly
The simple thought of the language made me flinch.

So passed my high school years. The senior prom
I missed, and the girls, and all the thrilling sports.
My teachers asked me, "Boy, where you *from?"*
"From deep in a savage forest of unknown words."
The dialogue went downhill after that,
But our positions were clear respectively: 30
They stood up for health and truth and light,
I stood up for Baudelaire and me.

The subject gets more and more embarrassing.
Should I mention the clumsy shrine I built

In the maple tree behind old Plemmons' spring?
Or how I played the young Artur to the hilt
In beer joints where the acrid farmers drank?
Or how I tried to make my eyes look *through?*
—I'd better not. Enough, that I stayed drunk
For eight hot years, and came up black and blue.   40

One trouble was that time was running out.
Rimbaud had finished "all that shit" before
He reached his nineteenth year. I had about
Nineteen short months to get down to the core.
I never did, of course. I wrote a bunch
Of junk I'm grateful to have burned; I read
Some books. But my courage was totally out to lunch.
Oh, Fred Fred Fred Fred Fred . . .

Remember when we met our freshman year?
Not something you'd want to repeat, I guess, for still   50
R. worked his will in me, a blue blear
Smoke poured forth. (That, and alcohol.)
(And an army of cranky opinions about whatever
Topic was brought up.) (And a hateful pose
Of expertise.) Jesus, was I clever!
And smelt myself as smelling like a rose.

I had a wish, "Mourir aux fleuves barbares,"
And to fulfill it could have stayed at home.
But down at Duke in 1954
(*I like Ike*) it carried weight with some   60
Few wild men and true who wanted to write
And even tried to write—God bless them
Everyone!—and who scheduled the night
For BEER and the explication of a POEM.

Well, you recall: Mayola's Chili House,
Annamaria's Pizza, Maitland's Top Hat,
The Pickwick, and that truly squalid place,
The Duchess, where the local whores stayed fat
On college boys, and the Blue Star, the I.
P.D. But the joint that really made us flip   70
Sat sunsoaked on Broad St., where we walked by
Rambeau's Barber Shop.

Those were the days! . . .—But they went on and on and
    on.
The failure I saw myself grew darker and darker.
And hearing the hard new myths from Bob Mirandon,
I got Rimbaud confused with Charlie Parker.
It was a mess, mon vieux. Finally
They kicked me out, and back to the hills I went.
But not before they'd taught me how to see
Myself as halfway halved and halfway blent.   80

Jim, we talked our heads off. What didn't we say?
We didn't say what it cost our women to prop
Our psyches up, we couldn't admit *the day*
And age belonged still to our fathers. One drop
Distillate of Carolina reality
Might have cured much, but they couldn't make us drink.
We kept on terribly seeing how to see,
We kept on terribly thinking how to think.

They turned me down for the army. I wanted it raw,
I wanted to find a wound my mother could love.   90
("Il a deux trous rouges au côté droit.")
I wanted Uncle Sugar to call my bluff . . .
No soap. I wound up hauling fertilizer,
Collecting bills, and trying to read Rimbaud
At night, and preaching those poems to David Deas or
Anyone else I thought might care to know.

The only good thing was that I got married.
And I watched the mountains until the mountains touched
My mind and partly tore away my fire-red
Vision of a universe besmirched.   100
I started my Concordance to Samuel Johnson,
And learned to list a proper footnote, got down
To reading folks like Pope and Bertrand Bronson,
And turned my back on the ashes of Paree-town.

But as my father said, "Fire's in the bloodstream."
The groaning it cost my muse to take off my edge
Still sounds in my sleep, rasps my furious dream.
—Tell you what, Jim: let's grow old and sage;

Let's don't wind up brilliant, young, and dead.
Let's just remember.
                              —Give my love to Jan.   110
Yours for terror and symbolism,
                                        ole Fred.
28 May 1971

MY GRANDFATHER'S CHURCH GOES UP

(Acts 2:1–47)
God is a fire in the head.
                    —Nijinsky

Holocaust, pentecost: what heaped heartbreak:

The tendrils of fire   forthrightly tasting
foundation to rooftree   flesh of that edifice . . .
Why was sear sent   to sunder those jointures,
the wheat-hued wood   wasted to heaven?
Both altar and apse   the air ascended
in sullen smoke.
                    (It was surely no sign
of God's salt grievance   but grizzled *Weird* grimly
and widely wandering.)
                    The dutiful worshipers
stood afar ghast-struck   as the green cedar shingles   10
burst outward like birds   disturbed in their birling.
Choir stall crushed inward   flayed planking in curlicues
back on it bending,   broad beams of chestnut
oak poplar and pine   gasht open paint-pockets.
And the organ uttered   an unholy *Omega*
as gilt pipes and pedals   pulsed into rubble.

How it all took tongue!   A total hosannah
this building burgeoned,   the black hymnals whispering
leaves lisping in agony   leaping alight,
sopranos' white scapulars   each singly singeing   20
robes of the baritones   roaring like rivers
the balcony bellowing   and buckling. In the basement

where the M.Y.F.   had mumbled for mercies
the cane-bottomed chairs   chirruped Chinese.
What a glare   of garish glottals
rose from the nave   what knar-mouthed natter!
And the transept tottered   intoning like tympani
as the harsh heat   held hold there.
The whole church resounded   reared its rare anthem
crying out Christ-mercy   to the cloud-cloven sky.   30

Those portents Saint Paul   foretold to us peoples
fresh now appeared: bifurcate fire-tongues,
and as of wild winds   a swart mighty wrestling,
blood fire and vapor   of smoke vastly vaulting,
the sun into darkness   deadened and dimmed,
wonders in heaven   signs wrought in the world:
the Spirit poured out   on souls of us sinners.
In this din as of drunkenness   the old men dreamed
                                                    dreams,
the daughters and sons   supernal sights saw.
God's gaudy grace   grasped them up groaning.   40
Doubt parched within them   pure power overtaking
their senses. Sobbing   like sweethearts bereft
the brothers and sisters   burst into singing.
Truly the Holy   Ghost here now halted,
held sway in their hearts   healed there the hurt.

Now over the narthex   the neat little steeple
force of the fire   felt furiously.
Bruit of black smoke   borne skyward
shadowed its shutters   swam forth in swelter.
It stood as stone   for onstreaming moments   50
then carefully crumpled   closed inward in char.
The brass bell within it   broke loose, bountifully
pealing, plunged   plangent to the pavement
and a glamour of clangor   gored cloudward gaily.

That was the ringing that wrung   remorse out of us
                                                    clean,
the elemental echo   the elect would hear always;
in peace or in peril   that peal would pull them.

Seventeen seasons   have since parted
the killing by fire   of my grandfather's kirk.
Moving of our Maker   on this middle earth   60
is not to be mind-gripped   by any men.

Here Susan and I   saw it, come
to this wood, wicker   basket and wool blanket
swung between us,   in sweet June
on picnic. Prattling   like parakeets
we smoothed out for our meal-place   the mild meadow
                                                   grasses
and spread our sandwiches   in the sunlit greensward.
Then amorously ate.   And afterward
lay languorous and   looking lazily.
Green grass and pokeweed   gooseberry bushes   70
pink rambling rose   and raspberry vine
sassafrass and thistle   and serrate sawbriar
clover and columbine   clung to the remnants,
grew in that ground   once granted to God.
Blackbirds and thrushes   built blithely there
the ferret and kingsnake   fed in the footing.
The wilderness rawly   had walked over those walls
and the deep-drinking forest   driven them down.

Now silence sang: swoon of wind
ambled the oak trees   and arching aspens.   80

In happy half-sleep   I heard or half-heard
in the bliss of breeze   breath of my grandfather,
vaunt of his voice   advance us vaward.
No fears fretted me   and a freedom followed
this vision vouchsafed,   victory of spirit.
He in the wind   wept not, but wonderfully
spoke softly   soothing to peace.
What matter he murmured   I never remembered,
words melted in wisps   washed whitely away;
but calm came into me   and cool repose.   90
Where Fate had fixed   no fervor formed;
he had accepted   wholeness of his handiwork.

Again it was given   to the Grace-grain that grew it,
had gone again   gleaming to Genesis

to the stark beginning   where the first stars burned.
Touchless and tristless   Time took it anew
and changed that church-plot   to an enchanted chrisom
of leaf and flower   of lithe light and shade.

Pilgrim, the past   becomes prayer
becomes remembrance rock-real   of Resurrection   100
when the Willer so willeth   works his wild wonders.

Kelly Cherry

Kelly Cherry was born in Baton Rouge, Louisiana, in 1940, raised in New York and Virginia, and educated at Mary Washington College, the University of Virginia, and the University of North Carolina-Greensboro. A writer with a serious philosophical bent, she once wrote, "Why, just to get from Tuesday to Thursday, you have to solve the problem of free will." She has published three books of poems, including Lovers and Agnostics *(1975) and* Relativity: A Point of View *(1977), and four novels, most recently* The Lost Traveller's Dream *(1984). Among her awards are a National Endowment for the Arts Fellowship, a Romnes Fellowship, and a Pushcart Prize. She is currently a professor of English at the University of Wisconsin.*

A SCIENTIFIC EXPEDITION IN SIBERIA, 1913

From the log

Week one: our expedition slowed,
     Faltered, stopped; we set up
Camp and dug in, but still it snowed
     And snowed, without let-up,

Until we thought we'd go insane.
          We literally lost our sense
Of balance, because sky and plain
          Were one omnipresence,

So dazzling white it could blind a man
          Or mesmerize his soul.   10
We lost sight of the horizon.
          There was one man, a Pole

Named Szymanowski, an expert on plants
          Of the early Pleistocene
Period, who dreamed of giants
          In the earth, swearing he'd seen

Them grow from snow like plants from dirt.
          We said that such dreams were
The price one pays for being expert,
          And laughed, but still he swore,   20

And still it snowed. The second week
          The ceaseless rush of wind
Was in our heads like ancient Greek,
          A curse upon our kind,

Or say: in our skulls like the drone
          Of bees swarming in a hive.
And we began to know that none,
          Or few, of us would survive.

Secretly, we sought the first signs
          Of sickness in each other,   30
Reading between the face's lines
          As a spy reads a letter,

But no one complained of fever,
          And suddenly the snow
Quit. You couldn't have proved it ever
          Fell, but for the wild show

Of evidence on the ground. Now
    The lid was lifted, and
Sun set icicled trees aglow
    With flame, a blue sky spanned   40

The hemisphere, and while we packed
    Our gear, we found we were
Singing, but Szymanowski backed
    Out, silent as the fur

On a fox . . . or the wolfish cur,
    Slinking like a shadow,
That stuck to our pack dogs like a burr.
    Where S. went, God may know,

But we went on to a frozen hill,
    A vast block of the past—   50
An ice cube for a drink in hell
    (If anything cools that thirst).

Inside, preserved like a foetus
    In formaldehyde, like
Life itself, staring back at us
    The mammoth creature struck

Poses for our cameras; then
    We got busy, and went
To work, and all seemed well for ten
    Days, and then some strange scent,   60

Not unpleasant, weighted the air,
    Sweet as fruit, and one dog
Stirred, and then another, and where
    I sat, keeping this log,

A steady dripping started up,
    Slowly at first, and then
Faster. I made my palms a cup
    To catch the flow, and when

I lapped the melted snow, I glanced
    Down, and saw how cold   70
Ground under my boot moved and danced
    In little streams: an old

Fear shook me and I ran to where
    The mammoth stood—freed from
Time and vulnerable to air.
    His curling tusks seemed some

Incredible extravagance,
    A creator's last spree.
His fixed stare held me in a trance,
    His reddish-brown, shaggy   80

Coat caught the sun like burnished oak,
    But he didn't move: was still
As if he'd been carved from a rock.
    Nothing supernatural

Was going to happen, and I breathed—
    Fresh meat on the hoof!—In
An instant, the pack dogs had covered
    Him like hungry ants spreading

Over a hatching egg, tearing
    Chunks of raw flesh from his side,   90
Snarling, snapping their jaws, baring
    Fangs that ripped his flank wide

Open. My hands, my boots were spattered
    With blood, and the dogs ate
Him up. That horror performed, we scattered
    Into the world, but late

In the afternoon, I saw a shadow
    At my heel, and I knew
The others were dead—numbed into slow
    Motion, and each a statue   100

Buried in ice. And then the clouds,
    Piled in the north and east
Like a funeral parlor's stack of shrouds,
    Darkened, sliding southwest,

And it snowed and has never stopped
    Snowing since, and I have
Come with blood in my mouth, my hands sopped
    With red snow, to speak and save.

John Ciardi

Born in Boston in 1916, John Ciardi holds degrees from Tufts and the University of Michigan. The recipient of the Prix de Rome and other awards, he is the author of many books of poetry, including Lives of X *(1971),* The Little That Is All *(1974), and* For Instance *(1979), and he is well-known for his translation of Dante's* The Divine Comedy *(1970) and his critical text* How a Poem Means *(1959). For many years he was the poetry editor of the* Saturday Review. *He lives in Metuchen, New Jersey.*

AT MY FATHER'S GRAVE

A leaf is not too little. A world may rest
in no more shade than spiders weave. Defend
the nit on every underside. I roost
on less than it, and I must yet be found
by the same bird that found St. Francis dead.
It's cold as nothing in the eye I see,
and anything's a wrap. Had I the deed

to all these stones, I'd burn it. Could I say
what world this is and, saying, let it be,
I'd keep as still as wormholes in a thought   10
and let it lack. A leaf could not blow by
my silence and find room to land. If that
is no real kindness for what sun I had
when I was warm, most kindness is a waste,
all kindness is too little. In my head
there are more teeth than mercies. I'll go west
and set the sun forever when I dare
disturb the leaf that's wedged against my door.

Amy Clampitt

Amy Clampitt was born in New Providence, Iowa, in 1920 and took a Doctor of Humane Letters degree from Grinnell College. She has worked as a waitress, file clerk, blurb writer, editor, researcher, and teacher. In 1982 she received a Guggenheim Fellowship, and in 1984 the Literature Award from the National Academy of Arts and Letters. Her books include Multitudes, Multitudes *(1974),* The Kingfisher *(1983),* The Summer Solstice *(1983),* A Homage to John Keats *(1984), and* What the Light Was Like *(1985). She lives in New York City.*

THE KINGFISHER

In a year the nightingales were said to be so loud
they drowned out slumber, and peafowl strolled screaming
beside the ruined nunnery, through the long evening
of a dazzled pub crawl, the halcyon color, portholed

by those eye-spots' stunning tapestry, unsettled
the pastoral nightfall with amazements opening.

Months later, intermission in a pub on Fifty-fifth Street
found one of them still breathless, the other quizzical,
acting the philistine, puncturing Stravinsky—"Tell
me, what *was* that racket in the orchestra about?"— 10
hauling down the Firebird, harum-scarum, like a kite,
a burnished, breathing wreck that didn't hurt at all.

Among the Bronx Zoo's exiled jungle fowl, they heard
through headphones of a separating panic, the bellbird
reiterate its single *chong,* a scream nobody answered.
When he mourned, "The poetry is gone," she quailed,
seeing how his hands shook, sobered into feeling old.
By midnight, yet another fifth would have been killed.

A Sunday morning, the November of their cataclysm
(Dylan Thomas brought in *in extremis* to St. Vincent's, 20
that same week, a symptomatic datum) found them
wandering a downtown churchyard. Among its headstones,
while from unruined choirs the noise of Christendom
poured over Wall Street, a benison in vestments,

a late thrush paused, in transit from some grizzled
spruce bog to the humid equatorial fireside: berry-
eyed, bark-brown above, with dark hints of trauma
in the stigmata of its underparts—or so, too bruised
just then to have invented anything so fancy,
later, re-embroidering a retrospect, she had supposed. 30

In gray England, years of muted recrimination (then
dead silence) later, she could not have said how many
spoiled takeoffs, how many entanglements gone sodden,
how many gaudy evenings made frantic by just one
insomniac nightingale, how many liaisons gone down
screaming in a stroll beside the ruined nunnery;

a kingfisher's burnished plunge, the color
of felicity afire, came glancing like an arrow

through landscapes of untended memory: ardor
illuminating with its terrifying currency   40
now no mere glimpse, no porthole vista
but, down on down, the uninhabitable sorrow.

Martha Collins

*Martha Collins was born in Des Moines, Iowa, in 1940 and educated at
Stanford and the University of Iowa. A Bunting fellow at Radcliffe from
1982 to 1983, she is currently director of the creative writing program at
the University of Massachusetts, Boston. She is the editor of* Critical Essays
on Louise Bogan *(1984) and the author of* The Catastrophe of Rainbows *(1985), a collection of poems.*

THE STORY WE KNOW

The way to begin is always the same. Hello,
Hello. Your hand, your name. So glad, Just fine,
and Good-bye at the end. That's every story we know,

and why pretend? But lunch tomorrow? No?
Yes? An omelette, salad, chilled white wine?
The way to begin is simple, sane, Hello,

and then it's Sunday, coffee, the *Times,* a slow
day by the fire, dinner at eight or nine
and Good-bye. In the end, this is a story we know

so well we don't turn the page, or look below   10
the picture, or follow the words to the next line:
The way to begin is always the same Hello.

But one night, through the latticed window, snow
begins to whiten the air, and the tall white pine.
Good-bye is the end of every story we know

that night, and when we close the curtains, oh,
we hold each other against that cold white sign
of the way we all begin and end. *Hello,*
Good-bye is the only story. We know, we know.

Peter Cooley

*Peter Cooley was born in Detroit in 1939 and educated at Shimer College,
the University of Chicago, and the University of Iowa. Since 1970 he has
been poetry editor for* The North American Review. *His books include*
The Company of Strangers *(1975),* The Room Where Summer Ends
(1979), and Nightseasons *(1983). At present he is a professor of English
at Tulane University.*

NAKED POETRY

Dear Harriet,
              The weather's warm today, the sea
flickering to land with gulls on the beach,
then raking it, claws drawn, hard.

Yes, this is my first verse epistle about sex
sent air mail special just to you.
Isn't that the poetry you'd have me write?

The water's mine as if I had a right
the elderly gave me, dead set against the sea
they never enter here late summer. They know you
in the closeups of us they soak up at the beach   10
since you left. They think it's only sex
I miss, like them, which makes it hard

explaining you away, although form's harder,
frankly, since I haven't written
one line lately till this poem. A blue movie, that's their sex,
their pretense we're still screwing in the sea
so they can cheer us, chaises at the beach
front row center. They whistle watching you

undressing, pinned back on a wave & you
letting me come—they push their fancy hard—,   20
a swizzle stick in gin, or fantasize the beach
stripped to a screen, a living theater sort of rite
embracing them. I need you. You can see
that by this letter; it swells back on sex

hiding the reputation of my sex
for centerfolds, skindrift. I know you
know I know the world is fictive, glass. See,
how this circles, brittle? Just because it's hard
to gravitate this poem doesn't mean you're right
to turn on form: glass is just sand & sand the beach   30

& you & I bodies forcing down the beach
equally & opposite & steady. Then, as for sex,
well, we had that & it was all right,
wasn't it, until the poetry crystalized & you
said I was pressing us for imagery & hardly
there. Come back. What I said about the sea

& the elderly, their movies at the beach
was sublimation pretending it's hard sex.
Screw poetry. Screw flicks. I want you. Write,

                                    XXX Henry

Jane Cooper

*Jane Cooper was born in Atlantic City, New Jersey, in 1924 and studied
at Vassar, the University of Wisconsin, and the University of Iowa. A
recipient of the Lamont Prize and Guggenheim and Ingram Merrill Foundation Fellowships, she is the author of* Weather of Six Mornings *(1969),*
Maps and Windows *(1974), and* Threads: Rosa Luxemburg from
Prison *(1979). She teaches at Sarah Lawrence College.*

THE FAITHFUL

Once you said joking slyly, "If I'm killed
I'll come to haunt your solemn bed,
I'll stand and glower at the head
And see if my place is empty still, or filled."

What was it woke me in the early darkness
Before the first bird's twittering?
A shape dissolving and flittering
Unsteady as a flame in a drafty house.

It seemed a concentration of the dark burning
By the bedpost at my right hand,   10
While to my left that no-man's land
Of sheet stretched palely as a false morning. . . .

All day I have been sick and restless. This evening
Curtained, with all the lights on,
I start up—only to sit down.
Why should I grieve after ten years of grieving?

What if last night I was the one who lay dead,
While the dead burned beside me
Trembling with passionate pity
At my blameless life and shaking its flamelike head?   20

IN THE LAST FEW MOMENTS CAME
THE OLD GERMAN CLEANING WOMAN

Our last morning in that long room,
Our little world, I could not cry
But went about the senseless chores
—Coffee and eggs and newspapers—
As if your plane would never fly,
As if we were trapped there for all time.

Wanting to fix by ritual
The marriage we could never share
I creaked to stove and back again.
Leaves in the stiffening New York sun   10
Clattered like plates; the sky was bare—
I tripped and let your full cup fall.

Coffee scalded your wrist and that
Was the first natural grief we knew.

Others followed after years:
Dry fodder swallowed, then the tears
When mop in hand the old world through
The door pressed, dutiful, idiot.

Cid Corman

*A writer whose work has been described as combining "an Oriental flavor"
with "Yankee toughness," Cid Corman was born in Boston in 1924 and
attended Tufts, the University of Michigan, the University of North Carolina, and the Sorbonne. Since 1951 he has been the editor of* Origin
*magazine and Origin Press. A long-time resident of Japan, he has published
many books, including* Livingdying *(1970),* For Dear Life *(1975), and*
Auspices *(1978).*

THE TORTOISE

Always to want to
go back, to correct
an error, ease a

guilt, see how a friend
is doing. And yet
one doesn't, except

in memory, in
dreams. The land remains
desolate. Always

the feeling is of   10
terrible slowness
overtaking haste.

Alfred Corn

---

*Alfred Corn was born in Bainbridge, Georgia, in 1943 and attended Emory
University and Columbia. His books are* All Roads at Once *(1976),* A
Call in the Midst of the Crowd *(1978),* The Various Light *(1980),
and* Notes from a Child of Paradise *(1984). His honors include the
Blumenthal and Levinson prizes from* Poetry *and an award from the
American Academy and Institute of Arts and Letters. He lives in New York
City and Vermont.*

REMEMBERING MYKENAI

Guides urged us, praised us up to the Lion Gate, its
Carved lintel "brought from twenty or possibly
   Two hundred miles away" and wedged in
   Place by the gods or a tyrant's hubris.

High up, the fallen muscular citadel,
Great blocks the winds had modeled and smoothed like the
   Hard flesh of some remembered Argive—
   Vengeful Orestes, the seed of Pelops?

Nearby, the beehive tomb lay, an underground
Dome sunk in gloom. Its resonance chilled us, as   10
   Trapped flies, whose droning stunned the eardrum,
   Sluggishly spiraled above our comments.

Stones, stone, the life they hewed; and the self a dark
Construct, both tomb and citadel. Why will a
   Dead hour, when change breeds mishap, rise to
   Strike us, metallic and harsh as noonday?

Rocks, thyme, the wind-scorched Peloponnese—to which
Years stretch in mute kilometers back. But those
   Strong measures taken, steps our feet took,
   Echo through ruins like yours, Mykenai.   20

Gregory Corso

*Gregory Corso was born in New York City in 1930. When he was seven-
teen, he was convicted of theft and sentenced to three years in jail, where he
began to write poetry. Later, he became a central figure in the Beat Movement.
Besides such collections of poetry as* Selected Poems *(1962),* Elegaic
Feelings American *(1970),* Earth Egg *(1974), and* Herald of the
Autochthonic Spirit *(1981), he has published a novel and several plays.
He currently lives in New York.*

BODY FISHED FROM THE SEINE

He floats down the Seine
The last victim of the FLN
He's Arab, he's soft, he's green
"He's a long time in the water been"
They're dragging him up now
Rope around his waist against the prow
Like a wet sponge he bounces and squirts
Somehow you feel though dead it hurts

I turned to Allen & Peter—what amazed them
Was not so much the sad victim   10
But how a big glass-top tourist boat
Stopped and had the tourists take note
They fresh from Eiffel and Notre-Dame
—A break of camera calm

Robert Creeley

Robert Creeley was born in Arlington, Massachusetts, in 1926. He studied at Harvard, Black Mountain College, and the University of New Mexico, and worked with the American Field Service in India and Burma. One of the principal figures of the Black Mountain Movement, he served as editor of the influential Black Mountain Review. *William Carlos Williams once said that Creeley had "the subtlest feeling for the measure that I encounter anywhere except in the verses of Ezra Pound." His* Collected Poems *appeared in 1983 and his* Collected Prose *in 1984. He teaches at the State University of New York at Buffalo.*

OH NO

If you wander far enough
you will come to it
and when you get there
they will give you a place to sit

for yourself only, in a nice chair,
and all your friends will be there
with smiles on their faces
and they will likewise all have places.

A WICKER BASKET

Comes the time when it's later
and onto your table the headwaiter
puts the bill, and very soon after
rings out the sound of lively laughter—

Picking up change, hands like a walrus,
and a face like a barndoor's,
and a head without any apparent size,
nothing but two eyes—

So that's you, man,
or me. I make it as I can,   10
I pick up, I go
faster than they know—

Out the door, the street like a night,
any night, and no one in sight,
but then, well, there she is,
old friend Liz—

And she opens the door of her cadillac,
I step in back,
and we're gone.
She turns me on—   20

There are very huge stars, man, in the sky,
and from somewhere very far off someone hands me a slice
      of apple pie,
with a gob of white, white ice cream on top of it,
and I eat it—

Slowly. And while certainly
they are laughing at me, and all around me is racket
of these cats not making it, I make it

in my wicker basket.

IF YOU

If you were going to get a pet
what kind of animal would you get.

A softbodied dog, a hen—
feathers and fur to begin it again.

When the sun goes down and it gets dark
I saw an animal in a park.

Bring it home, to give it to you.
I have seen animals break in two.

You were hoping for something soft
and loyal and clean and wondrously careful—   10

a form of otherwise vicious habit
can have long ears and be called a rabbit.

Dead. Died. Will die. Want.
Morning, midnight. I asked you

if you were going to get a pet
what kind of animal would you get.

BALLAD OF THE DESPAIRING HUSBAND

My wife and I lived all alone,
contention was our only bone,
I fought with her, she fought with me,
and things went on right merrily.

But now I live here by myself
with hardly a damn thing on the shelf,
and pass my days with little cheer
since I have parted from my dear.

Oh come home soon, I write to her.
Go screw yourself, is her answer. 10
Now what is that, for Christian word?
I hope she feeds on dried goose turd.

But still I love her, yes I do.
I love her and the children too.
I only think it fit that she
should quickly come right back to me.

Ah no, she says, and she is tough,
and smacks me down with her rebuff.
Ah no, she says, I will not come
after the bloody things you've done. 20

Oh wife, oh wife—I tell you true,
I never loved no one but you.
I never will, it cannot be
another woman is for me.

That may be right, she will say then,
but as for me, there's other men.
And I will tell you I propose
to catch them firmly by the nose.

And I will wear what dresses I choose!
And I will dance, and what's to lose! 30
I'm free of you, you little prick,
and I'm the one can make it stick.

Was this the darling I did love?
Was this that mercy from above
did open violets in the spring—
and made my own worn self to sing?

She was. I know. And she is still,
and if I love her? then so I will.
And I will tell her, and tell her right . . .

Oh lovely lady, morning or evening or afternoon.   40
Oh lovely lady, eating with or without a spoon.
Oh most lovely lady, whether dressed or undressed or
    partly.
Oh most lovely lady, getting up or going to bed or sitting
    only.

Oh loveliest of ladies, than whom none is more fair, more
    gracious, more beautiful.
Oh loveliest of ladies, whether you are just or unjust,
    merciful, indifferent, or cruel.
Oh most loveliest of ladies, doing whatever, seeing
    whatever, being whatever.
Oh most loveliest of ladies, in rain, in shine, in any
    weather.

Oh lady, grant me time,
please, to finish my rhyme.

J. V. Cunningham

*One of the indisputable masters of the epigram, J. V. Cunningham was born
in Cumberland, Maryland, in 1911 and grew up in Montana and Denver.
He received both undergraduate and graduate degrees from Stanford. His
books include* Collected Poems and Epigrams *(1971) and* Collected

Essays (1977). He taught at Brandeis University from 1953 until his retirement in 1980. He died in 1985.

THE AGED LOVER DISCOURSES IN THE FLAT STYLE

There are, perhaps, whom passion gives a grace,
Who fuse and part as dancers on the stage,
But that is not for me, not at my age,
Not with my bony shoulders and fat face.
Yet in my clumsiness I found a place
And use for passion: with it I ignore
My gaucheries and yours, and feel no more
The awkwardness of the absurd embrace.

It is a pact men make, and seal in flesh,
To be so busy with their own desires   10
Their loves may be as busy with their own,
And not in union. Though the two enmesh
Like gears in motion, each with each conspires
To be at once together and alone.

FOR MY CONTEMPORARIES

How time reverses
The proud in heart!
I now make verses
Who aimed at art.

But I sleep well.
Ambitious boys
Whose big lines swell
With spiritual noise,

Despise me not,
And be not queasy   10
To praise somewhat:
Verse is not easy.

But rage who will.
Time that procured me
Good sense and skill
Of madness cured me.

EPITAPH FOR SOMEONE OR OTHER

Naked I came, naked I leave the scene,
And naked was my pastime in between.

Philip Dacey

Philip Dacey was born in St. Louis, Missouri, in 1939 and educated at St. Louis University, Stanford, and the University of Iowa. From 1963 to 1965 he served in the Peace Corps. He is the author of How I Escaped from the Labyrinth and Other Poems *(1977),* The Boy Under the Bed *(1981),* Gerard Manley Hopkins Meets Walt Whitman in Heaven and Other Poems *(1982),* Fives *(1984), and co-editor of this anthology. He teaches at Southwest State University in Marshall, Minnesota.*

JACK, AFTERWARDS

It's difficult to say what it all meant.
The whole experience, in memory,
Seems like a story someone might invent
Who was both mad and congenitally cheery.

I have to remind myself, it happened to me.
The stalk's gone now, and Alma, the old cow;
And I fear only the dream with the shadow.

My mother had a lot to do with it.
In fact, you might say it was her beanstalk—
She scattered the seeds, I didn't, when she hit   10
My full hand and said all I was good for was talk.
She haunted me in those days: I couldn't walk
Anywhere without seeing her face,
Even on the crone in the giant's palace.

Throughout this whole time, my father was dead.
I think I must have felt his not-being-there
More than I would have his being-there. Instead
Of his snoring, his absence was everywhere.
So the old man with the beans, poor and threadbare
As he was, became the more important   20
To my boyish needs. Not to mention the giant.

Oddly enough, the beanstalk itself, which some
Might think the most wonderful part of all this,
Pales in time's perspective. Though my true home
Between the earth and sky, and though no less
Than magic, that stalk, in the last analysis,
Was but a means to an end. Yet, I must say,
I still recall the beanflowers' sweet bouquet.

Then there's the giant. What can be said? Nothing
And everything. Or this: if the truth be known   30
About someone so great, it was surprising
How vulnerable he seemed, and how alone.
Not that I wasn't frightened. I was, to the bone—
But it was his weakness, joined to such power,
I feared most, and fear now, any late hour.

The fruits of it all were gold, a hen, and a harp.
I wish I could say I miss my poverty,

When my appetite, if not my wit, was sharp,
But I don't. A little fat hasn't hurt me
Much. Still it's that strange harp's melody,   40
Beauty willing itself, not golden eggs,
Whose loss would leave me, I hope, one who begs.

Of everything, the strangest was to see
Alma the cow come back home at the end,
Her two horns wreathed in wild briony
And traveler's joy. Did the old man send
Her as a gift? She seemed, somehow, lightened.
I'd like to think I traded her away
To get her back, sea-changed, in such array.

So I sit here, my dying, blind mother   50
To tend to, and wonder how it was
I escaped, smiling, from such an adventure.
If events in those days conformed to laws,
I'd like to know—not least, nor only, because
What happened then still makes me ask, Why me?
Not even my mother knew, when she could see.

JILL, AFTERWARDS

He had this idea about the hill,
How at the top there would be water
Sweeter than any in any pail
Lugged previously, and to come down
Would be the easiest part of all.
I told him it was a kids' story.

Before I had knockers that story
Was making the rounds in my gang. Hell,
We laughed at it even then. We all

Knew better than to think sweet water   10
Could be had for the price of a pail
And a little legwork up and down

A hill that had been standing there, dawn
To dreary dawn, our whole life's story
Long. Not to mention the probabil-
ity such a thing as sweet water,
Hill or no hill, didn't exist. I'll
Give him credit for this, though: a wall

Couldn't have been more stubborn. He'd call
Me late at night even, to break down   20
My resistance. Okay, I said, I'll
Go. The truth is, he was cute. Starry-
eyed but cute. And I wondered whether
He had anything in his pants. Pale

Dawn found us taking turns with the pail
As we rose above the town. Not all
The money down there beats the water
We'll find, he said. Now I was poor, down
To a few bucks. It's no mystery
Money talks. Loud. But I climbed the hill.   30

To the top. And there was this big hole.
And deep. I got dizzy to look down
It. He had rope and let the pail fall
Yards and yards. 'Got something, he yelled, pull-
ing the catch in. Later, the story
He told, back in town, was the water

Spilled out. But the fact of the matter
Is I saw what he had. Nothing. Damn
If he didn't claim different, though. Al-
ways. Damn, too, if his pants weren't full.   40

I've got these kids to prove that story.
When they whine, I tell them: climb a hill.

RONDEL

A beautiful snow falls on a bed,
Amazing the man and woman there.
It falls between and over them where
Just before they lay close and naked.

They wonder if anything they said
Or did called down so cold through the air
This beautiful snow onto their bed
To amaze any who would love there;

They wonder if snowmen can be wed,
And if white is what they'll always wear,   10
And if lovers should sing or shiver
As they watch fall the uninvited
And beautiful snow onto their bed.

it has a hollow quality, [handwritten]

don't use the word beautiful [handwritten]

Glover Davis

Glover Davis was born in San Luis Obispo, California, in 1939. He holds degrees from California State University at Fresno and the University of Iowa. He has published two collections of poetry, Bandaging Bread *(1970)* and August Fires *(1978), and has recently completed a third,* Legend. *He teaches at San Diego State University.*

LOST MOMENTS

There is a darkness, dark
as a tunnel where a boat
rocks and its oarlocks creak
as chills settle in your throat.
If you can see the faint
pulse of a cigarette
or hear the murmuring plaint
of voices you might regret
lost moments in a shaft
of light that set the roses   10
trembling. Perhaps you laughed
at what the light imposes
on petals or your skin.
You smoked watching the pond
glaze gold and then went in.
Though dreams or darkness spawned
this place, it is no different
from the garden if you think
of your end, and of a current
through time you cannot blink   20
away as though it were
a lightless dream. It drifts
its deckled light through a pure
air. It leads and lifts
unless you think that this
tunnel of love is all
there is, then waters hiss
beneath the blades and oil
glistens on the crushed cups
and papers floating by.   30

THE BURIAL

The birds have stripped
the fig tree.
The fruit is ripped

and the bees
are hovering near
the loose skin.
I try to scare
birds with tin
can lids I string
like flashing   10
necklaces. A wing
beats a leaf
blue and the jays
erupt
through the leaf maze
but high up
where crown leaves
take   `
the sun, hawk
in a lake   20
of light, green sways.
Mockingbird
dives and red
from the blurred
feathers spreads
where the hawk climbs.
I remember
a curved beak
a black ember
for an eye   30
how the mate
would circle and cry
as I fit
the other
in a box.
When a shut
lid knocks
beneath my thumbs
and the dirt
rains down and numbs   40
my mind
I awake to find
my heart pumps
like a wing without air.

Peter Davison

Born in New York City in 1928, raised in Colorado, and educated at Harvard and Cambridge, Peter Davison has been an editor in book publishing houses since 1950. His books include The Breaking of the Day *(1964), which won the Yale Younger Poets Prize, and* Praying Wrong: New and Selected Poems 1957–1984 *(1985). He has for many years been the director of Atlantic Monthly Press and poetry editor of* The Atlantic.

THE COMPOUND EYE

For L. E. Sissman, 1928–1976

What an intolerable deal of history!
You were the fly upon a thousand walls,
the poet's eye with many hundred lenses,
master of every curiosity.
Marked down for death, nipped early at the heels,
you walked with shambling evasion, not in a hurry,
too proud to betray the merest smudge of panic.
Yet in your poems death lies never far
from the surface, knife beneath the water,
dark age pending. To stay alive for it   10
tubers and relics of each season's growth
must be tucked into order, time, and place.
Familiar phrases bowed beneath strange burdens
("a pleasure dome of Klees and Watteaus made"),
pleasures of a couplet coupled with
the nausea of chemotherapy.

Amid the disorder of illness, dying, death,
you put in order your arrested life.

Go, prince: peer owlish through the windowpane
betwixt the daintiness of your imagination   20
and all the tawdriness and disarray
our life is dressed in. From the postwar city
look out at the city of God, and then confess
how sweet was the disorder in the dress.

James Dickey

*Born in Atlanta, Georgia, in 1923 and educated at Vanderbilt, where he
was a star athlete, James Dickey served as a night fighter pilot in World War
II and the Korean War and worked as an advertising executive in Atlanta
and New York. He was awarded the National Book Award in 1966 for*
Buckdancer's Choice. *Among his other collections of verse are* Poems,
1957–1967 *(1967),* The Zodiac *(1976),* The Strength of Fields
(1979), and Puella *(1981). He is also the author of the best-selling novel*
Deliverance *(1970) and two volumes of criticism,* The Suspect in Poetry
(1964) and Babel to Byzantium *(1968). Currently he is writer-in-
residence at the University of South Carolina.*

ON THE HILL BELOW THE LIGHTHOUSE

Now I can be sure of my sleep;
I have lost the blue sea in my eyelids.
From a place in the mind too deep
For thought, a light like a wind is beginning.
   Now I can be sure of my sleep.

When the moon is held strongly within it,
The eye of the mind opens gladly.
Day changes to dark, and is bright,
And miracles trust to the body,
  When the moon is held strongly within it.   10

A woman comes true when I think her.
Her eyes on the window are closing.
She has dressed the stark wood of a chair.
Her form and my body are facing.
  A woman comes true when I think her.

Shade swings, and she lies against me.
The lighthouse has opened its brain.
A browed light travels the sea.
Her clothes on the chair spread their wings.
  Shade swings, and she lies against me.   20

Let us lie in returning light,
As a bright arm sweeps through the moon.
The sun is dead, thinking of night
Swung round like a thing on a chain.
  Let us lie in returning light.

Let us lie where your angel is walking
In shadow, from wall onto wall,
Cast forth from your off-cast clothing
To pace the dim room where we fell.
  Let us lie where your angel is walking,   30

Coming back, coming back, going over.
An arm turns the light world around
The dark. Again we are waiting to hover
In a blaze in the mind like a wind
  Coming back, coming back, going over.

  Now I can be sure of my sleep;
  The moon is held strongly within it.
  A woman comes true when I think her.

Shade swings, and she lies against me.
Let us lie in returning light; 40
Let us lie where your angel is walking,
Coming back, coming back, going over.

THE ISLAND

A light come from my head
Showed how to give birth to the dead
That they might nourish me.
In a wink of the blinding sea
I woke through the eyes, and beheld
No change, but what had been,
And what cannot be seen
Any place but a burnt-out war:
The engines, the wheels, and the gear
That bring good men to their backs 10
Nailed down into wooden blocks,
With the sun on their faces through sand,
And polyps a-building the land
Around them of senseless stone.
The coral and I understood
That these could come to no good
Without the care I could give,
And that I, by them, must live.
I clasped every thought in my head
That bloomed from the magical dead, 20
And seizing a shovel and rake,
Went out by the ocean to take
My own sweet time, and start
To set a dead army apart.
I hammered the coffins together
Of patience and hobnails and lumber,
And gave them names, and hacked
Deep holes where they were stacked.
Each wooden body, I took
In my arms, and singingly shook 30
With its being, which stood for my own
More and more, as I laid it down.

At the grave's crude, dazzling verge
My true self strained to emerge
From all they could not save
And did not know they could give.
I buried them where they lay
In the brass-bound heat of the day,
A whole army lying down
In animal-lifted sand.   40
And then with rake and spade
I curried each place I had stood
On their chests and on their faces,
And planted the rows of crosses
Inside the blue wind of the shore.
I hauled more wood to that ground
And a white fence put around
The soldiers lying in waves
In my life-giving graves.
And a painless joy came to me   50
When the troopships took to the sea,
And left the changed stone free
Of all but my image and me:
Of the tonsured and perilous green
With its great, delighted design
Of utter finality,
Whose glowing workman stood
In the intricate, knee-high wood
In the midst of the sea's blind leagues,
Kicked off his old fatigues,   60
Saluted the graves by their rank,
Paraded, lamented, and sank
Into the intelligent light,
And danced, unimagined and free,
Like the sun taking place on the sea.

BREATH

    Breath is on my face when the cloudy sun
        Is on my neck.
By it, the dangers of water are carefully
        Kept; kept back:

This is done with your father again
          In memory, it says.
Let me kneel on the boards of the rowboat,
          Father, where it sways

          Among the fins and shovel heads
                    Of surfaced sharks   10
And remember how I saw come shaping up
          Through lightening darks

          Of the bay another thing that rose
                    From the depths on air
And opened the green of its skull to breathe
          What we breathed there.

          A porpoise circled around where I
                    Lay in your hands
And felt my fear apportioned to the sharks,
          Which fell to sands   20

          Two hundred feet down within cold.
                    Looking over the side,
I saw that beak rise up beneath my face
          And a hole in the head

          Open greenly, and then show living pink,
                    And breath come out
In a mild, unhurried, unfathomable sigh
          That raised the boat

          And left us all but singing in midair.
                    Have you not seen,   30
Father, in Heaven, the eye of earthly things
          Open and breathe green,

          Bestowing comfort on the mortal soul
                    In deadly doubt,
Sustaining the spirit moving on the waters
          In hopeless light?

We arched and plunged with that beast to land.
    Amazing, that unsealed lung
Come up from the dark; that breath, controlled,
    Greater than song,   40

    That huge body raised from the sea
        Secretly smiling
And shaped by the air it had carried
    Through the stark sailing

    And changeless ignorance of brutes,
        So that a dream
Began in my closed head, of the curves and rolling
    Powers of seraphim,

    That lift the good man's coffin on their breath
        And bear it up,   50
A rowboat, from the sons' depleting grief
    That will not stop:

    Those that hide within time till the time
        Is wholly right,
Then come to us slowly, out of nowhere and anywhere
    risen,
        Breathlessly bright.

Thomas M. Disch

Thomas M. Disch was born in 1940 in Des Moines, Iowa, and "incarcerated till age 17 in various schools throughout Minnesota and educated at the public library." Besides numerous novels and collections of short stories, he has published three collections of poetry: The Right Way to Figure

Plumbing *(1972)*, Burn This *(1982)*, *and* Here I Am, There You Are, Where Were We *(1984)*, *which was a Poetry Book Society Choice in England. He lives in New York City.*

THE RAPIST'S VILLANELLE

She spent her money with such perfect style
The clerks would gasp at each new thing she'd choose.
I couldn't help myself—I had to smile

Or burst. Her slender purse was crocodile,
Her blouse was from Bendel's, as were her shoes.
She spent her money with such perfect style!

I loved her so! She shopped—and all the while
My soul that bustling image would perfuse.
I couldn't help myself: I had to smile

At her hand-knitted sweater from the Isle   10
Of Skye, at après-skis of bold chartreuse.
She spent her money with such perfect style.

Enchanted by her, mile on weary mile
I tracked my darling down the avenues.
I couldn't help myself. I had to smile

At how she never once surmised my guile.
My heart was hers—I'd nothing else to lose.
She spent her money with such perfect style
I couldn't help myself. I had to smile.

Alan Dugan

Alan Dugan was born in Brooklyn in 1923 and educated at Mexico City College. His first book, Poems, *won the 1961 Yale Younger Poets Prize and the 1962 National Book Award and Pulitzer Prize. His most recent book is* New and Collected Poems, 1961–1983 *(1984). In 1983 he received the Shelley Memorial Award, and in 1984 the Melville Cane Award. Noting Dugan's characteristic stoicism and cynicism, David Wojahn has said, "He carries sentiment the way that some women carry cans of Mace in their purses—it's only for use in times of duress, and even then he suspects that it won't be of much use." Nevertheless, Wojahn concludes, "he remains one of the most humane and genuinely comic American poets alive."*

ELEGY FOR A PURITAN CONSCIENCE

I closed my ears with stinging bugs
and sewed my eyelids shut
but heard a sucking at the dugs
and saw my parents rut.

I locked my jaw with rusty nails
and cured my tongue in lime
but ate and drank in garbage pails
and said these words of crime.

I crushed my scrotum with two stones
and drew my penis in   10
but felt your wound expect its own
and fell in love with sin.

POEM

What's the balm
for a dying life,
dope, drink, or Christ,
is there one?

I puke and choke
with it and find
no peace of mind
in flesh, and no hope.

It flows away
in mucous juice.   10
Nothing I can do
can make it stay,

so I give out
and water the garden: it
is all shit
for the flowers anyhow.

Stephen Dunn

Stephen Dunn was born in Forest Hills, New York, in 1939 and attended Hofstra University, the New School for Social Research, and Syracuse University. The recipient of two National Endowment for the Arts Fellowships and a Guggenheim Fellowship, he has published five collections of poetry, including A Circus of Needs *(1978),* Work and Love *(1981), and* Not Dancing *(1984). His sixth book,* Local Time, *won the National Poetry Series Open Competition and will be published in 1986. A former professional basketball player, he has taught at Columbia and the University of Washington and currently teaches at Stockton State College in Pomona, New Jersey.*

TANGIER

There's no salvation in elsewhere;
forget the horizon, the seductive sky.
If nothing's here, nothing's there.

I know. Once I escaped to Tangier,
took the same face, the same lie.
There's no salvation in elsewhere

when elsewhere has empty rooms, mirrors.
Everywhere: the capital I.
If nothing's here, nothing's there

unless, of course, your motive's secure;   10
not therapy, but joy,
salvation an idea left behind, elsewhere,

like overweight baggage or yesteryear.
The fundamental things apply.
If nothing's here, nothing's there—

I brought with me my own imperfect air.
The streets were noise. The heart dry.
There was no salvation elsewhere.
I came with nothing, found nothing there.

John Engels

John Engels was born in South Bend, Indiana, in 1931. A graduate of Notre Dame and the University of Iowa, he is the author of six collections of poetry, among them Weather-Fear: New & Selected Poems, 1958– 1982 *(1983) and* The Seasons in Vermont *(1983). He has held Gug-*

genheim and National Endowment for the Arts Fellowships and won two Pushcart Prizes and New England Review*'s Narrative Poetry Prize. He lives in North Williston, Vermont, and teaches at St. Michael's College.*

THE HOMER MITCHELL PLACE

The mountains carry snow, the season fails;
Jackstraw clapboard shivers on its nails,
The freezing air blows maple leaves and dust,
A thousand nails bleed laceries of rust,
Slates crack and slide away, the gutters sprout;
I wonder do a dead man's bones come out

Like these old lintels and wasp-riddled beams?
I ask in simple consequence of structure seen
In this old house, grown sturdy in its fall,
The brace and bone of it come clear of all   10
I took for substance, what I could not prove
From any measure of design or love.

Or is it rather that he falls away
To no articulation but decay,
However brightly leap the brass-hinged bone,
Beam and rafter, joist and cellar-stone?

Frederick Feirstein

Born in New York City in 1940, Frederick Feirstein was educated at the University of Buffalo, New York University, and the National Psychological Association for Psychoanalysis. His books include The Family Circle *(1973), a play, and three collections of poetry:* Survivors *(1976),* Manhattan Carnival *(1981), and* Fathering *(1982). Among his awards and honors are a Guggenheim Fellowship and the John Masefield Award. He lives in New York City and is a practicing psychotherapist.*

L'ART

Your clothes a dark pink heap, a dimming sky,
I bite the inside of your mocha thigh:
Matisse preferred to paint this scene, not I.

George Garrett

Born in 1929 in Orlando, Florida, and educated at Columbia and Princeton, George Garrett has written novels, short stories, and screenplays as well as poems. His many books include Collected Poems *(1984) and the novels* Death of a Fox *(1971) and* The Succession *(1983). The recipient of the Prix de Rome, a Ford Foundation grant, a Guggenheim Fellowship, and numerous other awards, he is currently director of the graduate program in creative writing at the University of Virginia.*

TIRESIAS

Speak to us who
are also split.
Speak to the two
we love and hate.

You have been both
and you have known
the double truth
as, chaste, obscene,

you were the lover
and the loved.   10
You were the giver
who received.

Now tell us how
we can be one
another too.
Speak to us who

in single wrath
cannot be true
to life or death.
Blinder than you.   20

Gary Gildner

*Gary Gildner was born in northern Michigan in 1938 and educated at
Michigan State University. He has published five collections of poetry, most
recently* Blue Like the Heavens: New and Selected Poems *(1984).*
The Crush, *his collection of short stories, appeared in 1983. A former
poet-in-residence at Reed College, he currently teaches at Drake University.*

MEETING MY BEST FRIEND FROM THE EIGHTH GRADE

He says when he comes in a bar
after beating Wyoming, say,
there's something like fur in the air
and people don't see him, they see a bear.

My best friend from the eighth grade is a coach.
He wants to Go Go Go Go—
He wants to Get There!—and gives me a punch.
His wife, in lime slacks, curls on the couch.

I ask him where
and thinking it over he pounds his palm; his eyes stare.   10
His wife passes peanuts, teases
his touchy hair.

He says never mind
and changes the subject to button-hooks, quick dives
—old numbers in our pimples we were famous for.
Nineteen years go by; he calls it a crime.

His wife cracks two more Buds, stretches, calls it
a night; we hear the door click.
Flushed, he flicks on the television . . .
We bend our beer cans like dummies, and sit.   20

From LETTERS FROM VICKSBURG

XII

Dear wife and bosom friend I hat seen hart
sites before I ever saw a battel
field   at Edwarts station hospitel
I fount out what it was to see a hert
the one that makes me dry hat lost his tong
the ball past thro his teeth and cut it off
and made his eyes and everything look rong
but heare theres times with the secesh thats grate
we dont shoot at them after dark and they
of corse dont shoot at us   the moon shines so   10
that we can see each other plain as day
we hav the right to go half ways acrost
and they can come half ways acrost to us
we leave our arms and some come cleare acrost

Allen Ginsberg

A leading figure in the Beat Movement and the San Francisco Renaissance, Allen Ginsberg was born in Newark, New Jersey, in 1926, the son of Naomi and lyric poet Louis Ginsberg. He attended Columbia University and worked as a laborer, sailor, and market analyst before publishing Howl and Other Poems *(1956), which overcame censorship trials to become one of the most widely read and translated books of the century. In 1965 he was crowned King of the Prague May Day festival and then expelled from Czechoslovakia. A political activist who has been on the FBI's list of security risks, he won the 1974 National Book Award for* The Fall of America. *His* Collected Poems *appeared in 1985 and an album of his songs,* First Blues, *was released in 1981. He lives on New York City's Lower East Side and teaches during the summer at the Naropa Institute in Colorado.*

From DON'T GROW OLD

FATHER DEATH BLUES

Hey Father Death, I'm flying home
Hey poor man, you're all alone
Hey old daddy, I know where I'm going

Father Death, Don't cry any more
Mama's there, underneath the floor
Brother Death, please mind the store

Old Aunty Death   Don't hide your bones
Old Uncle Death   I hear your groans
O Sister Death   how sweet your moans

O Children Deaths go breathe your breaths   10
Sobbing breasts'll ease your Deaths
Pain is gone, tears take the rest

Genius Death   your art is done
Lover Death your body's gone
Father Death   I'm coming home

Guru Death your words are true
Teacher Death I do thank you
For inspiring me to sing this Blues

Buddha Death, I wake with you
Dharma Death, your mind is true   20
Sangha Death, we'll work it through

Suffering is what was born
Ignorance made me forlorn
Tearful truths I cannot scorn

Father Breath once more farewell
Birth you gave was no thing ill
My heart is still, as time will tell.

July 8, 1976 (over Lake Michigan)

Louise Glück

Louise Glück was born in New York City in 1943 and raised on Long Island. She studied at Sarah Lawrence and Columbia. Her three collections are Firstborn *(1968),* The House on Marshland *(1975), and* Descending Figure *(1980). The recipient of grants from the Guggenheim*

Foundation, the Rockefeller Foundation, and the National Endowment for the Arts, she lives with her husband and son in Plainfield, Vermont, and teaches at Williams College.

BRIDAL PIECE

Our honeymoon
He planted us by
Water. It was March. The moon
Lurched like searchlights, like
His murmurings across my brain—
He had to have his way. As down
The beach the wet wind
Snored . . . I want
My innocence. I see
My family frozen in the doorway   10
Now, unchanged, unchanged. Their rice congeals
Around his car. He locked our bedroll
In the trunk for laughs, later, at the deep
End. Rockaway. He reaches for me in his sleep.

THE RACER'S WIDOW

The elements have merged into solicitude.
Spasms of violets rise above the mud
And weed and soon the birds and ancients
Will be starting to arrive, bereaving points
South. But never mind. It is not painful to discuss
His death. I have been primed for this,
For separation, for so long. But still his face assaults
Me, I can hear that car career again, the crowd coagulate
    on asphalt
In my sleep. And watching him, I feel my legs like snow
That let him finally let him go   10
As he lies draining there. And see
How even he did not get to keep that lovely body.

PHENOMENAL SURVIVALS OF DEATH IN NANTUCKET

I

Here in Nantucket does the tiny soul
Confront water. Yet this element is not foreign soil;
I see the water as extension of my mind,
The troubled part, and waves the waves of mind
When in Nantucket they collapsed in epilepsy
On the bare shore. I see
A shawled figure when I am asleep who says, "Our lives
Are strands between the miracles of birth
And death. I am Saint Elizabeth.
In my basket are knives."   10
Awake I see Nantucket, the familiar earth.

II

Awake I see Nantucket but with this bell
Of voice I can toll you token of regions below visible:
On the third night came
A hurricane; my Saint Elizabeth came
Not and nothing could prevent the rent
Craft from its determined end. Waves dent-
ed with lightning launched my loosed mast
To fly downward, I following. They do not tell
You but bones turned coral still smell   20
Amid forsaken treasure. I have been past
What you hear in a shell.

III

Past what you hear in a shell, the roar,
Is the true bottom: infamous calm. The doctor
Having shut the door sat me down, took ropes
Out of reach, firearms, and with high hopes

Promised that Saint Elizabeth carried
Only foodstuffs or some flowers for charity, nor was I
    buried
Under the vacation island of Nantucket where
Beach animals dwell in relative compatibility and peace.   30
Flies, snails. Asleep I saw these
Beings as complacent angels of the land and air.
When dawn comes to the sea's

                                IV

Acres of shining white body in Nantucket
I shall not remember otherwise but wear a locket
With my lover's hair inside
And walk like a bride, and wear him inside.
From these shallows expands
The mercy of the sea.
My first house shall be built on these sands,   40
My second in the sea.

Patricia Goedicke

Patricia Goedicke was born in Boston in 1931, raised in New Hampshire, and educated at Middlebury College and Ohio University. The recipient of the William Carlos Williams Award and other honors, she is the author of six collections, most recently The Trail that Turns on Itself *(1978),* The Dog that Was Barking Yesterday *(1980),* Crossing the Same River *(1980), and* The Wind of Our Going *(1985). A long-time resident of San Miguel de Allende in Mexico, she now lives in Missoula with her husband, writer Leonard Robinson, and teaches at the University of Montana.*

WISE OWL

An old black bird on a strand of silk,
Sidewise my father walks the white ice
Between two fields of snow.
It is night. The air is like thin milk,
Icicles click in the wind like dice,
His steps are crabbed and slow,

But dapper as a magpie with a game leg
The old brave gambler bets his hide
Against the glittering street,
Though the moon is a bright metallic egg,   10
The cold snaps at his twisted side,
And the snow flusters his feet.

Beside him the languorous featherbed fields
Dovecall comfort to the old crow:
If he would stop he would stay,
Lose and find himself softly concealed,
Sunk in the mothering mounded snow,
Nested the easiest way

But no. Not for this wise owl. The road
May dwindle away to an icy thread   20
But the dream of a new design
Mumbles and broods in his hunched head
Better luck next time, the gambler's goad
That keeps him along the lifeline.

So like a sparrow on a telephone wire
He balances down the tightrope track,
The road that must narrow as the night
Must finally constrict the flow of fire,
Harden, pinch the heart, and crack:
Ahead is the home light.   30

Albert Goldbarth

Albert Goldbarth was born in Chicago in 1948 and educated at the University of Illinois and the University of Iowa. Among his awards are two National Endowment for the Arts grants, a Guggenheim Fellowship, and the Jacob Glatstein Prize from Poetry. *His fifteen books include* January 31 *(1974), which was nominated for the National Book Award, and* Original Light: New & Selected Poems 1973–1983 *(1983). A new book,* Art & Sciences, *is scheduled for publication in 1986. He lives in Austin, where he teaches at the University of Texas.*

JOE GILLON HYPNOTIZES HIS SON

For my father

When you wake up, in your fourteenth year,
I'm forty, the attrition of a muscle fibre
in me will (*energy cannot be* etc.) appear
in you as a new flex. You'll write vers libre,
none of this constraint, hold what molests
you in your palm, swill whole decanters.
You'll understand the jokes about women's breasts
had something reverential at their centers.
A distance, thin as silver foil, will hiss
once, hover, then drop in the slot between us.   10
Now: how I dandle you, wipe the comma of piss
where it collects at your rim, promise you're a genus
better than I was, my cribside pace, my kiss . . .
You won't remember any of this.

THE PSYCHONAUT SONNETS: JONES

We sent him to one-with
a bull, he came back gibbering myth
and statistics on swans. Swans!
The medforce is puzzled: Jones
was a good mind-hopper. And there *is*
some connection. The goddess Nemesis's
annual solar revolving signaled a king
killed, literal or effigiate offering
to Neolithic Europe's spring crop; this
parallels a rebirth-cow/bull elsewhere, and Nemesis   10
is the deified function of the Grecian mortal
Leda—as Zeus came in a bull
to Europa, he took Leda with down
and pinion framing his lust; it is known

they thought the migratory v a pudenda symbol.
So: the transcendent incarnate, bull
and swan both. It's our only possible clue
to his mystic babbling. The technology is new
and mind-hoppers before him have slipped
in error but—well, listen to the transcript: 20

*

This is Jones. I've consolidated one-with in
the mind of a beef bull snorting its stockyard pen
virulent and damp, and am firmly in the Us
Stage. It would seem the bovine gregarious
principle applies—that is, a Jungian
shared knowledge fills this hardwood pen
with something like sense of history and future
re cattle, the fetus's first light, and the shadow of the
     butcher,

halve this brain like the moon: lit/dark. And
there is a swan in this bull. Please understand   30
I know this is not the kind of reportage
expected of me. But beating in this ribcage
is a swan—not a corporeal swan, but

the *presence* of swan, like the psychonaut
presence of me, Jones. I know I will live
through morning, then shit full five
percent of my body weight in fear, and fall
to the hammer. It is a fear like muscle
reflex. I can feel individual blood cells carom
wildly through brain; through *brain*. But the *mind* is calm   40
beneath that. The ancient Egyptians depicted souls
as winged—I now share in their Holy Apis-bull's

lore—and I think this spectre-swan in 1300
bellowing lbs. of beef says though I will be bled
to death, there is, in molecular bonding,
an impetus that will take wing
and continue. I realize that I give
something far removed from the quantitative
analysis I trained for. So: the floor is brick
that slipping won't damage my hide. There is a saltlick,   50
water, and a good night's rest,
that my heart pump normally after my tryst
with exsanguination, and empty me quick
and smooth. I will be slit through the dewlap, the stick
hole will pour, and my eyes will transmit heart
color for a moment, like light through Chartres

rose glass. And the swan, white
and yet invisible, like a leucocyte
in the red flow, will find release.
It was the bullock, of course, in Homeric Greece   60
that died each year in the king's stead, but
the swans that guided the chariot
his soul rode. Flesh and spirit share that root.
But, again, I know I disappoint the Institute,
so persevere: my electrocardiac index reads point.four
on the Lichtenstein scale. The killing floor
is a long, methodical, unfastening of layers
down to the viscera, those snot-jellied wares
destined for oleo. The head is cut free from the carcass
then hung by the trachea and esophagus   70

to prevent soiling of the head by the stomach
slops. Then they will saw the thick

altar of breastbone from its rib cathedral,
chisel cheek meat from jaw, and freeze. The smell
of it turns in my snout as hard as a lathe.
I request return from this one-with
immediately. I ask this with the living five.point.six
lb. tongue of a bull—an entire male Bewick's
Swan, or Whistling Swan, weighs as much. Metaphysics
may seem to you misplaced here, but is not. Two flicks   80
of the hatchet, the tongue-bone is severed. The tongue
is hand-washed, hooked, and hung
to drain. I can feel it swell. Return me: urgent! Each rung
on the drainrack trumpets swansong, swansong

Barbara L. Greenberg

*Barbara L. Greenberg was born in Boston in 1932. A graduate of Wellesley
and Simmons College, she writes fiction and drama as well as poetry. Among
her books are* The Spoils of August: Poems *(1974) and* Fire Drills:
Stories *(1982). She lives in Newton, Massachusetts.*

THE FAITHFUL WIFE

But if I *were* to have a lover, it would be someone
who could take nothing from you. I would, in conscience,
not dishonor you. He and I would eat at Howard Johnson's

which you and I do not enjoy. With him I would go
fishing because it is not your sport. He would wear blue

which is your worst color; he would have none of your
    virtues.

Not strong, not proud, not just, not provident, my lover
would blame me for his heart's distress, which you would
    never
think to do. He and I would drink too much and weep
    together

and I would bruise his face as I would not bruise your face   10
even in my dreams. Yes I would dance with him, but to a
    music
you and I would never choose to hear, and in a place

where you and I would never wish to be. He and I would
    speak
Spanish, which is not your tongue, and we would take
long walks in fields of burdock, to which you are allergic.

We would make love only in the morning. It would be
altogether different. I would know him with my other
    body,
the one that you have never asked to see.

Marilyn Hacker

*Born in New York City in 1942, Marilyn Hacker studied at Washington
Square College of New York University and the Art Students League. She
has lived in New York, Mexico City, San Francisco, and London, and
worked as a teacher, mail sorter, editor for a men's magazine, and an
antiquarian bookseller. Her first book,* Presentation Piece *(1974), which
employs a wide variety of traditional forms, won both the Lamont Prize and
the National Book Award. Subsequent books are* Separations *(1976),*

Taking Notice *(1980), and* Assumptions *(1985). She lives in Manhattan with her daughter, Iva, and edits* Thirteenth Moon, *a feminist literary journal.*

VILLANELLE

For D.G.B.

Every day our bodies separate,
exploded torn and dazed.
Not understanding what we celebrate

we grope through languages and hesitate
and touch each other, speechless and amazed;
and every day our bodies separate

us farther from our planned, deliberate
ironic lives. I am afraid, disphased,
not understanding what we celebrate

when our fused limbs and lips communicate   10
the unlettered power we have raised.
Every day our bodies' separate

routines are harder to perpetuate.
In wordless darkness we learn wordless praise,
not understanding what we celebrate;

wake to ourselves, exhausted, in the late
morning as the wind tears off the haze,
not understanding how we celebrate
our bodies. Every day we separate.

CANZONE

Consider the three functions of the tongue:
taste, speech, the telegraphy of pleasure,
are not confused in any human tongue;
yet, sinewy and singular, the tongue

accomplishes what, perhaps, no other organ
can. Were I to speak of giving tongue,
you'd think two things at least; and a cooked tongue,
sliced, on a plate, with caper sauce, which I give
my guest for lunch, is one more, to which she'd give
the careful concentration of her tongue   10
twice over, to appreciate the taste
and to express—it would be in good taste—

a gastronomic memory the taste
called to mind, and mind brought back to tongue.
There is a paucity of words for taste:
sweet, sour, bitter, salty. Any taste,
however multiplicitous its pleasure,
complex its execution (I might taste
that sauce ten times in cooking, change its taste
with herbal subtleties, chromatic organ   20
tones of clove and basil, good with organ
meats) must be described with those few taste-
words, or with metaphors, to give
my version of sensations it would give

a neophyte, deciding whether to give
it a try. She might develop a taste.
(You try things once; I think you have to give
two chances, though, to know your mind, or give
up on novelties.) Your mother tongue
nurtures, has the subtleties which give   30
flavor to words, and words to flavor, give
the by no means subsidiary pleasure
of being able to describe a pleasure
and recreate it. Making words, we give
the private contemplations of each organ
to the others, and to others, organ-

ize sensations into thoughts. Sentient organ-
isms, we symbolize feeling, give
the spectrum (that's a symbol) each sense organ
perceives, by analogy, to others. Disorgan-   40
ization of the senses is an acquired taste
we all acquire; as speaking beasts, it's organ-

ic to our discourse. The first organ
of acknowledged communion is the tongue
(tripartite diplomat, which after tongu-
ing a less voluble expressive organ
to wordless efflorescences of pleasure
offers up words to reaffirm the pleasure).

That's a primary difficulty: pleasure
means something, and something different, for each organ;   50
each person, too. I may take exquisite pleasure
in boiled eel, or blancmange—or not. One pleasure
of language is making known what not to give.
And think of a bar of lavender soap, a pleasure
to see and, moistened, rub on your skin, a pleasure
especially to smell, but if you taste
it (though smell is most akin to taste)
what you experience will not be pleasure;
you almost retch, grimace, stick out your tongue,
slosh rinses of ice water over your tongue.   60

But I would rather think about your tongue
experiencing and transmitting pleasure
to one or another multi-sensual organ
—like memory. Whoever wants to give
only one meaning to that, has untutored taste.

RONDEAU AFTER A TRANSATLANTIC
TELEPHONE CALL

Love, it was good to talk to you tonight.
You lather me like summer though. I light
up, sip smoke. Insistent through walls comes
the downstairs neighbor's double-bass. It thrums
like toothache. I will shower away the sweat,

smoke, summer, sound. Slick, soapy, dripping wet,
I scrub the sharp edge off my appetite.
I want: crisp toast, cold wine prickling my gums,
love. It was good

imagining around your voice, you, late-   10
awake there. (It isn't midnight yet
here.) This last glass washes down the crumbs.
I wish that I could lie down in your arms
and, turned toward sleep there (later), say, "Goodnight,
love. It was good."

SONNET ENDING WITH A FILM SUBTITLE

For Judith Landry

Life has its nauseating ironies:
The good die young, as often has been shown;
Chaste spouses catch Venereal Disease;
And feminists sit by the telephone.
Last night was rather bleak, tonight is starker.
I may stare at the wall till half-past-one.
My friends are all convinced Dorothy Parker
Lives, but is not well, in Marylebone.
I wish that I could imitate my betters
And fortify my rhetoric with guns.   10
Some day we women all will break our fetters
And raise our daughters to be Lesbians.
(I wonder if the bastard kept my letters?)
Here follow untranslatable French puns.

Donald Hall

Born in 1928 in New Haven, Connecticut, and educated at Harvard, Oxford, and Stanford, Donald Hall has received the Lamont Prize, a Guggenheim Fellowship, and other awards for his work. Among his books of poetry are The Alligator Bride: Poems New and Selected *(1969),*

The Town of Hill *(1975), and* Kicking the Leaves *(1978). His other
works include* Henry Moore: The Life and Work of a Great Sculptor
(1966), Remembering Poets *(1978), a memoir of Pound, Eliot, Frost,
and Dylan Thomas, and numerous anthologies and textbooks. After teaching
for ten years at the University of Michigan, he resigned to devote himself
full-time to writing poems, essays, stories, plays, reviews, and textbooks. He
now lives at Eagle Pond Farm near Danbury, New Hampshire, with his
wife, the poet Jane Kenyon.*

MY SON, MY EXECUTIONER

My son, my executioner,
 I take you in my arms,
Quiet and small and just astir,
 And whom my body warms.

Sweet death, small son, our instrument
 Of immortality,
Your cries and hungers document
 Our bodily decay.

We twenty-five and twenty-two,
 Who seemed to live forever,   10
Observe enduring life in you
 And start to die together.

THE LONG RIVER

The musk-ox smells
in his long head
my boat coming. When
I feel him there,
intent, heavy,

the oars make wings
in the white night,
and deep woods are close

on either side
where trees darken.   10

I rowed past towns
in their black sleep
to come here. I rowed
by northern grass
and cold mountains.

The musk-ox moves
when the boat stops,
in hard thickets. Now
the wood is dark
with old pleasures.   20

Mark Halperin

*Mark Halperin was born in New York City in 1940 and is a graduate
of Bard College and the University of Iowa. His first book,* Backroads, *was
published in 1976 and won the U.S. Award of the International Poetry
Forum, and his second book,* A Place Made Fast, *appeared in 1982. He
lives outside Ellensburg, Washington, and teaches at Central Washington
State College.*

JOHN CLARE

Sometimes there is a man—
I never feel him come,
but he is who I am
and I am someone.

He does not care to stay.
If we are both John Clare
why does he go away?
and where? and where?

Edward Harkness

Edward Harkness was born in Bremerton, Washington, in 1947 and grew up in Seattle. He earned a B.A. from the University of Washington and an M.F.A. from the University of Montana. He has published two collections, Long Eye Lost Wind Forgive Me *(1975) and* Fiddle Wrapped in a Gunny Sack *(1984). He lives in Seattle and teaches at Shoreline Community College.*

THE MAN IN THE RECREATION ROOM

The man in the recreation room is screaming
again. From season to graveside the moon turns blue.
How unhappy. How his mind moves dreaming

something blue with passion: three wings combing
space beyond a valley. What a view!
The man in the recreation room is screaming.

His hands have a mind of their own. He's palming
a gravestone. The moon has nothing to do.
How unhappy. How his mind moves dreaming

beyond a blue valley. His wings are flaming.   10
He's afraid his plans have fallen through,
the man in the recreation room screaming.

Past apples another starlight tries claiming
his eyesight. Lilacs die. All untrue.
How unhappy now? His mind moves dreaming

his hands slowly become his feet. The humming
in his head grows beautiful. Just for you
the man in the recreation room is screaming.
How unhappy. How his mind moves dreaming.

Charles O. Hartman

Born in Iowa City in 1949, Charles O. Hartman earned his A.B. at Harvard and his M.A. and Ph.D. at Washington University. He is the author of two poetry collections, Gravitation *(1982) and* The Pigfoot Rebellion *(1982), and a critical study,* Free Verse: An Essay on Prosody *(1980). He lives in Providence, Rhode Island, where he has recently finished* Downfall of the Straight Line, *a new collection of poems, and is working on a book about voice and improvisation in poetry, jazz, and song.*

DOUBLE MOCK SONNET

The locked lagoon is ice, the lake beyond
A mist, hypothesis. Between the pond
I see and the hard line where seeing stops,
A little strip of gray land strewn with props

Of the Hard Winter existential scene
We love to watch ourselves in for the mean
Comfort of claiming nothing left to lose—
The trees the lake's cold blusters disabuse
Of leaves, the stalks of grass pummeled to stubble—
Nevertheless bears up this load of trouble   10
Like any stupid beast. A species of
Nobility: subsume, subsume. As love
And life of dung and death, so we partake
Of both the frigid pond and the guessed lake.

A moment ago this stage was perfect, bare,
Inspiring like a Hardy heath, despair
The catchword of the landscape's monologue
(Soliloquy, I mean). Now there's a dog.
Though almost thin and low and nondescript
Enough to fit my fine pet of a script,   20
He's making too much noise. His barks assail
The silence, lake, trees, seagulls, his own tail,
Whatever. Single-voiced, he's nearly raised
An echo from the mist that hangs amazed.
However he affronts my counterfeit
Drama, he gets my thanks for making it
(Amid this wind-swept, sullen antonym)
Unnecessary to imagine him.

A LITTLE SONG

She beyond all others in deepest dreams comes
back. You shun sleep, lying in darkness, breath held,
hearing that voice over the rustling dry grass
        breathing in darkness.

Walk for miles each day, with a dog to watch, pen,
paper, ink, try, focus attention somewhere
else. But Mi, Sol, Re go the notes her voice slips
        into your blind heart.

Once you knew each inch of her body. No more.
Only one thing, caught in your faithful ear, still   10
lives. Your eyes lie. Even in dreams the face fades.
        Only a singing.

She's your cane these days. When you tap, she tells how
far you've strayed. Tap trees by the road, you hear how
hollow things are. Listen. You'll hear in high limbs
        voices of dry leaves.

William Hathaway

*Born in Madison, Wisconsin, in 1944 and raised in Ithaca, New York,
William Hathaway attended American College in Paris, Cornell, the University
of Montana, and the University of Iowa. He is the author of four
books of poetry:* True Confessions and False Romances *(1971),* A
Wilderness of Monkeys *(1975),* The Gymnast of Inertia *(1982), and*
Fish, Flesh & Fowl *(1985). He teaches at Louisiana State University at
Baton Rouge.*

WHY THAT'S BOB HOPE

The comedian, holding a chunk of flaming shale.
If only *Der Bingle* could see him now! He looked
so puffed and sleepy in that Texaco hardhat,
I could've popped a fuse. Well, like the oil,

here today and gone today. In *my* good old days
Hope was on Sullivan's "shew" so often us kids

dropped TV for longhair sex and smoking weeds.
What a mistake! But now we're past our wild phase

and Bob's back with this burning rock, funny
for a change. No, no old quips now about Dean's double   10
vision, Phyllis Diller's breasts or Sinatra's aging treble.
He says if we all squeeze the rock together real money

will drip out. We'll live real good and still afford a war
where he'll bust our boys' guts on tour in El Salvador.

Robert Hayden

Robert Hayden, who described writing a poem as "a form of prayer," was born in Detroit in 1913. He held degrees from Wayne State University and the University of Michigan, where he received the Hopwood Award. His other honors include the Grand Prize for the First World Festival of Negro Arts in Dakar, Senegal, in 1966. Among his books are Angle of Ascent: New and Selected Poems *(1975),* American Journal *(1980), and* Collected Prose *(1984). He also edited* Kaleidoscope: Poems by American Negro Poets *(1967) and co-edited* Afro-American Literature: An Introduction *(1971). He taught at the University of Michigan until his death in 1980.*

THE BALLAD OF NAT TURNER

Then fled, O brethren, the wicked juba
    and wandered wandered far
from curfew joys in the Dismal's night.
    Fool of St. Elmo's fire

In scary night I wandered, praying,
        Lord God my harshener,
speak to me now or let me die;
        speak, Lord, to this mourner.

And came at length to livid trees
        where Ibo warriors   10
hung shadowless, turning in wind
        that moaned like Africa,

Their belltongue bodies dead, their eyes
        alive with the anger deep
in my own heart. Is this the sign,
        the sign forepromised me?

The spirits vanished. Afraid and lonely
        I wandered on in blackness.
Speak to me now or let me die.
        Die, whispered the blackness.   20

And wild things gasped and scuffled in
        the night; seething shapes
of evil frolicked upon the air.
        I reeled with fear, I prayed.

Sudden brightness clove the preying
        darkness, brightness that was
itself a golden darkness, brightness
        so bright that it was darkness.

And there were angels, their faces hidden
        from me, angels at war   30
with one another, angels in dazzling
        combat. And oh the splendor,

The fearful splendor of that warring.
        Hide me, I cried to rock and bramble.
Hide me, the rock, the bramble cried. . . .
        How tell you of that holy battle?

The shock of wing on wing and sword
    on sword was the tumult of
a taken city burning. I cannot
    say how long they strove,   40

For the wheel in a turning wheel which is time
    in eternity had ceased
its whirling, and owl and moccasin,
    panther and nameless beast

And I were held like creatures fixed
    in flaming, in fiery amber.
But I saw I saw oh many of
    those mighty beings waver,

Waver and fall, go streaking down
    into swamp water, and the water   50
hissed and steamed and bubbled and locked
    shuddering shuddering over

The fallen and soon was motionless.
    Then that massive light
began a-folding slowly in
    upon itself, and I

Beheld the conqueror faces and, lo,
    they were like mine, I saw
they were like mine and in joy and terror
    wept, praising praising Jehovah.   60

Oh praised my honer, harshener
    till a sleep came over me,
a sleep heavy as death. And when
    I awoke at last free

And purified, I rose and prayed
    and returned after a time
to the blazing fields, to the humbleness.
    And bided my time.

Anthony Hecht

One of America's most accomplished formal poets, Anthony Hecht was born in New York City in 1923 and educated at Bard College and Columbia. During World War II, he served in the infantry. His many honors include the Prix de Rome and the Pulitzer Prize. The author of The Hard Hours *(1966),* Millions of Strange Shadows *(1977),* The Venetian Vespers *(1979), and other books, he lives in Rochester, New York, where he is John H. Deane Professor of Poetry and Rhetoric at the University of Rochester.*

THE END OF THE WEEKEND

A dying firelight slides along the quirt
Of the cast-iron cowboy where he leans
Against my father's books. The lariat
Whirls into darkness. My girl, in skin-tight jeans,
Fingers a page of Captain Marryat,
Inviting insolent shadows to her shirt.

We rise together to the second floor.
Outside, across the lake, an endless wind
Whips at the headstones of the dead and wails
In the trees for all who have and have not sinned.   10
She rubs against me and I feel her nails.
Although we are alone, I lock the door.

The eventual shapes of all our formless prayers,
This dark, this cabin of loose imaginings,
Wind, lake, lip, everything awaits

The slow unloosening of her underthings.
And then the noise. Something is dropped. It grates
Against the attic beams.
                    I climb the stairs,

Armed with a belt.
                    A long magnesium strip
Of moonlight from the dormer cuts a path   20
Among the shattered skeletons of mice.
A great black presence beats its wings in wrath.
Above the boneyard burn its golden eyes.
Some small grey fur is pulsing in its grip.

"MORE LIGHT! MORE LIGHT!"

For Heinrich Blücher and Hannah Arendt

Composed in the Tower before his execution
These moving verses, and being brought at that time
Painfully to the stake, submitted, declaring thus:
"I implore my God to witness that I have made no crime."

Nor was he forsaken of courage, but the death was
        horrible,
The sack of gunpowder failing to ignite.
His legs were blistered sticks on which the black sap
Bubbled and burst as he howled for the Kindly Light.

And that was but one, and by no means one of the worst;
Permitted at least his pitiful dignity;   10
And such as were by made prayers in the name of Christ,
That shall judge all men, for his soul's tranquillity.

We move now to outside a German wood.
Three men are there commanded to dig a hole
In which the two Jews are ordered to lie down
And be buried alive by the third, who is a Pole.

Not light from the shrine at Weimar beyond the hill
Nor light from heaven appeared. But he did refuse.
A Lüger settled back deeply in its glove.
He was ordered to change places with the Jews.   20

Much casual death had drained away their souls.
The thick dirt mounted toward the quivering chin.
When only the head was exposed the order came
To dig him out again and to get back in.

No light, no light in the blue Polish eye.
When he finished a riding boot packed down the earth.
The Lüger hovered lightly in its glove.
He was shot in the belly and in three hours bled to death.

No prayers or incense rose up in those hours
Which grew to be years, and every day came mute   30
Ghosts from the ovens, sifting through crisp air,
And settled upon his eyes in a black soot.

DOUBLE SONNET

I recall everything, but more than all,
Words being nothing now, an ease that ever
Remembers her to my unfailing fever,
How she came forward to me, letting fall
Lamplight upon her dress till every small
Motion made visible seemed no mere endeavor
Of body to articulate its offer,
But more a grace won by the way from all
Striving in what is difficult, from all
Losses, so that she moved but to discover   10
A practice of the blood, as the gulls hover,
Winged with their life, above the harbor wall,
Tracing inflected silence in the tall
Air with a tilt of mastery and quiver
Against the light, as the light fell to favor
Her coming forth; this chiefly I recall.

It is a part of pride, guiding the hand
At the piano in the splash and passage
Of sacred dolphins, making numbers human
By sheer extravagance that can command   20
Pythagorean heavens to spell their message
Of some unlooked-for peace, out of the common;
Taking no thought at all that man and woman,
Lost in the trance of lamplight, felt the presage
Of the unbidden terror and bone hand
Of gracelessness, and the unspoken omen
That yet shall render all, by its first usage,
Speechless, inept, and totally unmanned.

Michael Heffernan

Michael Heffernan was born in Detroit in 1942. After doing undergraduate work at the University of Detroit, he earned his M.A. and Ph.D. from the University of Massachusetts. He has been a Woodrow Wilson fellow, a Bread Loaf scholar, and the recipient of a National Endowment for the Arts Fellowship. His books are The Cry of Oliver Hardy *(1979) and* To the Wreakers of Havoc *(1984). He teaches at Pittsburg State University in Kansas.*

DAFFODILS

It wasn't the daffodils so much
as the idea of them that got
me. I was wandering by in my
own lonely manner like a cloud in the sky

feeling ugly and grim when out
of nowhere up blossomed a clutch

of yellow daffodils by the curb.
Bright things they were, good and sweet,
and I knew I liked them better than
music or money or my girl's friendly skin   10
the way they stood there by the street
nicer and newer and simpler

by far than anything I had seen
all morning. Oh it was fine
to know them! I said, You daffodils
put me in mind of the clean white windowsills
of a kitchen when I was nine
one April Saturday in 19

52—my grandmother's kitchen,
her fingers dangling with dough,   20
the odor of pie in the oven,
the windows white as the windows of Heaven,
as if the air were bright with snow,
and someone outside them, watching.

A COLLOQUY OF SILENCES

That calm above those trees in the gray spaces
among the crosswork of the twigs and branches
and thin birdwhistle piping into silence
with other further birds whistling in answer
among the selfsame silences. I answer:
we weren't meant to live among these spaces
except to scare our hearts out in the silence
that makes us wonder what the upper branches
of trees can have learned about the main branches
of wisdom and the sources of the answer   10

to the question about why all this silence
must persist among those elegant spaces
beyond the gray spaces around tree branches
where the silences of birds are the answer.

Judith Hemschemeyer

Judith Hemschemeyer was born in Sheboygan, Wisconsin, in 1935. She attended the University of Wisconsin and the University of Grenoble and is the author of I Remember the Room Was Filled with Light *(1973),* Very Close and Very Slow *(1975), and* Give What You Can *(1978). She lives in Orlando, Florida.*

I REMEMBER THE ROOM WAS FILLED WITH LIGHT

They were still young, younger than I am now.
I remember the room was filled with light
And moving air. I was watching him
Pick brass slivers from his hands as he did each night
After work. Bits of brass gleamed on his brow.
She was making supper. I stood on the rim
Of a wound just healing; so when he looked up
And asked me when we were going to eat
I ran to her, though she could hear. She smiled
And said 'Tell him . . .' Then 'Tell her . . .' On winged
    feet   10
I danced between them, forgiveness in my cup,
Wise messenger of the gods, their child.

William Heyen

*Born in Brooklyn in 1940 and educated at the State University of New York
at Brockport and at Ohio University, William Heyen has been a senior
Fulbright lecturer in American literature in Germany and a Guggenheim
fellow. He has also won the Eunice Tietjens Prize from* Poetry *and the
Witter Bynner Prize from the American Academy and Institute of Arts and
Letters. His books include* Depth of Field *(1970),* Long Island Light
(1979), Lord Dragonfly *(1981), and* Erika: Poems of the Holocaust
*(1984). He lives in Brockport, New York, where he teaches at the State
University of New York at Brockport and collects books.*

ARROWS

       That year spring snowmelt
   and rain had risen
into my cabin—
       for days I dredged silt,

       rock, and leaf-muck
   from the run-off ditch, built
a bank that felt
       right. My arms ached, my back

       warned me to stop.
   I knelt, a last time, to pick   10
up a half-stuck cedar stick.
       Its flat tip

       seemed notched,
   rounded sharp.
At its end, a shape
       emerged from washed clod

     clumped on this bluer-
  than-cedar wood, and glinted:
a quartz arrowhead.
     I knelt there   20

     as I kneel now, again,
  in time, the one interior river
bearing me, that hunter,
     you, and my frail cabin

     back like dreams into the deer's eye,
  the hawk's breast, the last chamber
of wolf- or bear-heart, where
     all arrows wait, rot, and fly.

RIDDLE

From Belsen a crate of gold teeth,
from Dachau a mountain of shoes,
from Auschwitz a skin lampshade.
Who killed the Jews?

Not I, cries the typist,
not I, cries the engineer,
not I, cries Adolf Eichmann,
not I, cries Albert Speer.

My friend Fritz Nova lost his father—
a petty official had to choose.   10
My friend Lou Abrahms lost his brother.
Who killed the Jews?

David Nova swallowed gas,
Hyman Abrahms was beaten and starved.
Some men signed their papers,
and some stood guard,

and some herded them in,
and some dropped the pellets,
and some spread the ashes,
and some hosed the walls,   20

and some planted the wheat,
and some poured the steel,
and some cleared the rails,
and some raised the cattle.

Some smelled the smoke,
some just heard the news.
Were they Germans? Were they Nazis?
Were they human? Who killed the Jews?

The stars will remember the gold,
the sun will remember the shoes,   30
the moon will remember the skin.
But who killed the Jews?

Edward Hirsch

*Edward Hirsch was born in Chicago in 1950 and educated at Grinnell
College and the University of Pennsylvania. He has received awards from the
Amy Lowell Foundation, the Ingram Merrill Foundation, and the National
Endowment for the Arts. His* For the Sleepwalkers (1981) *was nomi-
nated for a National Book Critics Circle Award. His second collection,* Wild
Gratitude, *is forthcoming in 1986. He teaches at the University of Houston.*

AT KRESGE'S DINER IN STONEFALLS, ARKANSAS

Every night, another customer.
One night it's a state trooper,
the next a truck driver going all the way
to Arlington, Georgia. Tonight

it's only a tourist, a northerner.
I prefer the truck driver.

You can trust a truck driver.
Tourists are effeminate, though good customers.
I hate it most on Thursday night
when that hog who wants me to go all the way   10
with him comes in; some state trooper!
I'd rather go to bed with a pig, a northerner!

Well, maybe not a northerner.
They do have peculiar ways.
Still, they're good customers.
I think I hate that fat trooper
as much as I hope my truck driver
comes back on Thursday night.

Only three more nights!
How long does it take a good driver—   20
'course he doesn't have a Buick like the trooper
or a sports car like that northerner—
to cross Georgia? If I didn't have a customer
I'd go all the way

to Georgia after him, all the way!
I bet I could send a message with that northerner.
You know truckers are the safest drivers.
He's not only my favorite customer
but I dream about him at night.
Maybe I could send a telegram with that trooper   30

but then I hate asking the trooper
for favors 'cause he wants favors on Thursday night.
Still, I wish he was here instead of that northerner.
You can make a life with a truck driver.
I wonder if he would ever take me away
with him. I wish he was my husband instead of my
        customer!

O maybe this Thursday night that truck driver, my favorite
    customer,
will push aside the trooper and flick ashes at the
    northerner,
o and maybe he will take me away.

Daniel Hoffman

*Daniel Hoffman was born in New York City in 1923. A graduate of
Columbia, he has taught at Columbia, Swarthmore, and since 1966, the
University of Pennsylvania. In 1967 he received a National Institute of Arts
and Letters Award. His books include* An Armada of Thirty Whales
(1954), which won the Yale Younger Poets Prize, Striking the Stones
(1967), The Center of Attention *(1974), and* Brotherly Love
(1981). He is also the author of several critical studies, including Form and
Fable in American Fiction *(1961) and* Poe Poe Poe Poe Poe Poe
Poe *(1972).*

IN THE DAYS OF RIN-TIN-TIN

In the days of Rin-Tin-Tin
There was no such thing as sin,
No boymade mischief worth God's wrath
And the good dog dogged the badman's path.

In the nights, the deliquescent horn of Bix
Gave presentiments of the pleasures of sex;
In the Ostrich Walk we walked by twos—
Ja-da, jing-jing, what could we lose?

The Elders mastered The Market, Mah-jongg,
Readily admitted the Victorians wrong,   10
While Caligari hobbled with his stick and his ghoul
And overtook the Little Fellow on his way to school.

John Hollander

*John Hollander was born in 1929 in New York City. He took his M.A.
at Columbia and his Ph.D. at Indiana University. The recipient of the Yale
Younger Poets Prize and the Bollingen Prize, he has published many books
of poetry, including* Spectral Emanations: New and Selected Poems
(1978), Blue Wine *(1979), and* Powers of Thirteen *(1983). He has
also written* Rhyme's Reason: A Guide to English Verse *(1981). He
currently teaches at Yale.*

From SONNETS FOR ROSEBLUSH

18

Why drink, why touch you now? If it will be
Gin from the beginning, ending there,
For me, in the unblaming rain we see
Outside your window, filling all the air?
If, in the marvellous middle of it all,
Gin-drops of sweat come splashing down like rain
On both our bodies? If, once each, we call
The other's name as if in final pain?
Why then go through with it, when to imagine
What we shall do, what we shall be, is still   10

The noblest work of all, the sovereign region
Enduring, green, beyond both wish and will?
Why, naked and trembling, act out such old laws?
Because because because because because.

David Brendan Hopes

*David Brendan Hopes was born in Akron, Ohio, in 1953 and educated at
Hiram College, Johns Hopkins, and Syracuse University. He has been a
parks naturalist, a professional singer, an actor, and since open-heart sur-
gery in 1976, a long-distance runner. He teaches at Hiram College and is
the author of* The Glacier's Daughter, *which won the 1981 Juniper Prize
and the 1982 Saxifrage Prize.*

LAMENT FOR TURLOUGH O'CAROLAN

Late it was in the night, with the wind
beating in a circle like a shot bird
and the bittern flapping from the reeds and
hammered down and in the flat black storm I heard
a harper harping for the dead
and I staring straight up in my bed.

You promised us next years like a farm
set about with orchards and a trim house
on it carved to the eaves with gryphons and
fine ladies, with twenty windows facing south.   10
And now in ghouly night, Turlough,
you put your bones to your lips and blow.

You promised a green tree and shade for
our journeys. You promised that it would be
seed time and summer and harvest unless
God Himself turned English. You must harp for me.
I want the paradise you sold
for a pocketful of peddlar's gold.

It's early in black morning I hear
the harp coming in like the wind off waves.   20
Where is your minstrelsy, Turlough? I walk
the same walk, stitch the old stitch. O be brave
my heart: the wind's not come quiet
though the harper's gone who lied through it.

Ben Howard

*Born in Iowa City in 1944, Ben Howard studied at the University of Leeds,
Drake, and Syracuse University, from which he received a Ph.D. in 1971.
He has published one book,* Father of Waters *(1979), and has recently
finished a second,* Northern Interior. *He lives in Alfred, New York, where
he teaches literature, writing, and classical guitar at Alfred University.*

THE DIVER

Listen, listen, and draw near:
Love is inexhaustible and full of fear.

He can't remain forever underwater,
Feeling his lungs contract and his shoulders tire
From pulling against a force which like a door
That will not open might induce despair

In one less willing to be compromised
By a power which he's never understood
Or dragged downstream, powerless and deprived
Of any willful course he might have had,

All for the sake of catching once or twice
A glimpse of elements unknown to him,   10
Which float in the dark and silence like the face
Of one in whose confusion he became

A self outside himself, and again a man,
Spent and cleansed in a chaos not his own.

Richard Howard

Widely esteemed for both his poetry and his more than one hundred translations from the French, Richard Howard was born in Cleveland in 1929 and educated at Columbia and the Sorbonne. He has received many awards for his work, including the 1970 Pulitzer Prize for Untitled Subjects *and the 1983 American Book Award for his translation of Baudelaire's* Les Fleurs du Mal. *His other books include the poetry collections* Fellow Feelings *(1976),* Misgivings *(1979), and* Lining Up *(1984), and his study of American poetry since World War II,* Alone with America *(1969). He lives in New York City, where he directs the Braziller Poetry Series and edits poetry for* Shenandoah.

PERSONAL VALUES

My dear Magritte, I have been ill. Again.
By now of course the symptoms are well known,
Signs which are taken or mistaken for
Wonders by the broken-winded mind, blown

Is the word all right, though all wrong is more
Like it: blown up and at the last gasp down
Until I cannot call my soul my own

During such uncalled-for occasions when
The torn mind turns into the body, then
Turns out, instants or ecstasies later,   10
To have been literally taken in.
Taken—was it always as well known—where?
You know, but you're not telling, not even
Telling tales out of school—André Breton

Himself could never persuade you to own
Up to what he called your "magic reason":
You refused to tell tales *in* school either.
In any case or, to be casual, in mine,
Each time the fit approaches, I repair
(To be fitted, you might say) to the one   20
Room there is no earthly obligation

To share, the place in which to be alone
Par excellence, par misère, a site no one
Has named properly because it must pair
The washing function with the wasting one,
Lore of the toilette with the toilet's lair.
This is where the thing chooses to come on,
Yet once I get inside, the room has gone,

Nowhere to be found: the four walls open
Up and away—the sky! Against which, seen   30
As if for the first (or last) time, appear
The comb in the corner, the soap near the green
Toothbrush glass, one huge matchstick on the floor
Where Marie must have missed it, all obscene
With enormity, much too big to mean

What the scale of mere habituation
Managed to confer upon them or shun
By not conferring. I wait for my seizure
With the patience of . . . a patient, at pains

To discover the glass beyond me, over   40
My head, the soap escaping by design,
The totem matchstick—like the comb, a sign

Of my illusions made illustrious: icon
And idol, texts of a new religion.
As I wait for the next spasm to spare
Or despair, dear René (which means *reborn*),
I send all my thanks for your more than fair
Copy of my condition. *Merci.* Where
Else could I find my life's illustration?

Barbara Howes

Barbara Howes was born in 1914 in New York City. A graduate of Bennington, she helped organize the Southern Tenant Farmers Union. Her poetry has been honored with a Guggenheim Fellowship and a National Institute of Arts and Letters Award, and her collection A Private Signal: Poems New & Selected *(1978) was nominated for the National Book Award. Her most recent book is* Moving *(1983).*

A RUNE FOR C.

Luck? I am upset. My dog is ill.
I am now in that grey shuttling trains go in for;
The sky clouds, it is hard to believe dawn will

Ever show up.—I look for omens:
Not birds broken, not Fords lashed around trees,
But some item showing that fate is open. . . .

Sometimes, far far down in the magical past
Of us all, in something that stutters, something that rises,
There is an intimation of luck just

Swinging over our way: a cat's paw loose   10
In the banister, a long train-run, and then,
Square and oil-shambled, blue between elms, the caboose!

EARLY SUPPER

Laughter of children brings
    The kitchen down with laughter.
While the old kettle sings
Laughter of children brings
To a boil all savory things.
    Higher than beam or rafter,
Laughter of children brings
    The kitchen down with laughter.

So ends an autumn day,
    Light ripples on the ceiling,   10
Dishes are stacked away;
So ends an autumn day,
The children jog and sway
    In comic dances wheeling.
So ends an autumn day,
    Light ripples on the ceiling.

They trail upstairs to bed,
    And night is a dark tower.
The kettle calls: instead
They trail upstairs to bed,   20

Leaving warmth, the coppery-red
   Mood of their carnival hour.
They trail upstairs to bed,
   And night is a dark tower.

DEATH OF A VERMONT FARM WOMAN

Is it time now to go away?
July is nearly over; hay
Fattens the barn, the herds are strong,
Our old fields prosper; these long
Green evenings will keep death at bay.

Last winter lingered; it was May
Before a flowering lilac spray
Barred cold for ever. I was wrong.
               Is it time now?

Six decades vanished in a day!   10
I bore four sons: one lives; they
Were all good men; three dying young
Was hard on us. I have looked long
For these hills to show me where peace lay . . .
               Is it time now?

Robert Huff

Born in Evanston, Illinois, in 1924 and educated at Wayne State University, Robert Huff gives credit for his poetic training "to the shores of Lake Michigan near Saugatuck, Michigan, and to the forests of the Northwest." He is the author of three books, including The Ventriloquist: New and

Selected Poems *(1977), and his poetry is recorded at the Library of Congress. He teaches at Western Washington State University in Bellingham.*

ALTHOUGH I REMEMBER THE SOUND

Although I remember the sound
The young snag made when I felled it,
It was not noise or music mattered then.
Briefly, the tree was silent on the ground.

Of what it was that mattered I recall
Simpiy, among the chips and dust
And keener near the center of the cut,
The sweet, new smell which rose after the fall.

Richard Hugo

Richard Hugo, who said his poems were often "triggered by something, a small town or an abandoned house, that I feel others would ignore," was born in 1923 in Seattle and educated at the University of Washington. A bombardier in the U.S. Army Air Corps during World War II, he worked for Boeing Aircraft Company for twelve years before taking a teaching position at the University of Montana. His books of poetry include What Thou Lovest Well, Remains American *(1975), which won the Theodore Roethke Memorial Poetry Prize, and* Making Certain It Goes On: The Collected Poems of Richard Hugo *(1984). He also published* The Triggering Town, *a collection of lectures and essays, and* Death and the Good Life, *a mystery novel, and served as editor of the Yale Series of Younger Poets from 1977 until his death in 1982.*

THE WAY A GHOST DISSOLVES

Where she lived the close remained the best.
The nearest music and the static cloud,
sun and dirt were all she understood.
She planted corn and left the rest
to elements, convinced that God
with giant faucets regulates the rain
and saves the crops from frost or foreign wind.

Fate assisted her with special cures.
Rub a half potato on your wart
and wrap it in a damp cloth. Close   10
your eyes and whirl three times and throw.
Then bury rag and spud exactly where
they fall. The only warts that I have now
are memories or comic on my nose.

Up at dawn. The earth provided food
if worked and watered, planted green
with rye grass every fall. Or driven wild
by snakes that kept the carrots clean,
she butchered snakes and carrots with a hoe.
Her screams were sea birds in the wind,   20
her chopping—nothing like it now.

I will garden on the double run,
my rhythm obvious in ringing rakes,
and trust in fate to keep me poor and kind
and work until my heart is short,
then go out slowly with a feeble grin,
my fingers flexing but my eyes gone gray
from cramps and the lack of oxygen.

Forget the tone. Call the neighbor's trumpet
golden as it grates. Exalt the weeds.   30
Say the local animals have class
or help me say that ghost has gone to seed.
And why attempt to see the cloud again—
the screaming face it was before it cracked
in wind from Asia and a wanton rain.

THE CHURCH ON COMIAKEN HILL

For Sydney Pettit

The lines are keen against today's bad sky
about to rain. We're white and understand
why Indians sold butter for the funds
to build this church. Four hens and a rooster
huddle on the porch. We are dark
and know why no one climbed to pray. The priest
who did his best to imitate a bell
watched the river, full of spirits, coil
below the hill, relentless for the bay.

A church abandoned to the wind is portent.   10
In high wind, ruins make harsh music.
The priest is tending bar. His dreams have paid
outrageous fees for stone and mortar.
His eyes are empty as a chapel
roofless in a storm. Greek temples seem
the same as forty centuries ago.
If we used one corner for a urinal,
he wouldn't swear we hadn't worshipped here.

The chickens cringe. Rain sprays chaos where
the altar and the stained glass would have gone   20
had Indians not eaten tribal cows
one hungry fall. Despite the chant,
salmon hadn't come. The first mass
and a phone line cursed the river.
If rain had rhythm, it would not be Latin.

Children do not wave as we drive out.
Like these graves ours may go unmarked.
Can we be satisfied when dead
with daffodils for stones? These Indians—
whatever they once loved or used for God—   30
the hill—the river—the bay burned by the moon—
they knew that when you die you lose your name.

THE FREAKS AT SPURGIN ROAD FIELD

The dim boy claps because the others clap.
The polite word, handicapped, is muttered in the stands.
Isn't it wrong, the way the mind moves back.

One whole day I sit, contrite, dirt, L.A.
Union Station, '46, sweating through last night.
The dim boy claps because the others clap.

Score, 5 to 3. Pitcher fading badly in the heat.
Isn't it wrong to be or not be spastic?
Isn't it wrong, the way the mind moves back.

I'm laughing at a neighbor girl beaten to scream   10
by a savage father and I'm ashamed to look.
The dim boy claps because the others clap.

The score is always close, the rally always short.
I've left more wreckage than a quake.
Isn't it wrong, the way the mind moves back.

The afflicted never cheer in unison.
Isn't it wrong, the way the mind moves back
to stammering pastures where the picnic should have
    worked.
The dim boy claps because the others clap.

T. R. Hummer

T. R. Hummer was born in Mississippi in 1950 and earned degrees at the University of Southern Mississippi and the University of Utah. His two books of poems are The Angelic Orders *(1982) and* The Passion of the Right-Angled Man *(1984). He has also edited, with Bruce Weigl,* The

Imagination as Glory: The Poetry of James Dickey *(1984), a collection of essays. He teaches at Kenyon College.*

THE RURAL CARRIER STOPS TO KILL
A NINE-FOOT COTTONMOUTH

Lord God, I saw the son-of-a-bitch uncoil
In the road ahead of me, uncoil and squirm
For the ditch, squirm a hell of a long time.
Missed him with the car. When I got back to him, he was
      all
But gone, nothing left on the road but the tip-end
Of his tail, and that disappearing into Johnson grass.
I leaned over the ditch and saw him, balled up now, hiss.
I aimed for the mouth and shot him. And shot him again.

Then I got a good strong stick and dragged him out.
He was long and evil, thick as the top of my arm.   10
There are things in this world a man can't look at without
Wanting to kill. Don't ask me why. I was calm
Enough, I thought. But I felt my spine
Squirm suddenly. I admit it. It was mine.

Thomas James

Thomas James was born in Joliet, Illinois, in 1946 and graduated from Northern Illinois University. After teaching English in a public school, he moved to Chicago, where he worked as an employment counselor for the state of Illinois. He published poems in various literary journals and was the

winner of the Theodore Roethke Prize from Poetry Northwest *in 1969.*
He committed suicide shortly after the publication of his first book of poems,
Letters to a Stranger, *in 1973.*

MUMMY OF A LADY NAMED
JEMUTESONEKH XXI DYNASTY

My body holds its shape. The genius is intact.
Will I return to Thebes? In that lost country
The eucalyptus trees have turned to stone.
Once, branches nudged me, dropping swollen blossoms,
And passionflowers lit my father's garden.
Is it still there, that place of mottled shadow,
The scarlet flowers breathing in the darkness?

I remember how I died. It was so simple!
One morning the garden faded. My face blacked out.
On my left side they made the first incision.   10
They washed my heart and liver in palm wine—
My lungs were two dark fruit they stuffed with spices.
They smeared my innards with a sticky unguent
And sealed them in a crock of alabaster.

My brain was next. A pointed instrument
Hooked it through my nostrils, strand by strand.
A voice swayed over me. I paid no notice.
For weeks my body swam in sweet perfume.
I came out scoured. I was skin and bone.
They lifted me into the sun again   20
And packed my empty skull with cinnamon.

They slit my toes; a razor gashed my fingertips.
Stitched shut at last, my limbs were chaste and valuable,
Stuffed with a paste of cloves and wild honey.
My eyes were empty, so they filled them up,
Inserting little nuggets of obsidian.
A basalt scarab wedged between my breasts
Replaced the tinny music of my heart.

Hands touched my sutures. I was so important!
They oiled my pores, rubbing a fragrance in.   30

An amber gum oozed down to soothe my temples.
I wanted to sit up. My skin was luminous,
Frail as the shadow of an emerald.
Before I learned to love myself too much,
My body wound itself in spools of linen.

Shut in my painted box, I am a precious object.
I wear a wooden mask. These are my eyelids,
Two flakes of bronze, and here is my new mouth,
Chiseled with care, guarding its ruby facets.
I will last forever. I am not impatient—   40
My skin will wait to greet its old complexions.
I'll lie here till the world swims back again.

When I come home the garden will be budding,
White petals breaking open, clusters of night flowers,
The far-off music of a tambourine.
A boy will pace among the passionflowers,
His eyes no longer two bruised surfaces.
I'll know the mouth of my young groom, I'll touch
His hands. Why do people lie to one another?

SNAKEBITE

Now I am getting light as cotton candy—
Out of the two red holes in my heel
Infinity pours, goodbye to all of me.
It was pleasant to watch my leg begin to swell;
An incredible headiness washed over me,
I didn't feel a thing. The color of a bluebottle,

The sky hit my skin like water from a pitcher.
I remember only a limber brown stick
Without any fangs, then the cool white stretcher
Where I became part of an unamusing joke   10
And the sun became a singular gold adder,
Which gathered its constricted shape and struck.

First I dream of wool, and then of water,
The bridge gone out under my footsoles.

Sleep eddies under everything pure as a colt's star.
These ladies in white speak a mouthful of bells.
They let the sleep rush out of me like air
Out of an innertube, smudging their white walls.

Watching milady through the wrong end of the telescope,
I suck the glass pencil at noonday.   20
Here is a pale horse, they say; this is his stirrup.
I ride on my own diminishing. I grow gray
In the mild contagion of my sleep.
The light spreads its thin skin and grows muddy.

They feed me through tubes and comfort me with needles.
Where are the nubile, white-winged ladies
Who populate these immaculate halls?
The young men who view me have sulphur-blue jaws
That do not complain. They bring me bottles
Of adamant, they move quietly as butterflies   30

And are upon me when I least expect it.
Everything I leave behind is ubiquitous,
Even the undependable broad daylight
Which grows thinner each time I raise my eyes
To watch the centuries stream from my foot
And the whole world rock backward into place.

Randall Jarrell

Called "the most heartbreaking poet of his generation" by Robert Lowell, Randall Jarrell was born in Nashville, Tennessee, in 1914 and raised in California. He received his education at Vanderbilt. During World War II he was a control tower operator in the U.S. Air Corps. He is the author of several collections of poetry, including **The Woman at the Washington**

Zoo (1960), which won the National Book Award, and The Complete
Poems *(1969), as well as the novel* Pictures from an Institution *(1954),
a collection of influential criticism,* Poetry and the Age *(1953), a translation of* Goethe's Faust: Part One *(1974), and several children's books.
He died in 1965 after being struck by a car.*

EIGHTH AIR FORCE

If, in an odd angle of the hutment,
A puppy laps the water from a can
Of flowers, and the drunk sergeant shaving
Whistles *O Paradiso!*—shall I say that man
Is not as men have said: a wolf to man?

The other murderers troop in yawning;
Three of them play Pitch, one sleeps, and one
Lies counting missions, lies there sweating
Till even his heart beats: One; One; One.
O murderers! . . . Still, this is how it's done: 10

This is a war. . . . But since these play, before they die,
Like puppies with their puppy; since, a man,
I did as these have done, but did not die—
I will content the people as I can
And give up these to them: Behold the man!

I have suffered, in a dream, because of him,
Many things; for this last saviour, man,
I have lied as I lie now. But what is lying?
Men wash their hands, in blood, as best they can:
I find no fault in this just man.   20

A CAMP IN THE PRUSSIAN FOREST

I walk beside the prisoners to the road.
Load on puffed load,
Their corpses, stacked like sodden wood,
Lie barred or galled with blood

By the charred warehouse. No one comes today
In the old way
To knock the fillings from their teeth;
The dark, coned, common wreath

Is plaited for their grave—a kind of grief.
The living leaf   10
Clings to the planted profitable
Pine if it is able;

The boughs sigh, mile on green, calm, breathing mile,
From this dead file
The planners ruled for them. . . . One year
They sent a million here:

Here men were drunk like water, burnt like wood.
The fat of good
And evil, the breast's star of hope
Were rendered into soap.   20

I paint the star I sawed from yellow pine—
And plant the sign
In soil that does not yet refuse
Its usual Jews

Their first asylum. But the white, dwarfed star—
This dead white star—
Hides nothing, pays for nothing; smoke
Fouls it, a yellow joke,

The needles of the wreath are chalked with ash,
A filmy trash   30
Litters the black woods with the death
Of men; and one last breath

Curls from the monstrous chimney. . . . I laugh aloud
Again and again;
The star laughs from its rotting shroud
Of flesh. O star of men!

Judson Jerome

Judson Jerome was born in Tulsa, Oklahoma, in 1927, and educated at the University of Oklahoma, the University of Chicago, and Ohio State University. For many years he has written a poetry column for Writer's Digest. *His books of poetry include* The Village and Other Poems *(1976),* Public Domain *(1977), and* Thirty Years of Poetry, 1949–1979 *(1979). He has also published plays, novels, textbooks, and a social commentary on communes. He lives in Maryland.*

EVE: NIGHT THOUGHTS

Okay, so the wheel bit was a grinding bore
and fire a risk in the cave, never mind the dogs
he brings home, and cows; but I can endure
his knocking rocks for sparks and rolling logs.
It's his words that get on my nerves, his incessant naming
of every bird or bug or plant, his odd
smirk as he commits a syllable, taming
Nature with categories—as though the Word were God.

Okay, so statements were bad enough,
and accusations crossing, spoiling digestion.   10
But then he invented the laugh.
Next day he invented the question.
I see it: he's busy building a verbal fence

surrounding life and me. But already I
counterplot: I'll make a poem of his sense.
By night, as he dreams, I am inventing the lie.

Denis Johnson

Denis Johnson was born in Munich, Germany, in 1949 and grew up in Tokyo, Manila, and Washington, D.C. A graduate of the University of Iowa, he has received two National Endowment for the Arts Fellowships for his poetry and the Sue Kauffman Prize for his fiction. Among his books are the poetry collections Inner Weather *(1976),* The Incognito Lounge *(1982), and* The Veil *(1985), and the novel* Angels *(1983). He lives in Wellfleet, Massachusetts, where he works as a free-lance writer and serves on the writing committee of the Fine Arts Work Center in Provincetown.*

PASSENGERS

The world will burst like an intestine in the sun,
the dark turn to granite and the granite to a name,
but there will always be somebody riding the bus
through these intersections strewn with broken glass
among speechless women beating their little ones,
always a slow alphabet of rain
speaking of drifting and perishing to the air,
always these definite jails of light in the sky
at the wedding of this clarity and this storm
and a woman's turning—her languid flight of hair   10
traveling through frame after frame of memory

where the past turns, its face sparking like emery,
to open its grace and incredible harm
over my life, and I will never die.

SWAY

Since I find you will no longer love,
from bar to bar in terror I shall move
past Forty-third and Halsted, Twenty-fourth
and Roosevelt where fire-gutted cars,
their bones the bones of coyote and hyena,
suffer the light from the wrestling arena
to fall all over them. And what they say
blends in the tarantellasmic sway
of all of us between the two of these:
harmony and divergence,   10
their sad story of harmony and divergence,
the story that begins
I did not know who she was
and ends *I did not know who she was.*

June Jordan

*June Jordan was born in Harlem in 1936 and grew up in Brooklyn. She
studied at Barnard and the University of Chicago. From 1970 to 1971 she
was a fellow at the American Academy in Rome, and since 1974 she has
been a contributing editor for* American Poetry Review. *Her novel* His
Own Where *was nominated for a National Book Award in 1971. Her
books of poetry include* Things I Do in the Dark: Selected Poems

(1977), Passion *(1980), and* Civil Wars *(1981). She teaches at the State
University of New York at Stony Brook.*

SUNFLOWER SONNET NUMBER ONE

But if I tell you how my heart swings wide
enough to motivate flirtations with the trees
or how the happiness of passion freaks inside
me, will you then believe the faithful, yearning freeze
on random, fast explosions that I place
upon my lust? Or must I say the streets are bare
unless it is your door I face
unless they are your eyes that, rare
as tulips on a cold night, trick my mind
to oranges and yellow flames around a seed   10
as deep as anyone may find
in magic? What do you need?

I'll give you that, I hope, and more
But don't you be the one to choose me: poor.

SUNFLOWER SONNET NUMBER TWO

Supposing we could just go on and on as two
voracious in the days apart as well as when
we side by side (the many ways we do
that) well! I would consider then
perfection possible, or else worthwhile
to think about. Which is to say
I guess the costs of long term tend to pile
up, block and complicate, erase away
the accidental, temporary, near
thing/pulsebeat promises one makes   10
because the chance, the easy new, is there
in front of you. But still, perfection takes
some sacrifice of falling stars for rare.
And there are stars, but none of you, to spare.

Donald Justice

A celebrated poet and teacher of poets, Donald Justice was born in 1925 in
Miami and educated at the University of Miami, Stanford, and the University of Iowa. He edited The Collected Poems of Weldon Kees (1962).
His own books of poems include The Summer Anniversaries (1960),
which won the Lamont Prize, Night Light (1967), Departures (1973),
and Selected Poems (1979), for which he was awarded the Pulitzer
Prize. He is currently on the faculty at the University of Florida.

FIRST DEATH

JUNE 12, 1933

I saw my grandmother grow weak.
When she died, I kissed her cheek.

I remember the new taste—
Powder mixed with a drying paste.

Down the hallway, on its table,
Lay the family's great Bible.

In the dark, by lamplight stirred,
The Void grew pregnant with the Word.

In black ink they wrote it down.
The older ink was turning brown.   10

From the woods there came a cry—
The hoot owl asking who, not why.

The men sat silent on the porch.
Each lighted pipe a friendly torch

Against the unknown and the known.
But the child knew himself alone.

JUNE 13, 1933

The morning sun rose up and stuck.
Sunflower strove with hollyhock.

I ran the worn path past the sty.
Nothing was hidden from God's eye.   20

The barn door creaked. I walked among
Chaff and wrinkled cakes of dung.

In the dim light I read the dates
On the dusty license plates

Nailed to the wall as souvenirs.
I breathed the dust in of the years.

I circled the abandoned Ford
Before I tried the running board.

At the wheel I felt the heat
Press upwards through the springless seat.   30

And when I touched the silent horn,
Small mice scattered through the corn.

JUNE 14, 1933

I remember the soprano
Fanning herself at the piano,

And the preacher looming large
Above me in his dark blue serge.

My shoes brought in a smell of clay
To mingle with the faint sachet

Of flowers sweating in their vases.   40
A stranger showed us to our places.

The stiff fan stirred in mother's hand.
Air moved, but only when she fanned.

I wondered how could all her grief
Be squeezed into one small handkerchief.

There was a buzzing on the sill.
It stopped, and everything was still.

We bowed our heads, we closed our eyes
To the mercy of the flies.

SESTINA: HERE IN KATMANDU

We have climbed the mountain.
There's nothing more to do.
It is terrible to come down
To the valley
Where, amidst many flowers,
One thinks of snow,

As formerly, amidst snow,
Climbing the mountain,
One thought of flowers,
Tremulous, ruddy with dew,   10
In the valley.
One caught their scent coming down.

It is difficult to adjust, once down,
To the absence of snow.

Clear days, from the valley,
One looks up at the mountain.
What else is there to do?
Prayer wheels, flowers!

Let the flowers
Fade, the prayer wheels run down.   20
What have they to do
With us who have stood atop the snow
Atop the mountain,
Flags seen from the valley?

It might be possible to live in the valley,
To bury oneself among flowers,
If one could forget the mountain,
How, never once looking down,
Stiff, blinded with snow,
One knew what to do.   30

Meanwhile it is not easy here in Katmandu,
Especially when to the valley
That wind which means snow
Elsewhere, but here means flowers,
Comes down,
As soon it must, from the mountain.

WOMEN IN LOVE

It always comes, and when it comes they know.
To will it is enough to bring them there.
The knack is this, to fasten and not let go.

Their limbs are charmed; they cannot stay or go.
Desire is limbo: they're unhappy there.
It always comes, and when it comes they know.

Their choice of hells would be the one they know.
Dante describes it, the wind circling there.
The knack is this, to fasten and not let go.

The wind carries them where they want to go,   10
Yet it seems cruel to strangers passing there.
It always comes, and when it comes they know
The knack is this, to fasten and not let go.

THE THIN MAN

I indulge myself
In rich refusals.
Nothing suffices.

I hone myself to
This edge. Asleep, I
Am a horizon.

IN THE ATTIC

There's a half hour towards dusk when flies,
Trapped by the summer screens, expire
Musically in the dust of sills;
And ceilings slope towards remembrance.

The same crimson afternoons expire
Over the same few rooftops repeatedly;
Only, being stored up for remembrance,
They somehow escape the ordinary.

Childhood is like that, repeatedly
Lost in the very longueurs it redeems.   10
One forgets how small and ordinary
The world looked once by dusklight from above . . .

But not the moment which redeems
The drowsy arias of the flies—
And the chin settles onto palms above
Numbed elbows propped on rotting sills.

Richard Katrovas

Richard Katrovas was born in Los Angeles in 1953 and educated at San Diego State University, the University of Arkansas, the University of Virginia, and the University of Iowa, where he received his M.F.A. in 1983. He is the author of two collections of poems, **Green Dragons** *(1984) and* **Snug Harbor** *(1985). He teaches at the University of New Orleans.*

ELEGY FOR MY MOTHER

Eleven years ago I left for good.
The earth has not cracked, nor the moon come down
to settle in among the lucid dead.
The fire in your vault drowns out the sound

of the gentle, screwing motion of the world.
Pitiful nights when caffeine wrecks my nerves
and I waver in the zone where murdered
children sing, I wonder if that flame deserves

anything sumptuous as your body.
From harm to harm, the nights link day to day,   10
and women pass through my life like water
washing my body's pent-up seeds away

and on that flowing forth from dark to dark
I navigate according to no star.
I strike a match and watch it burn, finding
in its one act of mercy what we are.

Greg Keeler

Born in Oklahoma in 1946, Greg Keeler now lives in Bozeman, Montana,
where he teaches at Montana State University. His two books are **Spring**
Catch *(1982) and* **The Far Bank** *(1984). Besides writing poetry, he also*
publishes and sings satirical country-western music.

AMERICAN FALLS

At 4:00 a.m., I drove to American Falls
through twenty miles of southern Idaho
to where the Snake stopped between canyon walls
behind the dam then roared out below.

Over the foaming forebay on catwalks
old men had already established themselves,
eyes fixed on current-bent rods, backs
bent to the spray. And from the swells

they pulled flopping rainbows, huge balloons
of flesh. They used nightcrawlers, sucker-meat on   10
cheap hooks with lots of weight. I fished spoons
that only worked for a thin hour of dawn.

Between cement walls and the turbines, the fish
were ours or chopped up before the river
was itself again. And the old men, fresh
for death, knew this better than I, whether

or not they showed me their stringers.
No one had to mention humility under the
terrible sound of water getting thinner
with one place to go. When we'd see   20

Union Pacific scream over the top of the dam,
it was only a whisper to us, like the lines
in our fingers, whistling a secret hymn
deep into the howl, searching for signs ·

of present-tense rainbows. The smoke
of a phosphate plant rose with dead fish
above the banks, always out to tell us no
and keep us trying, flicking our wrists

toward flux. Now it's all framed. They're dead.
Their clusters of fat trout swam out of time.   30
A smooth new dam is there instead—
no forebay, just water in a hard, thin line.

Weldon Kees

Born in Beatrice, Nebraska, in 1914 and educated at the University of Nebraska, Weldon Kees was a poet, fiction writer, critic, jazz pianist and composer, photographer, filmmaker, and abstract expressionist painter. He disappeared in 1955. His car was found near the Golden Gate Bridge, but because he had talked both of suicide and of living abroad under an assumed name, his fate remains uncertain. His books include The Collected Poems of Weldon Kees *(1962) and* The Ceremony & Other Stories *(1984).*

FOR MY DAUGHTER

Looking into my daughter's eyes I read
Beneath the innocence of morning flesh
Concealed, hintings of death she does not heed.
Coldest of winds have blown this hair, and mesh
Of seaweed snarled these miniatures of hands;
The night's slow poison, tolerant and bland,
Has moved her blood. Parched years that I have seen
That may be hers appear: foul, lingering
Death in certain war, the slim legs green.
Or, fed on hate, she relishes the sting   10
Of others' agony; perhaps the cruel
Bride of a syphilitic or a fool.
These speculations sour in the sun.
I have no daughter. I desire none.

From FIVE VILLANELLES

1

The crack is moving down the wall.
Defective plaster isn't all the cause.
We must remain until the roof falls in.

It's mildly cheering to recall
That every building has its little flaws.
The crack is moving down the wall.

Here in the kitchen, drinking gin,
We can accept the damndest laws.
We must remain until the roof falls in.

And though there's no one here at all,   10
One searches every room because
The crack is moving down the wall.

Repairs? But how can one begin?
The lease has warnings buried in each clause.
We must remain until the roof falls in.

These nights one hears a creaking in the hall,
The sort of thing that gives one pause.
The crack is moving down the wall.
We must remain until the roof falls in.

X. J. Kennedy

X. J. Kennedy was born in Dover, New Jersey, in 1929 and "began scribbling early, publishing at the age of twelve a science-fiction magazine called Terrifying Test-Tube Tales.*" He studied at Seton Hall University, Columbia, the Sorbonne, and the University of Michigan, served as poetry editor of the* Paris Review *from 1961 to 1964, and co-edited* Counter/ Measures *from 1972 to 1974. His poetry collections include* Nude Descending a Staircase, *which won the 1961 Lamont Prize,* Growing Into Love *(1969),* Breaking & Entering *(1971),* Emily Dickinson in Southern California *(1974), and* Cross Ties: Selected Poems *(1985). He is also the author of a popular textbook,* Introduction to Poetry *(1966). He lives in Bedford, Massachusetts, with his wife, Dorothy.*

NUDE DESCENDING A STAIRCASE

Toe upon toe, a snowing flesh,
A gold of lemon, root and rind,
She sifts in sunlight down the stairs
With nothing on. Nor on her mind.

We spy beneath the banister
A constant thresh of thigh on thigh—
Her lips imprint the swinging air
That parts to let her parts go by.

One-woman waterfall, she wears
Her slow descent like a long cape   10
And pausing, on the final stair
Collects her motions into shape.

RONDEL

Violation on a theme by Charles d'Orléans

The world is taking off her clothes
    Of snowdrift, rain, and strait-laced freeze
    And turns, to show forth by degrees
The bosom of a Rose La Rose.

There's not a bud nor bird, Lord knows,
    Can stay still in boughs' balconies.
The world is taking off her clothes
    Of snowdrift, rain, and strait-laced freeze.

Brooklet grown great from melting snows
    Wears a G-string of ice to tease   10
    And, sequined, river's last chemise
Undone in a shudder goes.
The world is taking off her clothes.

NOTHING IN HEAVEN FUNCTIONS AS IT OUGHT

Nothing in Heaven functions as it ought:
Peter's bifocals, blindly sat on, crack;
His gates lurch with the cackle of a cock,
Not turn with a hush of gold as Milton had thought;
Gangs of the slaughtered innocents keep huffing

The nimbus off the Venerable Bede
Like that of an old dandelion gone to seed;
And the beatific choir keep breaking up, coughing.

But Hell, sleek Hell hath no freewheeling part:
None takes his own sweet time, none quickens pace.   10
Ask anyone, How come you here, poor heart?—
And he will slot a quarter through his face,
You'll hear an instant click, a tear will start
Imprinted with an abstract of his case.

Galway Kinnell

A poet who has described his work as a "struggle against the desire for heaven," Galway Kinnell was born in 1927 in Providence, Rhode Island, and raised in Pawtucket. He studied at Princeton and the University of Rochester. His numerous honors include an Award of Merit Medal from the Academy and Institute of Arts and Letters and the 1983 Pulitzer Prize and American Book Award for his Selected Poems. *Among his other volumes of poetry are* What a Kingdom It Was *(1960),* The Book of Nightmares *(1971), and* Mortal Acts, Mortal Words *(1980). He has also published a novel,* Black Light *(1965), and translations of François Villon, Yves Bonnefoy, and Yvan Goll. He is currently Distinguished Professor of English at New York University.*

FOR WILLIAM CARLOS WILLIAMS

When you came and you talked and you read with your
Private zest from the varicose marble
Of the podium, the lovers of literature
Paid you the tribute of their almost total

Inattention, although someone when you spoke of a pig
Did squirm, and it is only fair to report another gig-

gled. But you didn't even care. You seemed
Above remarking we were not your friends.
You hung around inside the rimmed
Circles of your heavy glasses and smiled and   10
So passed a lonely evening. In an hour
Of talking your honesty built you a tower.

When it was over and you sat down and the chair-
man got up and smiled and congratulated
You and shook your hand, I watched a professor
In neat bow tie and enormous tweeds, who patted
A faint praise of the sufficiently damned,
Drained spittle from his pipe, then scrammed.

TO CHRIST OUR LORD

The legs of the elk punctured the snow's crust
And wolves floated lightfooted on the land
Hunting Christmas elk living and frozen;
Inside snow melted in a basin, and a woman basted
A bird spread over coals by its wings and head.

Snow had sealed the windows; candles lit
The Christmas meal. The Christmas grace chilled
The cooked bird, being long-winded and the room cold.
During the words a boy thought, is it fitting
To eat this creature killed on the wing?   10

He had killed it himself, climbing out
Alone on snowshoes in the Christmas dawn,
The fallen snow swirling and the snowfall gone,
Heard its throat scream as the gunshot scattered,
Watched it drop, and fished from the snow the dead.

He had not wanted to shoot. The sound
Of wings beating into the hushed air

Had stirred his love, and his fingers
Froze in his gloves, and he wondered,
Famishing, could he fire? Then he fired.   20

Now the grace praised his wicked act. At its end
The bird on the plate
Stared at his stricken appetite.
There had been nothing to do but surrender,
To kill and to eat; he ate as he had killed, with wonder.

At night on snowshoes on the drifting field
He wondered again, for whom had love stirred?
The stars glittered on the snow and nothing answered.
Then the Swan spread her wings, cross of the cold north,
The pattern and mirror of the acts of earth.   30

THE FUNDAMENTAL PROJECT OF
TECHNOLOGY

"A flash! A white flash sparkled!"
—Tatsuichiro Akizuki, *Concentric Circles of Death*

Under glass: glass dishes which changed
in color; pieces of transformed beer bottles;
a household iron; bundles of wire become solid
lumps of iron; a pair of pliers; a ring of skull-
bone fused to the inside of a helmet; a pair of eyeglasses
taken off the eyes of an eyewitness, without glass,
which vanished, when a white flash sparkled.

An old man, possibly a soldier back then,
now reduced down to one who soon will die,
sucks at the cigaret dangling from his lip, peers   10
at the uniform, scorched, of some tiniest schoolboy,
sighs out bluish mists of his own ashes over
a pressed tin lunch box well crushed back then when
the word *future* first learned, in a white flash, to jerk tears.

On the bridge outside, in navy black, a group
of schoolchildren line up, hold it, grin at a flash-pop,

swoop in a flock across grass, see a stranger, cry,
hello! hello! hello! and soon, *goodbye! goodbye! goodbye!*
having pecked up the greetings that fell half unspoken
and the going-sayings that those who went the morning   20
it happened a white flash sparkled did not get to say.

If all a city's faces were to shrink back all at once
from their skulls, would a new sound come into existence,
audible above moans eaves extract from wind that smoothes
the grass on graves; or raspings heart's-blood greases still;
or wails infants trill born already skillful at the grandpa's
          rattle;
or infra-screams bitter-knowledge's speechlessness
memorized, at that white flash, inside closed-forever
          mouths?

To de-animalize human mentality, to purge it of obsolete
evolutionary characteristics, in particular of death,   30
which foreknowledge terrorizes the contents of skulls with,
is the fundamental project of technology; however,
pseudologica fantastica's mechanisms require:
if you would establish deathlessness you must eliminate
those who die; a task attempted, when a white flash
          sparkled.

Unlike the trees of home, which continually evaporate
along the skyline, the trees here have been enticed down
toward world-eternity. No one knows which gods they
          enshrine.
Does it matter? Awareness of ignorance is as devout
as knowledge of knowledge. Or more so. Even though not
          knowing,   40
sometimes we weep, from surplus of gratitude, even though
          knowing,
twice already on earth sparkled a flash, a white flash.

The children go away. By nature they do. And by
          memory—
in scorched uniforms, holding tiny crushed lunch tins.
All the pleasure-groans of each night call them to return,
          satori

their ghostliness back into the ashes, in the momentary
    shrines,
the thankfulness of arms, from which they will go
again and again, until the day flashes and no one lives
to look back and say, a flash, a white flash sparkled.

Peter Klappert

Peter Klappert was born in Rockville, New York, in 1942. He was educated at Cornell and the University of Iowa. His first book, Lugging Vegetables to Nantucket, *won the Yale Younger Poets Prize in 1971. His later books are* Circular Stairs, Distress in the Mirrors *(1975),* Non Sequitur O'Connor *(1977), and* The Idiot Princess of the Last Dynasty *(1981).*

ELLIE MAE LEAVES IN A HURRY

There's some who say she put death up her dress
and some who say they saw her pour it down.
It's not the sort of thing you want to press

so we just assumed she planned on leaving town
and gave her money for the first express.
She had some family up in Puget Sound.

Well we are married men. We've got interests.
You can't take children out like cats to drown.
It's not the sort of thing you want to press.

We didn't know she'd go and pour death down,   10
though most of us had heard of her distress.
We just assumed she planned on leaving town.

There's some of us who put death up her dress
but she had family up in Puget Sound.
We gave her money for the first express.

Well we are married men. We've got interests.
Though most of us had heard of her distress.
You can't take children out like cats to drown,
it's just the sort of news that gets around.

Etheridge Knight

Etheridge Knight was born in Corinth, Mississippi, in 1933. He served in the Korean War and spent eight years in Indiana State Prison for armed robbery. He has said, "I died in Korea from a shrapnel wound and narcotics resurrected me. I died in 1960 from a prison sentence and poetry brought me back to life." A past editor of Motive *and co-editor of* Black Box, *he has received a Guggenheim Fellowship. His books include* Poems from Prison *(1968),* Belly Song *(1973),* Born of a Woman *(1980), and the anthology* Black Voices from Prison *(1970).*

HAIKU

1

Eastern guard tower
glints in sunset; convicts rest
like lizards on rocks.

2

The piano man
is stingy at 3 am
his songs drop like plum.

3

Morning sun slants cell.
Drunks stagger like cripple flies
On Jailhouse floor.

4

To write a blues song   10
is to regiment riots
and pluck gems from graves.

5

A bare pecan tree
slips a pencil shadow down
a moonlit snow slope.

6

The falling snow flakes
Can not blunt the hard aches nor
Match the steel stillness.

7

Under moon shadows
A tall boy flashes knife and   20
Slices star bright ice.

8

In the August grass
Struck by the last rays of sun
The cracked teacup screams.

9

Making jazz swing in
Seventeen syllables AIN'T
No square poet's job.

Ted Kooser

*Born in Ames, Iowa, in 1939 and educated at Iowa State University and
the University of Nebraska, Ted Kooser now lives in Lincoln, Nebraska,
where he is vice-president of Lincoln Benefit Life Company. The primary aim
of his poetry, he has said, is "presenting a regional picture of the midwest."*

He is the publisher of Windflower Press *and the editor of the popular*
Windflower Home Almanac of Poetry *(1980). His most recent volumes*
of poetry are Sure Signs: New and Selected Poems *(1980), and* One
World at a Time *(1985).*

ANNIVERSARY

At dinner, in that careful rouge of light
of five or six martinis, you could pass
for Ginger Rogers; we could dance all night
on tiny tabletops as slick as glass
in flying, shiny shoes. As Fred Astaire,
my wrinkles grow distinguished as we dine,
my bald spot festers with the growth of hair,
I grow intelligent about the wine.
But such high life is taxing; urgencies
excuse us from the table. Hand in hand   10
we seek the restrooms, trembling at the knees,
and find our grins grown horrid in that land
of flare-lit, glaring mirrors. Through the wall
you flush your toilet like a lonely call.

WILD PIGS

There's four square miles of timber, mostly oak,
just north of here; the only stand of trees
much bigger than a wind-break up or down
the county, and it's thick as thatch, so thick
two fellows shot themselves by accident
just getting through the brush along the road.
The place is full of deer, and pheasants, and quail
like swarms of horseflies in a dairy barn.
And, listen up: they say there's pigs in there,
wild pigs, the size of hunting dogs, with tusks   10

that'll snap a fellow's shin-bone like a twig.
The story goes that in the Civil War
some farmer from Missouri drove them here
to keep the army from conscripting them.
They say he fed them acorns through the war,
and when he went to drive them home again
in '65 they wouldn't go. No Sir;
they liked those acorns! Oh, he tried and tried
to get them out; hired herders, set a fire,
shot some of them for something, God knows why.   20
Although he caught a few of them, some stayed
and multiplied, and got as wild as wolves.
They're up there now, if anybody'd look.

BEER BOTTLE

In the burned-
out highway
ditch the throw-

away beer
bottle lands
standing up

unbroken,
like a cat
thrown off

of a roof   10
to kill it,
landing hard

and dazzled
in the sun,
right side up;

sort of a
miracle.

Judith Kroll

Judith Kroll was born in Brooklyn in 1943. She holds degrees from Smith and Yale, and from 1968 to 1975 she taught at Vassar. Since 1975 she has been living in India, writing and translating Kannada bhakti poems with the partial support of an American Institute of Indian Studies Fellowship. She has twice received National Endowment for the Arts Fellowships and is the author of a book of poems, In the Temperate Zone *(1973), and a critical study,* Chapters in a Mythology: The Poetry of Sylvia Plath *(1976).*

SESTINA

Is this the object:
not to let things pass
without noticing,
without being in control,
at least of a clear sight?
There are so many things worth nothing.

I sit hour after hour, doing nothing—
dreaming of India, a far green object,
a blinding sun hung on the edge of my sight.
One moment I think I am writing, the next I pass   10
into infinite fields, and a sky whose control
rains absolute, unnoticing.

I try to think—but find myself noticing
each word sealed off from its thought by a round nothing.
Something is out of control;
I do not even object,
unaware that the hours pass,
that the present moment is buried from sight

by this vision of me in India, allowing my sight
to filter off in the distance, noticing   20
my feet pass over the lawn, my eyes pass
over and over the garden, settling on nothing.
Such a relief, sight without object.
Such a relief, to let control

be a process like breathing; to let control
lie in the targets of sight,
lie, if anywhere, lost in the heart of the object,
and to let the effort of noticing
soak like rain in that tree, that flower, that nothing.
Every moment something is coming to pass.   30

I remember a high brown mountain: a pass
cut through it, jagged, holding in control
the animals, trees, underbrush, and sky—nothing
escaped, not even my sight;
and the pass extinguished itself at a temple on top, without
      noticing
it had used itself up, it had reached its object.

Is this the object: to pass,
without noticing, beyond control,
beyond fixed sight, beyond nothing?

Maxine Kumin

The 1973 winner of the Pulitzer Prize for Poetry, Maxine Kumin was born in Philadelphia in 1925 and earned bachelor's and master's degrees from Radcliffe. At one time an Olympic-caliber swimmer, she has published many collections of poetry, most recently Our Ground Time Here Will Be

Brief: New and Selected Poems *(1982). She has also written several novels and some twenty books for children (three co-authored with Anne Sexton). She lives on Hillside Farm in New Hampshire, where she and her husband raise horses.*

MORNING SWIM

Into my empty head there come
a cotton beach, a dock wherefrom

I set out, oily and nude
through mist, in chilly solitude.

There was no line, no roof or floor
to tell the water from the air.

Night fog thick as terry cloth
closed me in its fuzzy growth.

I hung my bathrobe on two pegs.
I took the lake between my legs.   10

Invaded and invader, I
went overhand on that flat sky.

Fish twitched beneath me, quick and tame.
In their green zone they sang my name

and in the rhythm of the swim
I hummed a two-four-time slow hymn.

I hummed *Abide with Me.* The beat
rose in the fine thrash of my feet,

rose in the bubbles I put out
slantwise, trailing through my mouth.   20

My bones drank water; water fell
through all my doors. I was the well

that fed the lake that met my sea
in which I sang *Abide with Me.*

JANUARY 25TH

All night in the flue like a trapped thing,
like a broken bird,
the wind knocked unanswered.
Snow fell down the chimney, making
the forked logs spit
ashes of resurrected crickets.
By 3 A.M. both stoves were dead.
A ball of steel wool
froze to the kitchen window sill,
while we lay back to back in bed,   10

two thin survivors. Somewhere in a small dream,
a chipmunk uncorked from his hole
and dodged along the wall.
My love, we live at such extremes
that when, in the leftover spite of the storm,
we touch and grow warm,
I can believe I saw
the ground release
that brown and orange commonplace
sign of thaw.   20

Now daylight the color of buttermilk
tunnels through the coated glass.
Lie still; lie close.
Watch the sun pick
splinters from the window flowers.
Now under the ice, under twelve knee-deep layers
of mud in last summer's pond
the packed hearts of peepers are beating
barely, barely repeating
themselves enough to hang on.   30

Stanley Kunitz

A poet who seeks to "embrace the great simplicities," Stanley Kunitz was born in Worcester, Massachusetts, in 1905 and educated at Harvard, where he received the Garrison Medal for Poetry. Among his many books are Selected Poems, 1928–1958, *for which he received the 1959 Pulitzer Prize,* The Poems of Stanley Kunitz, 1928–1978 *(1979), and* The Wellfleet Whale *(1983). A collection of essays,* A Kind of Order, A Kind of Folly, *appeared in 1975. A former editor of the Yale Series of Younger Poets, he is currently a member of the writing committee at the Fine Arts Work Center in Provincetown, Massachusetts.*

THREE FLOORS

Mother was a crack of light
and a gray eye peeping;
I made believe by breathing hard
that I was sleeping.

Sister's doughboy on last leave
had robbed me of her hand;
downstairs at intervals she played
Warum on the baby grand.

Under the roof a wardrobe trunk
whose lock a boy could pick   10
contained a red Masonic hat
and a walking stick.

Bolt upright in my bed that night
I saw my father flying;

the wind was walking on my neck,
the windowpanes were crying.

AN OLD CRACKED TUNE

My name is Solomon Levi,
the desert is my home,
my mother's breast was thorny,
and father I had none.

The sands whispered, *Be separate,*
the stones taught me, *Be hard.*
I dance, for the joy of surviving,
on the edge of the road.

Joan LaBombard

*Born in San Francisco in 1920 and educated at the University of California
at Los Angeles, Joan LaBombard has won a Borestone Mountain Poetry
Prize and an award from the Poetry Society of America. Her* Calendar
Poems *appeared in 1985. She lives in Los Angeles.*

BY THE BEAUTIFUL OHIO

Now at the dark's perpetual descent,
I remember the hoses, looped like snakes,
The arcs of silver spilled in little lakes,
All that rainbow bridge to summer, bent

Under the hanging stars. They swung so low
Our shirt-sleeved fathers grazed them long ago:
Giants with silver whips, who could crack down
A shower of stars to cool our parching lawn.

That time of summer, there was always time.
Shrill voices counting: *twenty, ready or not,*   10
And bodies light as moths or a firefly's
Glimmer among the elms and then wink out,
Or at the statue-maker's sudden whim,
Swing from his hand in easy equipoise,
Creating marble myths of girls and boys,
While the water falls like silver over them.

Our porches bloomed with shy and spinster aunts,
Daisy, Olivia, Elizabeth—
Their names a nosegay or an orchard's breath.
Among the potted ferns and bric-a-brac   20
They fluttered fans or flirted gauzy sleeves,
Caged in a latticework of trumpet leaves,
And made a constant litany of talk
Till porches darkened and the cage went black.

And in the smothered furnace of the street
A moony Ford goes by on muffled wheels;
Boys and their mongrels spin like catherine wheels.
Under the maples where their elders wilt
One banjo plucks a tune, and two guitars
Follow the tinny plinking charitably   30
And as another fumbles for the key,
The gloomed catalpas blaze with sudden stars.

Come home. The coast is clear. The river's voice
Ravels the labyrinth of space and time.
The blurred canoes, the dance pavilion swim
In wrinkled splendor on the water's face
And the riding lights of towns along that shore
Hang like a chain of tears we bargained for
When first we set our small boats bobbing free,
And never dreamed the river flowed away.   40

Joseph Langland

*A believer in the importance of "the singing voice, even in the harshest poem,"
Joseph Langland was born in Spring Grove, Minnesota, in 1917 and grew
up in Iowa. Educated at Santa Ana College and the University of Iowa, he
has taught at the University of Wyoming and the University of Massachusetts. His books include* The Green Town *(1956),* The Wheel of Summer *(1963), which received the Melville Cane Award, and* Any Body's
Song *(1980), a National Poetry Series selection.*

CONVERSATIONS FROM CHILDHOOD: THE VICTROLA

Lo, Here the Gentle Lark

When Alma Gluck
sang in high soprano,
   Lo,
Here the Gentle Lark,

on the scratched
ten-inch 78 record
to the old Victrola,

that little dog
was always listen-
      ing
in the old horn.

Flutes sang, she sang—
larks singing together—
and he began.

The Dog in the Horn

You dumb bloke,
you think steel needles
      can go
ten records without a mark?

Yeah, we watched
how the grooves got scored,
afraid the mended rota

would lose a cog.
We even tried group
      whistling
when the thing was gone.   10

Money went bang,
depression came, dry weather,
no crops. Man!

And though time
goes terribly round
  & round
I am singing, still.

Yessiree, I'm
looking for the tone
  and sound
of the world's goodwill.

Sydney Lea

Sydney Lea was born in Philadelphia in 1942 and studied at Yale, from which he received his Ph.D. in 1972. The founder and co-editor of New England Review/Bread Loaf Quarterly, *he is on the faculty of Middlebury College and the Bread Loaf Writers' Conference. His poems have been collected in* Searching the Drowned Man *(1980) and* The Floating Candles *(1982). He is also the author of a critical study,* Gothic to Fantastic *(1981).*

ISSUES OF THE FALL

All the plenitude of a sudden so changed! Like quick cartoons of a thought,
   a feeling. Small beasts turned milkwhite from brown. Pale in air,
      fluff—the lingering milkweed pinwheels off. High up,
        fern blackens where buck and doe are getting
         ready: he scents the musk at her light-
          haired whorl of entry. Risen,
           darkened goslings
            chuckle,
            mourn
         in pairs. And so on.   10

I'm thinking of animation, and these last statements of consequence
from old Summer: tired as the 'pecker's scarcening jabs, thumps
at a long season's end. Hollow. Bored. But it's deep,
    it is almost infernal, the time restored
      to the speeding mind by such a time,
        each year repeated as now
          it's repeated before
            the curtain
              falls
        again. Of snow.   20

Before into new and back. Old into after. I speak of transformation,
my own and others': A childhood theatre, Disney, and my Mother
ceasing to be merely Mother, but not yet another
    woman, fantasy so altering the very nature
      of things that I and the world might
        fall through the vortex—so
          frequent a figure
           in the moving
            pictures—
          I to become   30

fowl or animal. Gifted with the power to speak in defiance of all
I had been taught to think was true, was natural. I would learn
the words, moves. "You don't even know down from up,"
    an older girl had told me in an early hard
      day at school. The liquid sound
        of kisses above me like
          the suck of straws
           at milkshakes,
             Good
          and Plenty, spare evil   40

scent that dropped from the balcony. I mustn't ever climb there! Why, then
did they call it "colored heaven"? On the screen, locked in an embrace,
    Mickey and Minnie sigh, chuckle at Pluto, Pluto
      somehow swallows a whistle. There's a cry
        from deep inside: someone older
          might imagine the far wail
           of a soul on its way
             to hell.
            Hard
          laughter down dark   50

air. Which I will join, damnation be damned! Or salvation. And yet it's far
from funny, it's frightful, this sad high summons from low beastly bowels,
attended by beasts. I tremble, but long to rise or tumble
among them. Mother coaxes me back to silence,
briefly. The camera's tricks make up
a finale: buds transformed
to pale angels, whirling
earthward,
taking
on animal guise.   60

There are rare tears in Mother's eyes at these wonderful speeding frames.
Uncertain how to respond, I whistle. The milk of childhood drains.

THERE SHOULD HAVE BEEN

For Alastair Reid

With evening the groom and bride in groundfog
should have mounted the flatbed wagon, drawn
into the orchard by a vast dappled bullock.
Deer—tall stag, keen doe—should have come

so lacily gliding you'd have trouble to tell
their shapes apart from the onrushing mist.
An uncle was seated beside me. He held
white folds of my shirtcollar locked in a fist.

He rumbled: "My dancing days are all over,"
showing the blue stub under his knee   10
where skin like a windfall plum's was gathered.
I started. He gathered me back to see.

The buck's high rack would be velvet by rights,
would sparkle—I thought—with beads of the fog
in the firelight. Because there should have been firelight,
costume, concertina, song.

A wattled aunt secretly loosened a stay.
They could have been lovely, the bride and the groom,
waltzing together on pale tumbled blooms.
I thought how a falling star might display   20

the company's tears, good bubbles of wine,
the rings of emerald newts on the pond
in mating embrace. The close room was stained,
the hallways were humid, with beer and with rum.

The uncle insisted on hauling the needle
back to the same first groove, every dance.
He hummed a rough note under Ella Fitzgerald's
Love For Sale. The party winced

at his crippled taste. Outside the rain
delivered howls from the turnpike, hammers,   30
drills and curses of masons and carpenters
working all night on "Whispering Pines,

Half-Acre Estates"—they were "Coming Soon"—
across the fields. My father started
the rust-pitted Chevy for home at one.
Leg propped on the seat, my uncle farted

and snored. My mother angled her nose
to the window. The asphalt wrinkled with steam.
There should have been some way of escape
for the lumpish opossum pair on the road,   40

dazed as the couple I'd saved from the cake,
jacked in their tracks by the onrushing beams.

THE FLOATING CANDLES

For my brother Mahlon (1944–1980)

You lit a firebrand:
old pine was best.
It lasted, the black
pitch fume cast odors
that, kindling a campfire
or such, today
can bring tears. You held
the torch to one dwarf
candle stub then another
and others till each   10

greased cup filled up
and the stiff wicks stood.
Ten minutes a candle,
but we were young
and minutes seemed long
as the whole vacation.
We chafed and quarreled.
The colors bled
like hues in jewels.
At last we carried   20
a tub of the things
down the path to the Swamp
Creek pond through seed-
heavy meadows where katydids
whined like wires
in mid-August air's
dense atmosphere.
An hour before bedtime.
Reluctant grownups
would trail behind,   30
bearing downhill
the same dull patter
and cups brimful
of rye, which they balanced
with the same rapt care
that balanced our load.
The bullfrogs twanged
till you touched a wick
with the stick, still flaming,
then quieted. We heard them   40
plop in the shallows,
deferring to fire,
and heard in the muck
turtles coasting in flight.
The night brought on
a small breeze to clear
the day that all day
had oppressed us, to dry
the sweat that our purposeful
hour had made,   50
to spread the glims

like dreamboats of glory
in invisible current.
That slow tug drew
the glowing flotilla
south to the dam.
The bank brush—hung
with gemmy bugs—shone
and made great shadows
as the candles slipped by,   60
erasing the banal
fat stars from the surface.
This was, you could say,
an early glimpse
of a later aesthetic.
Nonsense. We know
it was cruder than that
and profounder, far.
It showed us the way
the splendid can flare   70
despite the flow
of the common. Now,
despite the persistence
of heat and quarrel,
the thickness of wives
and children and time,
such shinings on water
are fact. Or sublime.

Al Lee

*Al Lee was born in 1938 in Louisville, Kentucky, and is a graduate of Yale
and the University of Iowa. From 1962 to 1964 he served in the Peace Corps
in Ghana. He is the author of* Time *(1974) and editor of* The Major

Young Poets *(1971)*. *He lives in Maplewood, New Jersey, and teaches*
English at the New Jersey Institute of Technology in Newark.

BESIDE MY GRANDMOTHER

Mam-maw's losing touch at last: her face
is neutralizing in the early gloom
of mid-November. But hanging on because
        of drab & milky bottles her room
withdraws into, she croaks for doctors whom
        the pinpricks in her junkie's arm
retired by calming her coronary storm.

Her eighty years become twelve hours today.
Clustered diamonds weigh upon her hands.
No one but me attends her as the gray   10
        outside & in her walls extends
across her muzzled eyes until she bends
        into her heyday froth again.
Her tears are salty on her sandy skin.

Her second husband's home & coughing blood
like a lame house dog choking on a tack.
Her bachelor youngest son dusts off the road
        & calls it quits, wobbling back
with his tail between his legs, down on his luck
        at 51, & mama cries   20
to see her brother slink like a lost cause.

"Lie back & rest! I am your fair-haired boy.
Everything I've touched has turned to gold,"
I tell this woman bedded with a noise
        inside her ears, which are as filled
as her bed is violent & deathly cold.
        Her memory becomes a cell.
"Stop it," she says, "the hammering in the hall."

Barbara Lefcowitz

Born in New York City in 1935, Barbara Lefcowitz holds a B.A. from Smith, an M.A. from the State University of New York at Buffalo, and a Ph.D. from the University of Maryland. She is the author of A Risk of Green *(1978) and* The Wild Piano *(1981).*

EMILY DICKINSON'S SESTINA FOR MOLLY BLOOM

At times I almost believed it: madness
the only way to say yes,
to stumble into shapes of night
that gape open
like abandoned wells—
This would work like no other

disguise—yet I chose another
route, neither mad
nor well
enough to shout yes!   10
when morning scissor-blades opened
my sack of night

full of valentines to death—Night
whose curve of darkness I preferred to other
hours' slanting light that would open
all my closed lives—not the madly
flowered darkness that would make *you* say yes!
but—I might as well

admit it—the well-
sealed kind of night   20

where I could nod yes
to another
sputter of benign madness
from the loaded gun of an open

wound whose red opening
was never stanched well
enough; if only I hadn't feared the mad
shudder-burst & bloom demanded by your night
I would have become another
woman, spread open like a figtree in my father's
        northern garden, Yes   30

or—yes!
a house with its shutters open
to another
throng of lovers climbing my well-
flowered hair night after night,
all Amherst going mad,

its quartz contentment split open by the pulsing night—
Molly, as well become you as another—
Yes, and my heart going like mad and yes saying yes
        I will yes!   40

David Lehman

*David Lehman was born in 1948 in New York City and attended Co-
lumbia and Cambridge. Besides his poetry collections* Some Nerve *(1973)
and* Day One *(1979), he has edited* Beyond Amazement: New Essays
on John Ashbery *(1980) and, with Charles Berger,* James Merrill:

Essays in Criticism *(1984). Among his awards are two Ingram Merrill grants and a Book-of-the-Month Club Creative Writing Fellowship. He teaches in the Department of Comparative Literature at Columbia and reviews books for* Newsweek.

TOWARDS THE VANISHING POINT

Various nostalgias: rock, scissor, and paper:
Cardinals and opposing orioles in the April rain:
No pain: a brain perfectly in tune with the newspaper,
Like a commuter in love with a computer, and with the
    paper
On which he neatly jots down, in blue
Ballpoint ink, opposing arguments on the burning issue of
    paper
Money and the inflationary rate. Alas, what good are
    paper
Airplanes for traveling down streets longer than the cities
Of which they are a part? Yet we elect to live in these
    cities,
Our faces greeted by windswept pieces of paper,   10
Fragments of flowers: a life in which to pause
Is both a luxury and a defeat, and not to pause

Unthinkable, for it makes resumption possible, though each
    pause
Requires its own because. All newspapers
Are plausible; therefore none are. (Pause.)
As he wiped the dirt off him, he paused
Momentarily, in a daze: it had begun to rain,
But he did not feel a drop. The pause
Brought no applause in its wake, like the pause
Of a parenthesis, bracketing blank space, or like the parting
    blue   20
Sea of the biblical tale, emptiness between blue
Walls, held back in an eternal pause.

What happens next? Up the twisting alleys of these
     mountainous cities,
Motorcycles murder sleep. "Who runs our cities?

I mean, who really runs them? Not that all our cities
Have turned into mortuaries and airports, but . . ." A
     pause
With the grace of sleep ensued, bringing relief to the cities
Of our discontent, our cities
On and off the plain, committed on paper
To the building of sanitary new cities   30
On the same old sites, only cleansed now of the truth that
     can poison our cities
With the truth, lovely as roses in a light rain
Or the migration of starlings on a day made quiet by rain.
Paris and Florence are examples of cities
That know but one moment of ignition, when the blue
Of collars and stockings is erased, replaced by the blue

Of a hero's bruised skin, until everything is as blue
As what you see out of plane windows blurred by rain.
There are those who regard Picasso's blue
Period as anomalous, but the chronic push-and-pull of blue   40
Clouds and a chameleon sky, during a thunderous pause
In a storm, delights even implacable critics of blue,
Who prefer the red of berries and blood to the icier sheen
     of blue.
Adrift, marooned, yet equipped with sufficient paper
For the task, we experience the familiar white of the paper
As an invitation to a lifetime of urges for the blue:
The sea receives us as it does the rain:
Our tears are made superfluous by the rain.

We remember them fondly: fog equals snow plus rain:
Evening in the city equals blue sky minus blue: 50
If dirges and laments could put off death, it would rain:
If laughter could cure insomnia, it would rain:
You could share in the malevolent joy of cities
As enemy clouds drop their payload of rain:
On the battlefields of Waterloo it would rain

And on the apartment houses of Watergate, rain without
    pause:
It would rain forty days and forty nights without pause:
And after it stopped, nostalgia for the rain
Would set in, and editorials in our daily papers
Would recommend that we set fire to the paper   60

And no longer write poems on paper
But on a surface like water, during a pause
Between waves. We would live in unfamiliar cities,
Our pleasure the promise of babies in blue,
Our weather the invention of rain.

Brad Leithauser

Born in Detroit in 1953, Brad Leithauser attended Harvard and Harvard Law School. From 1980 to 1983 he lived in Japan. He has received an Ingram Merrill Award, an Amy Lowell Fellowship, a Guggenheim Fellowship, and a MacArthur Foundation Prize Fellowship. His books include Hundreds of Fireflies *(1982), a collection of poetry, and* Equal Distance *(1985), a novel.*

A QUILLED QUILT, A NEEDLE BED

    Under the longleaf pines
The curved, foot-long needles have
Woven a thatchwork quilt—threads,
Not patches, windfall millions
Looped and overlapped to make
The softest of needle beds.

The day's turned hot, the air
Coiling around the always
Chill scent of pine. As if lit
From below, a radiance   10
Warmer yet more clement than
The sun's, the forest-carpet

Glows. It's a kind of pelt:
Thick as a bear's, tawny like
A bobcat's, more wonderful
Than both—a maize labyrinth,
Spiraling down through tiny
Chinks to a caked, vegetal

Ferment where the needles
Crumble and blacken. And still   20
The mazing continues . . . whorls
Within whorls, the downscaling
Yet-perfect intricacies
Of lichens, seeds and crystals.

Denise Levertov

*One of the most influential proponents and developers of Coleridge's theory
of organic form, Denise Levertov was born in Ilford, Essex, England, in
1923 and educated at home. She emigrated to the United States in 1948,
after marrying the American writer Mitchell Goodman. Although she never
attended Black Mountain College, she has been associated with the Black
Mountain Movement. A former poetry editor of* The Nation, *she has
received many honors, including the Morton Dauwen Zabel Award, the*

Shelley Memorial Award, and a Guggenheim Fellowship. Her Collected
Poems *appeared in 1983. She lives in Maine.*

BEDTIME

We are a meadow where the bees hum,
mind and body are almost one

as the fire snaps in the stove
and our eyes close,

and mouth to mouth, the covers
pulled over our shoulders,

we drowse as horses drowse afield,
in accord; though the fall cold

surrounds our warm bed, and though
by day we are singular and often lonely.   10

OBSESSIONS

Maybe it is true we have to return
to the black air of ashcan city
because it is there the most life was burned,

as ghosts or criminals return?
But no, the city has no monopoly
of intense life. The dust burned

golden or violet in the wide land
to which we ran away, images
of passion sprang out of the land

as whirlwinds or red flowers, your hands   10
opened in anguish or clenched in violence
under that sun, and clasped my hands

in that place to which we will not return
where so much happened that no one else noticed,
where the city's ashes that we brought with us
flew into the intense sky still burning.

Philip Levine

*Philip Levine was born in Detroit in 1928 and educated at Wayne State
University, the University of Iowa, and Stanford. His awards include a
Guggenheim Fellowship, the Lenore Marshall Award, the National Book
Critics Circle Award, and the first American Book Award. Among his
books are* Ashes: Poems Old and New *(1979),* 7 Years from Somewhere *(1979),* One for the Rose *(1981),* Selected Poems *(1984),
and* Sweet Will *(1985). Through all the considerable changes in his
poetry over the years, at least one thing has remained constant, according to
Levine: "I try to pay homage to the people who taught me my life was a
holy thing." He currently divides his time between Fresno, California,
where he teaches at California State University, and Boston, where he
teaches at Tufts.*

ANIMALS ARE PASSING FROM OUR LIVES

It's wonderful how I jog
on four honed-down ivory toes
my massive buttocks slipping
like oiled parts with each light step.

I'm to market. I can smell
the sour, grooved block, I can smell
the blade that opens the hole
and the pudgy white fingers

that shake out the intestines
like a hankie. In my dreams   10
the snouts drool on the marble,
suffering children, suffering flies,

suffering the consumers
who won't meet their steady eyes
for fear they could see. The boy
who drives me along believes

that any moment I'll fall
on my side and drum my toes
like a typewriter or squeal
and shit like a new housewife   20

discovering television,
or that I'll turn like a beast
cleverly to hook his teeth
with my teeth. No. Not this pig.

NIGHT THOUGHTS OVER A SICK CHILD

Numb, stiff, broken by no sleep,
I keep night watch. Looking for
signs to quiet fear, I creep
closer to his bed and hear
his breath come and go, holding
my own as if my own were
all I paid. Nothing I bring,
say, or do has meaning here.

Outside, ice crusts on river
and pond; wild hare come to my   10
door, pacified by torture.

No less ignorant than they
of what grips and why, I am
moved to prayer, the quaint gestures
which ennoble beyond shame
only the mute listener.

No one hears. A dry wind shifts
dry snow, indifferently;
the roof, rotting beneath drifts,
sighs and holds. Terrified by   20
sleep, the child strives toward
consciousness and the known pain.
If it were mine by one word
I would not save any man,

myself or the universe
at such cost: reality.
Heir to an ancestral curse
Though fallen from Judah's tree,
I take up into my arms my hopes,
my son, for what it's worth give   30
bodily warmth. When he escapes
his heritage, then what have

I left but false remembrance
and the name. Against that day
there is no armor or stance,
only the frail dignity
of surrender, which is all
that can separate me now
or then from the dumb beast's fall,
unseen in the frozen snow.   40

FOR FRAN

She packs the flower beds with leaves,
Rags, dampened paper, ties with twine
The lemon tree, but winter carves
Its features on the uprooted stem.

I see the true vein in her neck
And where the smaller ones have broken
Blueing the skin, and where the dark
Cold lines of weariness have eaten

Out through the winding of the bone.
On the hard ground where Adam strayed,   10
Where nothing but his wants remain,
What do we do to those we need,

To those whose need of us endures
Even the knowledge of what we are?
I turn to her whose future bears
The promise of December air—

My living wife, Frances Levine,
Mother of Theodore, John, and Mark,
Out of whatever we have been
We will make something for the dark.   20

John Logan

*John Logan, who has defined poetry as "a reaching, an anonymous loving,"
was born in Red Oak, Iowa, in 1923. He received a bachelor's degree in
zoology from Coe College, a master's degree in English from the University
of Iowa, and did graduate work in philosophy at Georgetown, Notre Dame,
and Berkeley. He served as poetry editor for* The Nation *and also founded
and, with Milton Kessler, edited* Choice. *The recipient of a Morton
Dauwen Zabel Award, the William Carlos Williams Award, and other
honors, he has published many books, most recently* Only the Dreamer Can
Change the Dream: Selected Poems *(1981).*

SHORE SCENE

There were bees about. From the start I thought
The day was apt to hurt. There is a high

Hill of sand behind the sea and the kids
Were dropping from the top of it like schools
Of fish over falls, cracking skulls on skulls.
I knew the holiday was hot. I saw
The August sun teeming in the bodies
Logged along the beach and felt the yearning
In the brightly covered parts turning each
To each. For lunch I bit the olive meat: 10
A yellow jacket stung me on the tongue.
I knelt to spoon and suck the healing sea . . .
A little girl was digging up canals
With her toes, her arm hanging in a cast
As white as the belly of a dead fish
Whose dead eye looked at her with me, as she
Opened her grotesque system to the sea . . .
I walked away; now quietly I heard
A child moaning from a low mound of sand,
Abandoned by his friend. The child was tricked,   20
Trapped upon his knees in a shallow pit.
(The older ones will say you can get out.)
I dug him up. His legs would not unbend.
I lifted him and held him in my arms
As he wept. Oh I was gnarled as a witch
Or warlock by his naked weight, was slowed
In the sand to a thief's gait. When his strength
Flowed, he ran, and I rested by the sea . . .
A girl was there. I saw her drop her hair,
Let it fall from the doffed cap to her breasts   30
Tanned and swollen over wine red woolen.
A boy, his body blackened by the sun,
Rose out of the sand stripping down his limbs
With graceful hands. He took his gear and walked
Toward the girl in the brown hair and wine
And then past me; he brushed her with the soft,
Brilliant monster he lugged into the sea . . .
By this tide I raised a small cairn of stone
Light and smooth and clean, and cast the shadow
Of a stick in a perfect line along   40
The sand. My own shadow followed then, until
I felt the cold swirling at the groin.

TO A YOUNG POET WHO FLED

Your cries make us afraid, but we love your delicious music!
—Kierkegaard

So you said you'd go home to work on your father's farm.
We've talked of how it is the poet alone can touch
with words, but I would touch you with my hand, my lost
    son,
to say good-bye again. You left some work, and have gone.
You don't know what you mean. Oh, not to me as a son,
for I have others. Perhaps too many. I cannot
answer all the letters. If I seem to brag, I add
I know how to shatter an image of the father
(twice have tried to end the yearning of an orphan son,
but opened up in him, and in me, another wound).   10
No—I say this: you don't know the reason of your gift.
It's not the suffering. Others have that. The gift of tears
is the hope of saints, Monica again and Austin.
I mean the gift of the structure of a poet's jaw,
which makes the mask that's cut out of the flesh of his face
a megaphone—as with the goat clad Greeks—to ampli-
fy the light gestures of his soul toward the high stone seats.
The magic of the mouth that can melt to tears the rock
of hearts. I mean the wand of tongues that charms the exile
of listeners into a bond of brothers, breaking   20
down the lines of lead that separate a man from a
man, and the husbands from their wives, in these old,
    burned glass
panels of our lives. The poet's jaw has its tongue ripped
as Philomel, its lips split (and kissed beside the grave),
the jawbone patched and cracked with fists and then with
    the salve
of his fellows. If they make him bellow,, like a slave
cooked inside the ancient, brass bull, still that small
    machine
inside its throat makes music for an emperor's guest
out of his cries. Thus his curse: the poet cannot weep
but with a public and musical grief, and he laughs   30
with the joys of others. Yet, when the lean blessings come,

they are sweet, and great. My son, I could not make your
    choice.
Let me take your hand. I am too old or young to say,
"I'd rather be a swineherd in the hut, understood
by swine, than be a poet misunderstood by men."

William Logan

Born in Boston in 1950, William Logan is a graduate of Yale and the
University of Iowa. He spent two years in England as an Amy Lowell Poetry
Traveling Scholar and currently directs the creative writing program at the
University of Florida. He is the author of Dream of Dying *(1979),*
Sad-Faced Men *(1982), and* Difficulty *(1984).*

TATIANA KALATSCHOVA

Only a woman of this measure
Suits the industry model.
Among the headless torsos she stands
Unyielding and calm as a perfect

Saint about to be burned, as they sew
The cloth around her bones
Unlike anyone else's bones,
Being noble, Russian, a measure

For all the dresses to be sewn
In her common size. When she models,   10
The designers become accustomed to the perfect
Blonde posture her body takes as it stands

In their dresses. She understands
The satisfaction in bones
That year to year perfect
Their proportions. Take her measure:

From it they have made mannequins, models
Named for a dead czar's daughter, who sewed
As her sisters and servants sewed
Rubies into pillows, and then were made to stand   20

In the basement to be bloodied by the model
Soldiers who poured acid on their bones.
This Tatiana dances to a different measure,
The hem and drape of perfect

Design. She need not perfect
The techniques of the peasant, to sew
Bolt and bolt of cloth without measure,
To harvest the corn when it stands,

To find in a chicken the bones
Thin as the bones of a model.   30
But any woman, whether a model
To industry or blessed with imperfect

Proportions, knows that skin will weaken her bones.
When the czar is murdered, let it not end so
Quickly, she might say, unless she understands
That silence is itself a measure:

Robert Lowell

*A member of the famous family that includes poets James Russell and Amy
Lowell, Robert Lowell was born in Boston in 1917 and educated at Harvard, Kenyon, and Louisiana State University. During World War II he*

*was jailed for resisting the draft. One of the most honored poets of his time,
he received the Pulitzer Prize, the National Book Award, the National Book
Critics Circle Award, the Bollingen Poetry Translation Award, and the
Copernicus Award, and in 1963 he was elected by the American Academy
and Institute of Arts and Letters to the chair vacated by Robert Frost. His
books include* Lord Weary's Castle *(1946),* Life Studies *(1959),*
Imitations *(1961),* For the Union Dead *(1964),* Selected Poems
(1976), and Day By Day *(1977). He died in 1977.*

MR. EDWARDS AND THE SPIDER

I saw the spiders marching through the air,
Swimming from tree to tree that mildewed day
  In latter August when the hay
    Came creaking to the barn. But where
      The wind is westerly,
Where gnarled November makes the spiders fly
Into the apparitions of the sky,
  They purpose nothing but their ease and die
Urgently beating east to sunrise and the sea;

What are we in the hands of the great God?   10
It was in vain you set up thorn and briar
  In battle array against the fire
    And treason crackling in your blood;
      For the wild thorns grow tame
And will do nothing to oppose the flame;
Your lacerations tell the losing game
  You play against a sickness past your cure.
How will the hands be strong? How will the heart endure?

A very little thing, a little worm,
Or hourglass-blazoned spider, it is said,   20
  Can kill a tiger. Will the dead
    Hold up his mirror and affirm
      To the four winds the smell

And flash of his authority? It's well
If God who holds you to the pit of hell,
Much as one holds a spider, will destroy,
Baffle and dissipate your soul. As a small boy

On Windsor Marsh, I saw the spider die
When thrown into the bowels of fierce fire:
There's no long struggle, no desire   30
To get up on its feet and fly—
It stretches out its feet
And dies. This is the sinner's last retreat;
Yes, and no strength exerted on the heat
Then sinews the abolished will, when sick
And full of burning, it will whistle on a brick.

But who can plumb the sinking of that soul?
Josiah Hawley, picture yourself cast
Into a brick-kiln where the blast
Fans your quick vitals to a coal—   40
If measured by a glass
How long would it seem burning! Let there pass
A minute, ten, ten trillion; but the blaze
Is infinite, eternal: this is death,
To die and know it. This is the Black Widow, death.

IN THE CAGE

The lifers file into the hall,
According to their houses—twos
Of laundered denim. On the wall
A colored fairy tinkles blues
And titters by the balustrade;
Canaries beat their bars and scream.
We come from tunnels where the spade
Pick-axe and hod for plaster steam
In mud and insulation. Here
The Bible-twisting Israelite   10
Fasts for his Harlem. It is night,
And it is vanity, and age
Blackens the heart of Adam. Fear,
The yellow chirper, beaks its cage.

WATER

It was a Maine lobster town—
each morning boatloads of hands
pushed off for granite
quarries on the islands,

and left dozens of bleak
white frame houses stuck
like oyster shells
on a hill of rock,

and below us, the sea lapped
the raw little match-stick   10
mazes of a weir,
where the fish for bait were trapped.

Remember? We sat on a slab of rock.
From this distance in time,
it seems the color
of iris, rotting and turning purpler,

but it was only
the usual gray rock
turning the usual green
when drenched by the sea.   20

The sea drenched the rock
at our feet all day,
and kept tearing away
flake after flake.

One night you dreamed
you were a mermaid clinging to a wharf-pile,
and trying to pull
off the barnacles with your hands.

We wished our two souls
might return like gulls   30
to the rock. In the end,
the water was too cold for us.

Thomas Lux

Thomas Lux was born in Northampton, Massachusetts, in 1946 and educated at Emerson College and the University of Iowa. Before taking his current position at Sarah Lawrence, he taught at Oberlin and the University of Houston. A former associate editor of Field, *he is the author of* Memory's Handgrenade *(1972),* The Glassblower's Breath *(1976),* Sunday *(1979), and* Tarantulas on the Lifebuoy *(1983).*

ALL THE SLAVES

All the slaves within me
are tired or nearly dead.
They won't work for money,
not for a slice of bread.

Tired or nearly dead,
half underwater, wanting
merely a slice of bread:
the inner slaves, singing.

Half underwater, wanting
only a few flippers to swim,   10
the inner slaves, singing
the depth-charges within.

Only a few flippers to swim!
And a sensor to sense the sound
of the depth-charges within—
that's all they ask for aloud.

A sensor to sense the sound,
a hearer to hear the small aurals:
that's all they ask for aloud.
They're slaves with slaves' morals.   20

Hearers hearing small aurals,
they won't work for money.
They're slaves with slaves' morals,
all these slaves within me.

Mekeel McBride

*Born in 1950, Mekeel McBride has been a visiting professor at Princeton
and currently teaches at the University of New Hampshire. Her books include*
No Ordinary World *(1979) and* The Going Under of the Evening
Land *(1983).*

A BLESSING

From what, sometimes, seems an arbitrary
form or discipline often come two words
that rhyme and, in the rhyming, fully marry
the world of spoons and sheets and common birds
to another world that we have always known,
where the waterfall of dawn does not drown
even the haloed gnat, where we are shown
how to find and hold the pale day moon, round
and blessed in the silver lake of a coffee spoon.

Thomas McGrath

Born on a farm in North Dakota in 1916, Thomas McGrath was educated
at the University of North Dakota, Louisiana State University, and Oxford,
where he was a Rhodes scholar. During World War II he served in the Air
Force in the Aleutians. The founder and first editor of Crazy Horse *maga-*
zine, he has written many books, among them New and Selected Poems
(1964), Letter to an Imaginary Friend *(1969),* The Movie at the End
of the World *(1972),* Passages Toward the Dark *(1982), and* Echoes
Inside the Labyrinth *(1983).*

THE END OF THE WORLD

The end of the world: it was given to me to see it.
Came in the black dark, a bulge in the starless sky,
A trembling at the heart of the night, a twitching of the
    webby flesh of the earth.
And out of the bowels of the street one beastly,
    ungovernable cry.

Came and I recognized it: the end of the world.
And waited for the lightless plunge, the fury splitting the
    rock.
And waited: a kissing of leaves: a whisper of man-killing
    ancestral night—
Then: a tinkle of music, laughter from the next block.

Yet waited still: for the awful traditional fire,
Hearing mute thunder, the long collapse of sky.   10
It falls forever. But no one noticed. The end of the world
    provoked
Out of the dark a single and melancholy sigh

From my neighbor who sat on his porch drinking beer in
    the dark.
No: I was not God's prophet. Armageddon was never
And always: this night in a poor street where a careless
    irreverent laughter
Postpones the end of the world: in which we live forever.

Sandra McPherson

*Born in 1943 in San Jose, California, and educated at San Jose State College
and the University of Washington, Sandra McPherson has been awarded
fellowships from the National Endowment for the Arts and the Ingram
Merrill Foundation. She has taught at the University of Iowa and Berkeley
and currently teaches in the Oregon Writers Workshop in Portland. Her
books are* Elegies for the Hot Season *(1970),* Radiation *(1973),* The
Year of Our Birth *(1978),* Sensing *(1980), and* Patron Happiness
(1983).

LAMENT, WITH FLESH AND BLOOD

I do not know much about innocence
But it seems you are responsible
For this evening lake's young blue that laments
How fishermen joke and loons laugh. Sybil
Of leeches, you're young but you're scary,
Dangling your thin, taut, clarifying legs
At fish cleanings in the estuary.
Fog stars the knives that slip out pike eggs.
Blue's future is black. The present is rain.
The past is rain the wind blows back.   10

Still you sit—Audubon, catch that blue vein!—
A tiny funnel bisecting your cheek.
I want you to run to me with your kiss.
Still you brood in the lake like wild rice.

TRIOLET

She was in love with the same danger
everybody is. Dangerous
as it is to love a stranger,
she was in love. With the same danger
an adulteress risks a husband's anger.
Stealthily death enters a house:
she was in love with that danger.
Everybody is dangerous.

Charles Martin

Charles Martin was born in New York City in 1942 and educated at Fordham and the State University of New York at Buffalo. He has received an Ingram Merrill Fellowship and is the author of Room for Error *(1978) and* Passages from Friday *(1983) and the translator of* The Poems of Catullus *(1979).*

SHARKS AT THE NEW YORK AQUARIUM

Suddenly drawn through the thick glass plate
And swimming among them, I imagine
Myself as, briefly, part of the pattern
Traced in the water as they circulate

Endlessly, obeying the few laws
That thread the needle of their simple lives:
One moment in a window of serrated knives,
Old-fashioned razors and electric saws.
And then the sudden, steep, sidewinding pass:
No sound at all. The waters turning pink,   10
Then rose, then red, after a long while clear.
And here I am again, outside the tank,
Uneasily wrapped in our atmosphere!
Children almost never tap on the glass.

SIGNS

THIS PARK IS PUBLIC PROPERTY AND SHOULD
NOT WILL NOT CANNOT PLEASE OBEY
THE TREES WHOSE BRANCHES FLOURISH AS YOU WOULD
SCHOOLCHILDREN ON A TRIP OR HOLIDAY

BECAUSE OF ON THE LAWNS IS NOT ALLOWED
AND WILL BE VIOLATED BY THE TREES
GROWING IN SECTIONS WHERE THE NEWLY PLOWED
ARE NOT PERMITTED THEREFORE THEREFORE "PLEASE"

CURB YOUR SOFTBALL IS RESTRICTED TO
DESIGNATED AREAS THE ROSES   10
EXPOSING THEMSELVES TO THOSE "JUST PASSING
     THROUGH"
WILL ALL BE PUNISHED AFTER THIS PARK CLOSES

PLEASE REMEMBER ITS FOR OTHERS TOO
BEFORE YOU LEAVE FOR HOME PLEASE PICK UP ALL
SLEDDING BIKING JOGGING WATCHING YOU
DAILY AT FIVE WEEKENDS AT NIGHTFALL

Peter Meinke

Peter Meinke was born in Brooklyn in 1932 and earned degrees at Hamilton College, the University of Michigan, and the University of Minnesota. His collections include Lines from Neuchatel *(1974), which won the Poetry Society of America's Gustav Davidson Award,* The Night Train and the Golden Bird *(1977),* The Rat Poems *(1978), and* Trying to Surprise God *(1981). He lives in St. Petersburg, Florida, where he directs the writing workshop at Eckerd College.*

ATOMIC PANTOUM

In a chain reaction
the neutrons released
split other nuclei
which release more neutrons

The neutrons released
blow open some others
which release more neutrons
and start this all over

Blow open some others
and choirs will crumble   10
and start this all over
with eyes burned to ashes

And choirs will crumble
the fish catch on fire
with eyes burned to ashes
in a chain reaction

The fish catch on fire
because the sun's force
in a chain reaction
has blazed in our minds   20

Because the sun's force
with plutonium trigger
has blazed in our minds
we are dying to use it

With plutonium trigger
curled and tightened
we are dying to use it
torching our enemies

Curled and tightened
blind to the end   30
torching our enemies
we sing to Jesus

Blind to the end
split up like nuclei
we sing to Jesus
in a chain reaction

William Meredith

*William Meredith was born in New York City in 1919. A graduate of
Princeton, he served as a Navy aviator during World War II and the
Korean War and worked as a reporter for the* New York Times *and opera
critic for* The Hudson Review. *His awards include the Yale Younger*

Poets Prize and the Loines Award. Among his books are Earth Walk: New
and Selected Poems *(1970),* Hazard, the Painter *(1975), and* The
Cheer *(1979). He has also translated Apollinaire's* Alcools *(1964).
Since 1955 he has been a member of the faculty of Connecticut College.*

EFFORT AT SPEECH

For Muriel Rukeyser

Climbing the stairway gray with urban midnight,
Cheerful, venial, ruminating pleasure,
Darkness takes me, an arm around my throat and
        Give me your wallet.

Fearing cowardice more than other terrors,
Angry I wrestle with my unseen partner,
Caught in a ritual not of our own making,
        panting like spaniels.

Bold with adrenalin, mindless, shaking,
God damn it, no! I rasp at him behind me,   10
Wrenching the leather wallet from his grasp. It
        breaks like a wishbone,

So that departing (routed by my shouting,
Not by my strength or inadvertent courage)
Half of the papers lending me a name are
        gone with him nameless.

Only now turning, I see a tall boy running,
Fifteen, sixteen, dressed thinly for the weather.
Reaching the streetlight he turns a brown face briefly
        phrased like a question.   20

I like a questioner watch him turn the corner
Taking the answer with him, or his half of it.
Loneliness, not a sensible emotion,
        breathes hard on the stairway.

Walking homeward I fraternize with shadows,
Zig-zagging with them where they flee the streetlights,
Asking for trouble, asking for the message
                    trouble had sent me.

All fall down has been scribbled on the street in
Garbage and excrement: so much for the vision   30
Others taunt me with, my untimely humor,
                    so much for cheerfulness.

Next time don't wrangle, give the boy the money,
Call across chasms what the world you know is.
Luckless and lied to, how can a child master
                    human decorum?

Next time a switch-blade, somewhere he is thinking,
I should have killed him and took the lousy wallet.
Reading my cards he feels a surge of anger
                    blind as my shame.   40

Error from Babel mutters in the places,
Cities apart, where now we word our failures:
Hatred and guilt have left us without language
                    who might have held discourse.

James Merrill

James Merrill was born in New York City in 1926, served in the U.S. Army, and attended Amherst College. Among the many awards he has received are the Bollingen Prize, the Pulitzer Prize, and twice, the National Book Award. He is the author of two novels, two plays, and thirteen collections of poetry, most recently From the First Nine: Poems 1947–

1976 *(1982),* The Changing Light at Sandover *(1982) and* Late
Settings *(1985). The current editor of the Yale Series of Younger Poets,
he divides his time between homes in Stonington, Connecticut, and Key West,
Florida.*

A RENEWAL

Having used every subterfuge
To shake you, lies, fatigue, or even that of passion,
Now I see no way but a clean break.
I add that I am willing to bear the guilt.

You nod assent. Autumn turns windy, huge,
A clear vase of dry leaves vibrating on and on.
We sit, watching. When I next speak
Love buries itself in me, up to the hilt.

MIRROR

I grow old under an intensity
Of questioning looks. *Nonsense,*
I try to say, *I cannot teach you children
How to live.—If not you, who will?*
Cries one of them aloud, grasping my gilded
Frame till the world sways. *If not you, who will?*
Between their visits the table, its arrangement
Of Bible, fern and Paisley, all past change,
Does very nicely. If ever I feel curious
As to what others endure,   10
Across the parlor *you* provide examples,
Wide open, sunny, of everything I am
Not. You embrace a whole world without once caring
To set it in order. That takes thought. Out there
Something is being picked. The red-and-white bandannas
Go to my heart. A fine young man
Rides by on horseback. Now the door shuts. Hester
Confides in me her first unhappiness.
This much, you see, would never have been fitted

Together, but for me. Why then is it   20
They more and more neglect me? Late one sleepless
Midsummer night I strained to keep
Five tapers from your breathing. *No,* the widowed
Cousin said, *let them go out.* I did.
The room brimmed with gray sound, all the instreaming
Muslin of your dream . . .

Years later now, two of the grown grandchildren
Sit with novels face-down on the sill,
Content to muse upon your tall transparence,
Your clouds, brown fields, persimmon far   30
And cypress near. One speaks. *How superficial
Appearances are!* Since then, as if a fish
Had broken the perfect silver of my reflectiveness,
I have lapses. I suspect
Looks from behind, where nothing is, cool gazes
Through the blind flaws of my mind. As days,
As decades lengthen, this vision
Spreads and blackens. I do not know whose it is,
But I think it watches for my last silver
To blister, flake, float leaf by life, each milling-   40
Downward dumb conceit, to a standstill
From which not even you strike any brilliant
Chord in me, and to a faceless will,
Echo of mine, I am amenable.

SWIMMING BY NIGHT

A light going out in the forehead
Of the house by the ocean,
Into warm black its feints of diamond fade.
Without clothes, without caution

Plunging past gravity—
Wait! Where before
Had been floating nothing, is a gradual body
Half remembered, astral with phosphor,

Yours, risen from its tomb
In your own mind,   10
Haunting nimbleness, glimmerings a random
Spell had kindled. So that, new-limned

By this weak lamp
The evening's alcohol will feed
Until the genie chilling bids you limp
Heavily over stones to bed,

You wear your master's robe
One last time, the far break
Of waves, their length and sparkle, the spinning globe
You wear, and the star running down his cheek.   20

W. S. Merwin

W. S. Merwin was born in 1927 in New York City and raised in Union City, New Jersey, and Scranton, Pennsylvania. He began writing as a small child, composing hymns for his father, who was a Presbyterian minister. A graduate of Princeton, Merwin lived for many years in France, England, Mexico, and elsewhere, and has translated widely from Latin, French, Spanish, Portuguese, and Russian literature. He has received the Yale Younger Poets Prize, the P.E.N. Prize for Translation, the Bollingen Prize, the Pulitzer Prize, and many other honors. His numerous collections include The Lice *(1967),* Selected Translations 1948–1968 *(1968),* The Carrier of Ladders *(1970),* The First Four Books of Poems *(1975),* The Compass Flower *(1977), and* Opening the Hand *(1983).*

THE DRUNK IN THE FURNACE

For a good decade
The furnace stood in the naked gully, fireless
And vacant as any hat. Then when it was
No more to them than a hulking black fossil
To erode unnoticed with the rest of the junk-hill
By the poisonous creek, and rapidly to be added
To their ignorance,

They were afterwards astonished
To confirm, one morning, a twist of smoke like a pale
Resurrection, staggering out of its chewed hole,   10
And to remark then other tokens that someone,
Cosily bolted behind the eye-holed iron
Door of the drafty burner, had there established
His bad castle.

Where he gets his spirits
It's a mystery. But the stuff keeps him musical:
Hammer-and-anvilling with poker and bottle
To his jugged bellowings, till the last groaning clang
As he collapses onto the rioting
Springs of a litter of car-seats ranged on the grates,   20
To sleep like an iron pig.

In their tar-paper church
On a text about stoke-holes that are sated never
Their Reverend lingers. They nod and hate trespassers.
When the furnace wakes, though, all afternoon
Their witless offspring flock like piped rats to its siren
Crescendo, and agape on the crumbling ridge
Stand in a row and learn.

GRANDFATHER IN THE OLD MEN'S HOME

Gentle at last, and as clean as ever,
He did not even need drink any more,
And his good sons unbent and brought him

Tobacco to chew, both times when they came
To be satisfied he was well cared for.
And he smiled all the time to remember
Grandmother, his wife, wearing the true faith
Like an iron nightgown, yet brought to birth
Seven times and raising the family
Through her needle's eye while he got away   10
Down the green river, finding directions
For boats. And himself coming home sometimes
Well-heeled but blind drunk, to hide all the bread
And shoot holes in the bucket while he made
His daughters pump. Still smiled as kindly in
His sleep beside the other clean old men
To see Grandmother, every night the same,
Huge in her age, with her thumbed-down mouth, come
Hating the river, filling with her stare
His gliding dream, while he turned to water,   20
While the children they both had begotten,
With old faces now, but themselves shrunken
To child-size again, stood ranged at her side,
Beating their little Bibles till he died.

RIVER SOUND REMEMBERED

That day the huge water drowned all voices until
It seemed a kind of silence unbroken
By anything: a time unto itself and still;

So that when I turned away from its roaring, down
The path over the gully, and there were
Dogs barking as always at the edge of town,

Car horns and the cries of children coming
As though for the first time through the fading light
Of the winter dusk, my ears still sang

Like shells with the swingeing current, and   10
Its flood echoing in me held for long
About me the same silence, by whose sound

I could hear only the quiet under the day
With the land noises floating there far-off and still;
So that even in my mind now turning away

From having listened absently but for so long
It will be the seethe and drag of the river
That I will hear longer than any mortal song.

Robert Mezey

Robert Mezey was born in Philadelphia in 1935 and educated at Kenyon, the University of Iowa, and Stanford. He won the 1960 Lamont Prize for The Lovemaker *and recently received an American Academy and Institute of Arts and Letters Award. Besides* The Lovemaker, *his many books include* The Door Standing Open: New and Selected Poems, 1954–1969 *(1970),* Couplets *(1978), and* Selected Translations *(1981). With Stephen Berg, he edited the influential anthologies* Naked Poetry *and* New Naked Poetry. *He teaches at Pomona College in Claremont, California.*

MY MOTHER

My mother writes from Trenton,
a comedian to the bone
but underneath serious
and all heart. 'Honey,' she says,
'be a mensch and Mary too,

its no good, to worry, you
are doing the best you can
your Dad and everyone
thinks you turned out very well
as long as you pay your bills   10
nobody can say a word
you can tell them, to drop dead
so save a dollar it can't
hurt—remember Frank you went
to highschool with? he still lives
with his wife's mother, his wife
works while he writes his books and
did he ever sell a one
the four kids run around naked
36, and he's never had,   20
you'll forgive my expression
even a pot to piss in
or a window to throw it,
such a smart boy he couldnt
read the footprints on the wall
honey you think you know all
the answers you dont, please, try
to put some money away
believe me it wouldn't hurt
artist shmartist life's too short   30
for that kind of, forgive me,
horseshit, I know what you want
better than you, all that counts
is to make a good living
and the best of everything,
as Sholem Aleichem said,
he was a great writer did
you ever read his books dear,
you should make what he makes a year
anyway he says some place   40
Poverty is no disgrace
but its no honor either
that's what I say,
                    love,
                        Mother'

Jane Miller

Jane Miller was born in New York in 1949 and educated at the University of Iowa. She is the author of Many Junipers, Heartbeats *(1980),* The Greater Leisures *(1983), which was a National Poetry Series selection, and, with Olga Broumas,* Black Holes, Black Stockings *(1985). She lives in Provincetown, Massachusetts, and teaches at Freehand, a school for woman writers and photographers.*

TIME; OR, HOW THE LINE ABOUT CHAGALL'S *LOVERS* DISAPPEARS

Man Ray is blowing out fuses in a French room
wired for minimum current.
Ours is more like a shy moment
in blue,

the pale light that witnesses three sleighs
asleep against a large pine.
So much is some distance
away:

the pond recently black with wild duck locks its inch
of ice;   10
and then the goose
in which a quarter of an hour is brought to despair.

Next week we shall say "three years"
as if there were such
white peaches,
in Russia, perhaps, but not here.

Here is our bedroom where doubt maintains
a yellow bedframe and, fortunately,
that spare key.
Therefore the door; we go through like Vico's spiral, like a
    village moved to   20

tears by a passing train.
Past the effect of moonlight, if not the moon,
its steel bells interrupting the dialectic.
Your brown eyes darling, why must they be so black?

You're asleep in the fourth dimension
like an almond
tree in the mild
winter sun of the Mediterranean.

I crawl under you, careless
where destinies have a way of not sounding   30
serious. Speech is death
who can but laugh and pipe a flute,

who loves you.

Vassar Miller

*Vassar Miller, who has said that "Poetry may be the expiring breath of God
drawn out to eternity," was born in Houston in 1924 and educated at the
University of Houston. She has published several collections of poetry, most
recently* Selected & New Poems *(1982), and an anthology,* Despite
This Flesh: The Disabled in Stories and Poems *(1985). A former poet
laureate of Texas, she lives in Houston.*

WITHOUT CEREMONY

Except ourselves, we have no other prayer;
Our needs are sores upon our nakedness.
We do not have to name them; we are here.
And You who can make eyes can see no less.
We fall, not on our knees, but on our hearts,
A posture humbler far and more downcast;
While Father Pain instructs us in the arts
Of praying, hunger is the worthiest fast.
We find ourselves where tongues cannot wage war
On silence (farther, mystics never flew)   10
But on the common wings of what we are,
Borne on the wings of what we bear, toward You,
Oh Word, in whom our wordiness dissolves,
When we have not a prayer except ourselves.

Gary Miranda

Gary Miranda was born in Bremerton, Washington, in 1938 and raised in Seattle. He did undergraduate work at various Jesuit seminaries and graduate work at San Jose State University and the University of California at Irvine. He is the author of Listeners at the Breathing Place *(1978), which was nominated for the Pulitzer Prize,* Grace Period *(1983), and a translation of Rilke's* Duino Elegies *(1981). He has won nine awards from the Poetry Society of America, and in 1978 was chosen by* The Atlantic *to serve as poet-in-residence at Robert Frost's house in Franconia, New Hampshire. He lives in Portland, Oregon, where he works as a graphic artist.*

HORSE CHESTNUT

I fell from one once. Judy Cole
used to put five of them, whole,
in her mouth. My brothers ran to tell
my mother: It's Gary—he fell
from a tree but he isn't dead
yet. As I write, there is one outside
my window. I have a weakness, still, for
women with large mouths. The doctor
put two fingers into my head,
tingly with novocaine, and said   10
to my mother: Look, you can see
where the skull is chipped. Sometimes we
made pipes, or necklaces. My mother
groaned and looked away. I could never
figure out what connection they had
with horses.

Later, Judy Cole was named Miss
Seattle. Mostly, what I remember is
blood all around and me lying
there thinking: so this is dying.   20
Every one of them has two inside,
like testicles. I wasn't afraid
really, just convinced. By the time I began
to think I loved her we had been
children too long for it to matter.
Sixteen stitches. I saw her once later,
when she was married. My mother
said: I don't want to see you near
that tree again—understand? I still tend
to confuse dying and love. And   30
no one I've ever loved has died,
exactly.

LOVE POEM

A kind of slant—the way a ball will glance
off the end of a bat when you swing for the fence

and miss—that is, if you could watch that once
up close and in slow motion; or the chance
meanings, not even remotely intended, that dance
at the edge of words, like sparks. Bats bounce
just so off the edges of the dark at a moment's
notice, as swallows do off sunlight. Slants

like these have something to do with why "angle"
is one of my favorite words, whenever it chances   10
to be a verb; and with why the music I single
out tonight—eighteenth century dances—
made me think just now of you untangling
blueberries, carefully, from their dense branches.

THE MAGICIAN

For an uncle, drowned at sea

I remember you at the bathroom mirror
practicing sleight-of-hand,
trying to master all the angles
like a guilty husband.

Or I think of the time you nearly drowned
at Wilderness. My father
pumped your chest long past necessity
and a crowd gathered

and I was sure your breath was a toy
no tears could buy.   10
But you came back, a regular
Houdini.

By now you are an accepted fact,
even to the fish. Dead,
you are as unastonishing
as love that has outworn its need.

It will do no good to toss in your sleep,
accumulating patter.
Because, uncle, there is no crowd
and it does not matter   20

that death has taught you to hold your breath
for years at a turn.
It is a trick
anyone can learn.

Judith Moffett

*Judith Moffett was born in Louisville, Kentucky, in 1942 and grew up in
Cincinnati. She earned a Ph.D. in American Civilization from the Univer-
sity of Pennsylvania, where she now teaches. She has received awards from
the Ingram Merrill Foundation, The Swedish Academy, and the National
Endowment for the Arts. Her books of poetry are* Keeping Time *(1976)
and* Whinny Moor Crossing *(1984), and she has published a translation
of Hjalmar Gullberg's* Gentleman, Single, Refined and Selected
Poems 1937–1959 *(1979), which won her the Columbia Translation
Prize, and a critical study,* James Merrill: An Introduction to the
Poetry *(1984).*

NOW OR NEVER

I They gave me in my kindergarten year
What seemed irrelevant, an Old Maid deck.
Gems, wrinkled skin, strange glasses on a stick,
Long gloves, pressed lips, and horrible orange hair,
No child, no husband ever to be hers,
That gaunt crone wasn't anything like me!
I got her meaning fast: *ignominy*
Is being single in a game of pairs.

How could I have imagined singleness,
Who called my mother's spinster aunt an old   10
"Witch-widder" heartlessly and was corrected
(A "maiden lady")? Nor had I suspected,
A child myself, that yearning for a child
Can raven even old maids like avarice.

II   Each morning of my tenth summer *swears Memory*
      mythologizing as usual our washer disgorged a pulpy
            heap
      of wet white strong cheap
      fabric, ropy, smelling of soap, which it was my
      job to untwist, shake out, nip
      onto the lines high in windy sun   20
      it never rained two corners to a clothespin,
      then prop still higher. *Flap*   Flap.

      I plucked them down
      stiffened, fragrant, mounding the basket knee-
      high, to be cleverly doubled to eight
      neat thicknesses by me each afternoon.
      Diaper service was costly, convenient Pampers yet
      to be invented. I was the diaper service. *Me*

III   Those were the clean ones, but I don't think
      I minded any of it;   30
      a fragrance must exonerate,
      somehow, a stink.

      I've sloshed hundreds of filled diapers in
      toilet bowls, not breathing;
      what I remember is a sheathing
      of powder on the changeling's clean skin.

      And milkiness, patting his back
      against my draped shoulder. For this, I see
      the laundered airy diapers of Memory
      peeling like lightning off the stack.   40

Not, not ever now, the crusty sour-
milk ones I very well know there were.

IV There had to be. Doctors: "Your baby has
pyloric stenosis," a valve constriction which meant
he threw up a lot. Eventually he went
back to the hospital and was dosed with drops.

My mother broke to me the fabulous news
she was "expecting" (at last! after the years of hopes
and disappointing miscarriages!) in the Maternity
Shoppe of a big downtown department store: 50

"What's a 'maternity dress'?" "For ladies to wear
while they're pregnant." "Who're *you* buying one
        for?" "Me!"

I used to say, back in the irresponsible Fifties,
I wanted "a big family." Though I was one of the
        tree-
dwelling, androgynous little girls dolls bore,
I always liked even upchucky babies.

V   And all that windy, sunny diaper-summer—
His first, my tenth—I'd go out with our baby,
My little, little brother, walking. Maybe
His live weight on my heart induced the murmur   50
I always, lately, seem to hear. Returning
I'd feed him formula and sing, the rocker
Groaning a metronomic cadence, Shaker
Wisdom: *we come round right* I sang *by turning.*

Recalling what this battered snapshot shows,
The flannelette cocoon my sharp elbows
Bracket so bonily, a wash of joy
Transfigures all that gawkiness and spreads
Luminous circles right around both heads,
Mine, frowsy, and the fragile skull of the boy.   60

VI so late as 65 a man has time   small
    wonder age obsesses   my own
    how inconceivably 31
    pelvis stiffening ova going stale

    Charlotte Brontë
    died at 39 of TB
    and the complications of a first pregnancy
    having it would have killed her anyway

    Eunice Kennedy Shriver
    handily started her large family at 32   70
    you don't know   can't know   you

    fret   you're apprehensive   terrified
    demons called mongolism and difficult birth invade
    your peace   *now* you conclude *or never*

MEZZO CAMMIN

I mean to mark the Midway Day
With soundings in this verse-form. Say,
        Muse, how you hate it!
I know your taste for excess. But
These jingly rhymes must undercut,
        Counter, deflate it.

I trust them, and I can't trust you
To practice self-restraint. In lieu
        Of building
Some Watts Tower to my fulcrum age   10
I've shut you in this little cage;
        Start gilding!

The stanzas should be varied slightly,
Thus: some more and some less tightly
        Nipped at the waist
And ankles, odd lines fitting an extra s-
Yllable in, or with a dextrous
        Flick of the wrist

Some rhymes set slant, and so forth; still
It's tight, you'll have to try, Muse. Trill   20
      Like a canary,
Bright jailbird; swing your wee trapeze!
Come come, don't sulk. Laudamus, please,
      Not miserere.

At 21, by now, what did
I want/expect? At least one kid,
      More like a triad;
The man; to've written books in whose
Thickets a troubled child could lose
      Itself, as I had.   30

Might I have made a kid-glove fit
Of wifery and kiddy lit
      And being Mother—
Slipped chipper as a Chinese foot
Stunted into my doll-size boot—
      Or sensed I'd smother

And howling burst the seams—or ripened
Like a summer squash? It's happened;
      The odd wife sprouts
In marriage as in fertilizer.   40
Single, shall I be full-size, or . . . ?
      —Doubts or no doubts

"The family experience"—
Engrossing, commonplace; one's chance
      To mother better
Than Mother did—I've missed that; I'm
Too old, now, to begin in time
      At last. A matter

I hope will come to matter less,
Though there's no question childlessness   50
      Bears harder
Than spinsterhood. Since all the strong
Kind types go off the market young,
      It's murder

To find one single, able, willing,
Sane, and minimally appealing
        Body/work/wit;
But still there's *time.* "Too old"'s what's poignant.
Only one other disappointment
        Overpowers that: 60

Losing the Baptists: wash of grief.
(A hamstring harped on loud enough
        Already.)
Not even Jesus, Ethicist
Survives this far; if not the Christ,
        Nobody.

O *Kinder, Kirche,* let me go,
How can I bless you now? I know,
        I trust, the center
That holds, holds more than family   70
And faith, and warms a place for me
        In deep mid-winter.

Start Spinster Lib? We spinsters pull
Up stakes and fly to Istanbul
        On low-cost charters!
Of the past ten I've wangled three
Years foreign; and mobility
        Is just for starters.

Spinsters who spend the night don't phone;
Spinsters go trekking on their own   80
        And have a swell time.
One, on a solitary jaunt,
Comes close to people couples don't,
        Glued in the birdlime

Of one another's omnipresence.
—Fresh views, late talk, warmth; tumescence
        Also (which thrives
On talk), unlooked-for, not surprising,
Nice. Nice way of improvising
        Alternate lives.   90

Then, after breakfast, off you go. It's
No bad thing for "nature poets"
    To solo through.
Though hiking with a friend is splendid,
Hike got less of me than friend did
    When one came too.

In every sense you're more acute
Alone. You note what's what en route,
    You're not distracted.
Plus (irony) so long as you're   100
Abroad upon the tumbling moor
    Where Life's enacted—

So perilous, so gorse-gilt, so
Abundant—friendships seem godsent.
    Always, you're shaken—
Joy is a shock; you're . . . *reverent.*
By tough old-maid wayfarers no
    True friend gets taken

For granted; nor do loving's other
Faces blear through custom either.   110
    Spinsters have learnt
To value what they can't get used to—
Values many a wife's reduced to,
    Wishing she weren't!

Too cramped, she envies (irony)
Us bachelor girls, so long less free
    Than outcast! Yearning
To spread roots in a roomy plot,
We crumpled them into some pot
    And went sojourning.   120

The life abroad calls into question
Style, assumptions Yank and Christian,
    Habits (how you—
"Two-handed engine"?—fork your plateful);
Forces thought and choice. I'm grateful.
    The road from Lou-

isville to Lund was passing strange
But now I'm through I wouldn't change,
    Cresting this peak age,
For kids and home. A Lu:uhv'le shut   130
Mind, close and smoky as a hut,
    Came with the package.

Things have the disadvantages,
It's claimed, of their advantages—
    Of light and air, then.
I think so. No one gets it all.
The grass is green here too; I call
    My draw a fair one.

TWININGS ORANGE PEKOE

The gas ring's hoarse exhaling wheeze,
Voice of blue flamelets, licks the kettle's
Copper underbelly, which crouches
Closer, concentrates, by degrees

Begins spellbound to match that pressure
And dragon tone. Breath crowds the slim
Tranced throat that cannot close or scream;
It spouts a rushing *whooo* of pleasure.

The brown potbellied pot, top doffed,
Reveals its scalded insides' tender   10
Nursery blue, from which a cloud
Exudes, and from its spout a slender

Curl. It sweats and loves the *tch*
A lid makes popping off a tin,
The fragrance deep as leafmold, rich
As pipe tobacco, coffee, cocoa;

Loves the spoon's dry *scroop,* the skin-
Tight leafheap scattered in its breast
(A tannic prickle); the swift boiling
Flashflood, spoonswirl, settling flight; loves best   20

The steeping in the dark: blind alchemy:
Tap water, and an acid that cures leather
Stains cups and eats through glazes, pregnantly
Stewing together,

To arch forth in a stream as brown and bright
And smoky as an eye, strain marbling up
Through milk and sugar in a stoneware cup,
White white on white.

N. Scott Momaday

A leading figure in Native American literature, N. Scott Momaday was born in Lawton, Oklahoma, in 1934, and grew up on a number of Indian reservations in the Southwest. After undergraduate study at the University of New Mexico, he took M.A. and Ph.D. degrees from Stanford. His books include the Pulitzer Prize-winning novel House Made of Dawn *(1968), an autobiography,* The Names: A Memoir *(1976), and two collections of poetry,* Angle of Geese and Other Poems *(1974) and* The Gourd Dancer *(1976). He currently teaches at the University of Arizona.*

COMPARATIVES

Sunlit sea,
the drift of fronds,
and banners
of bobbing boats—
the seaside
of any day—
except: this
cold, bright body
of the fish

upon the planks,   10
the coil and
crescent of flesh
extending
just into death.

Even so,
in the distant,
inland sea,
a shadow runs,
radiant,
rude in the rock: 20
fossil fish,
fissure of bone
forever.
It is perhaps
the same thing,
an agony
twice perceived.

It is most like
wind on waves—
mere commotion,   30
mute and mean,
perceptible—
that is all.

Richard Moore

*Richard Moore was born in Greenwich, Connecticut, in 1927. He served
as a pilot in the Air Force, attended Yale and Trinity College, and now lives
in Belmont, Massachusetts, and teaches at the New England Conservatory
of Music. He is the author of four books:* A Question of Survival *(1971),*
Word from the Hills *(1972),* Empires *(1982), and* The Education
of a Mouse *(1983).*

FRIENDS

O how lightly in youth we achieved our disinterested
    friendships!
  It was so easy to give
                  when we were nothing ourselves—
shapeless, indefinite, rarefied—great souls filling the
    cosmos.
  But we were bound to contract,
                  doomed to solidify, friend.
Gravity, centered in each, draws out of the infinite spaces
  all things down to its own
                  niggardly miserable earth.

Robert Morgan

Robert Morgan was born in Hendersonville, North Carolina, in 1944 and grew up in nearby Zirconia in the Blue Ridge Mountains. He earned degrees from the Universities of North Carolina at Chapel Hill and Greensboro. The recipient of three National Endowment for the Arts Fellowships and the Eunice Tietjens Prize from Poetry, *he has published several collections, including* Zirconia Poems *(1969),* Red Owl *(1972),* Land Diving *(1976),* Trunk & Thicket *(1978), and* Groundwork *(1979). He teaches at Cornell.*

CHANT ROYAL

Born in a notch of the high mountains where
a spring ran from under the porch, on
the second of April just one hundred years
ago this month, my grandpa was a weak one
to start with, premature, weighed a scant
two pounds twelve ounces. So fragile the aunt
who tended him that first night feared to move

him except for feeding and the changing of
diapers. He slept near the fire in a shoebox
with one end cut out. Against the odds he would prove   10
adequate for survival, withstanding all knocks.

Because he was puny his mother would rear
him sheltered, keep him beside her out of the sun
and rain alike, feed him molasses and sulfur in fear
of worms and would let him walk, not run,
to the gap with the others to stand on the slant
bars while the cows were milked in elegant
twilight. Pious and hard, she showed her love
through strictness and was known to reprove
him for the least resistance. She tried raw fox   20
grape juice and teas of the yarb grannies, strove,
adequate for survival, withstanding all knocks,

to find faith healers, quacks, to cure
her youngest. A cousin wrote of Dr. Wilson
down near Greenville. They took the wagon one clear
morning and reached the town just as the moon
rose full. The man at the door said, "I can't
see you this late," but examined and began to rant
on the virtues of tobacco ("Give him a chew.") then shove
and shoo them out. That night they drove   30
all the way back. No telling what unlocks
the vitality: from that day he began to grow and rove
adequate for survival, withstanding all knocks.

Frampold as any mountain branch he hunted bees and deer,
carried to mill on Cold Friday and learned the fun
of shivarees and drinking. Saw his father appear
walking through the pasture toward him and beckon,
then vanish when he spoke like any hant,
and die within the month. He heard a panther
scream and follow as he came back through the cove   40
from hogkilling, and sat up nights by the stove
while his brother crisised with fever and tried to mock
death before it cooled him. Nobody who saw the dove
was adequate for survival, withstanding all knocks.

Out sanghunting he met Mrs. Capps and her
daughter sawing crosscut. The girl could stun
with her beauty, hiding bare feet under leaves. Inner

currents stirred. He quit drinking, came to church, and
  won
her after three weeks courting. But they lived in want
the first year; a child died. He made his covenant   50
one cold night in the orchard and a trove
came in acres for sale cheap on the creek above
the Andrews place. There he sank a well through rock,
weathered debt, depression, set groves,
adequate for survival, withstanding all knocks.

Envoi

Guardian ghost, inhere herein. Before Jove
may this music honor his example, improve
my time as he invested his, and no less unorthodox
discover significance in the bonds his fate wove
adequate for survival, withstanding all knocks.   60

Howard Moss

*Howard Moss was born in 1922 in New York City and educated at the
University of Wisconsin and Columbia. He is the author of twelve books of
poems, including* Selected Poems, *for which he received the 1972 National Book Award,* Buried City *(1975),* A Swim Off the Rocks
(1976), Notes from the Castle *(1980),* Rules of Sleep *(1984), and*
New Selected Poems *(1985). Since 1950 he has been the poetry editor
of* The New Yorker.

FINDING THEM LOST

Thinking of words that would save him, slanting
Off in the air, some cracked, some bent;
Finding them lost, he started saying
Some other words he never meant.

The green went back and forth in waves
As if his heart pumped out the lawn
In blood, not grass. A bench sailed down,
Becoming the bench he sat upon,

Staring out at the crazy garden,
With its women washed out to milky shades,   10
Or pressed through the trees' accordion,
While the past jerked past in lantern slides,

Badly lit, of images unbidden,
Faces, arms, and forgotten eyes
That, peeping through the leaves, half hidden,
Turned on and off like fireflies.

Fire and flies. *That* was it,
He thought, as the nurse bloomed, coming, coming
Straight through a tree to hold his hand.
Holding hers, he felt blood drumming   20

Through the twined bones of where they met.
It was three months the stubborn grass
Wouldn't rise up to meet his foot,
Or rising up, caught him unawares.

How to get back to pure imagination,
He asked the nerves of work and love,
And both networks of such importance,
He dreamed them. But what was he dreaming of?

Sleep, it was sleep, that found him napping
When the delicious dew of sweat   30
Brought forth the baby he'd been hiding
Wrapped in his skin, maybe his heart.

And what the mirror gave back was him
Finally, tired and very old.
"My life, begin . . ." But it didn't, wouldn't,
Though grass was grass and no bench sailed

Down to a garden to support him
And no one walked through a tree to hold
His hand. But a green lawn pulses in him.
Home, he still dreams of going home.   40

TO THE ISLANDS

Afflicted by order, the minimalist disease,
We leave for the islands and something wilder,
The ocean simmering, reading Jean Rhys
By hurricane lamp in a cottage the builder

Forgot to finish. Or he ran out of money.
At least it isn't dirty, old New York,
Crunch and siren. And when we get lonely,
Bird watching, a phonograph, a nature walk

Come to the rescue. But the ship shipwrecks
On rocks unforeseen. The sun won't come out.   10
Old standbys don't work, like drink, or sex,
Boredom a poison with no antidote,
And just when we think of getting the hell out,
The beautiful scapegoats arrive by boat.

Stanley Moss

Stanley Moss was born in New York in 1925 and educated at Trinity College, Yale, and abroad. He served on the editorial staffs of Botteghe Oscure, New Directions, *and* The New American Review. *He is the recipient of a Rockefeller grant and the author of* The Wrong Angel *(1966) and* Skull of Adam *(1978). He lives in New York City, where he works as an art dealer and publisher of Sheep Meadow Press.*

PRAYER

Give me a death like Buddha's. Let me fall
over from eating mushrooms Provençal,
a peasant wine pouring down my shirt-front,
my last request not a cry but a grunt;
kicking my heels to heaven, may I succumb
tumbling into a rose bush after a love
half my age; though I'm deposed, my tomb
shall not be empty, may my belly show above
my coffin like a distant hill, my mourners come
as if to pass an hour in the country,   10
to see the green, that old anarchy.

Howard Nemerov

Howard Nemerov was born in 1920 in New York City. After graduating from Harvard, he joined the Royal Canadian Air Force and flew in England in World War II. His most recent books are The Collected Poems, *which won the Pulitzer Prize and the National Book Award in 1978,* Sentences *(1980),* Inside the Onion *(1984), and* New and Selected Essays *(1985). He lives in St. Louis, where he is Edward Mallinckrodt Distinguished University Professor of English at Washington University.*

A PRIMER OF THE DAILY ROUND

A peels an apple, while B kneels to God,
C telephones to D, who has a hand
On E's knee, F coughs, G turns up the sod
For H's grave, I do not understand
But J is bringing one clay pigeon down

While K brings down a nightstick on L's head,
And M takes mustard, N drives into town,
O goes to bed with P, and Q drops dead,
R lies to S, but happens to be heard
By T, who tells U not to fire V   10
For having to give W the word
That X is now deceiving Y with Z,
Who happens just now to remember A
Peeling an apple somewhere far away.

THE GOOSE FISH

On the long shore, lit by the moon
To show them properly alone,
Two lovers suddenly embraced
So that their shadows were as one.
The ordinary night was graced
For them by the swift tide of blood
That silently they took at flood,
And for a little time they prized
        Themselves emparadised.

Then, as if shaken by stage-fright   10
Beneath the hard moon's bony light,
They stood together on the sand
Embarrassed in each other's sight
But still conspiring hand in hand,
Until they saw, there underfoot,
As though the world had found them out,
The goose fish turning up, though dead,
        His hugely grinning head.

There in the china light he lay,
Most ancient and corrupt and grey.   20
They hesitated at his smile,
Wondering what it seemed to say
To lovers who a little while
Before had thought to understand,
By violence upon the sand,
The only way that could be known
        To make a world their own.

It was a wide and moony grin
Together peaceful and obscene;
They knew not what he would express,   30
So finished a comedian
He might mean failure or success,
But took it for an emblem of
Their sudden, new and guilty love
To be observed by, when they kissed,
    That rigid optimist.

So he became their patriarch,
Dreadfully mild in the half-dark.
His throat that the sand seemed to choke,
His picket teeth, these left their mark   40
But never did explain the joke
That so amused him, lying there
While the moon went down to disappear
Along the still and tilted track
    That bears the zodiac.

BRAINSTORM

The house was shaken by a rising wind
That rattled window and door. He sat alone
In an upstairs room and heard these things: a blind
Ran up with a bang, a door slammed, a groan
Came from some hidden joist, and a leaky tap,
At any silence of the wind, walked like
A blind man through the house. Timber and sap
Revolt, he thought, from washer, baulk and spike.
Bent to his book, continued unafraid
Until the crows came down from their loud flight   10
To walk along the rooftree overhead.
Their horny feet, so near but out of sight,
Scratched on the slate; when they were blown away
He heard their wings beat till they came again,
While the wind rose, and the house seemed to sway,
And window panes began to blind with rain.
The house was talking, not to him, he thought,

But to the crows; the crows were talking back
In their black voices. The secret might be out:
Houses are only trees stretched on the rack.   20
And once the crows knew, all nature would know.
Fur, leaf and feather would invade the form,
Nail rust with rain and shingle warp with snow,
Vine tear the wall, till any straw-borne storm
Could rip both roof and rooftree off and show
Naked to nature what they had kept warm.

He came to feel the crows walk on his head
As if he were the house, their crooked feet
Scratched, through the hair, his scalp. He might be dead
It seemed, and all the noises underneath   30
Be but the cooling of the sinews, veins,
Juices, and sodden sacks suddenly let go;
While in his ruins of wiring, his burst mains,
The rainy wind had been set free to blow
Until the green uprising and mob rule
That ran the world had taken over him,
Split him like seed, and set him in the school
Where any crutch can learn to be a limb.

Inside his head he heard the stormy crows.

John Frederick Nims

Born in Muskegon, Michigan, in 1913, John Frederick Nims received his
B.A. and M.A. from Notre Dame and his Ph.D. in comparative literature
from the University of Chicago. He served as editor of Poetry for many years.
The recipient of the 1982 Academy of American Poets Fellowship, he has
published numerous collections of poetry, most recently Selected Poems

(1982). He has also written Western Wind *(1974, 1983), a well-known poetry textbook, and edited* The Harper Anthology of Poetry *(1981). He teaches at the Chicago campus of the University of Illinois.*

LOVE AND DEATH

And yet a kiss (like blubber)'d blur and slip,
Without the assuring skull beneath the lip.

Frank O'Hara

A proponent of "personism," the attempt to put the poem "squarely between the poet and the person" to whom it is addressed, Frank O'Hara was born in Baltimore in 1926 and grew up in Massachusetts. He attended the New England Conservatory of Music, Harvard, and the University of Michigan, where he won the Hopwood Award. He was associated with John Ashbery, Kenneth Koch, and other members of the New York Poets. He worked as an editor for Art News *and as curator of the international program at the Museum of Modern Art in New York. His books include* The Collected Poems *(1971) and* Poems Retrieved *(1977). He died in 1966 after being struck by a dune buggy on Fire Island. Upon his death, his family and friends established the Frank O'Hara Foundation for Poetry and Art to recognize and assist writers and other artists.*

TO THE POEM

Let us do something grand
just this once   Something

small and important and
unAmerican   Some fine thing

will resemble a human hand
and really be merely a thing

Not needing a military band
nor an elegant forthcoming

to tease spotlights or a hand
from the public's thinking   10

But be   In a defiant land
of its own a real right thing

POEM

At night Chinamen jump
on Asia with a thump

while in our willful way
we, in secret, play

affectionate games and bruise
our knees like China's shoes.

The birds push apples through
grass the moon turns blue,

these apples roll beneath
our buttocks like a heath   10

full of Chinese thrushes
flushed from China's bushes.

As we love at night
birds sing out of sight,

Chinese rhythms beat
through us in our heat,

the apples and the birds
move us like soft words,

we couple in the grace
of that mysterious race.   20

YOU ARE GORGEOUS AND I'M COMING

Vaguely I hear the purple roar of the torn-down Third Avenue
    El
it sways slightly but firmly like a hand or a golden-downed
    thigh
normally I don't think of sounds as colored unless I'm
    feeling corrupt
concrete Rimbaud obscurity of emotion which is simple and
    very definite
even lasting, yes it may be that dark and purifying wave,
    the death of boredom
nearing the heights themselves may destroy you in the pure
    air
to be further complicated, confused, empty but refilling,
    exposed to light

With the past falling away as an acceleration of nerves
    thundering and shaking
aims its aggregating force like the Métro towards a realm
    of encircling travel
rending the sound of adventure and becoming ultimately
    local and intimate   10
repeating the phrases of an old romance which is constantly
    renewed by the
endless originality of human loss the air the stumbling quiet
    of breathing
newly the heavens' stars all out we are all for the captured
    time of our being

AUBADE

To Jimmy Schuyler

A million stars are dreaming out
the murderous whims of the apples.
Sinking like celestas in the dawn
already growing faint, beyond temples

whose silent throbbing dictates
a green life to my waking heart. Bids
the bones that decorate this shore
become the pearl of loved eyelids'

sunlight, withdrawn until unseen
at night, when like the cat's hand,   10
the sea, they warmly flutter near
upon the belly of the sable sand.

A meaning of my life volleys
thus into the sky to rest, breathes
upon these vessels by the sea,
to be wrought in the frothing waves.

Carole Oles

Carole Oles was born in New York City in 1939 and earned degrees at Queens College and Berkeley. Her books include The Loneliness Factor *(1979),* Quarry *(1983), and* Night Watches *(1985). She has received the Poetry Society of America's Gertrude B. Claytor Prize, a National Endowment for the Arts Fellowship, and other awards. She teaches at the Boston campus of the University of Massachusetts.*

A MANIFESTO FOR THE FAINT-HEARTED

Don't curse your hands,
the tangle of lines
there. Look how
in the deepening snow
your feet make blue fish
no one can catch.

Don't take personally
the defection of leaves.
You can't be abandoned
by what you never owned.   10
Spring will give back more
green than you can bear.

Don't rest by the hearth
when all you're worth
tells you *Run!*
If the fires within
strangle, not even suns
will comfort your bones.

You're not so special.
The jungle's full of animals   20
whose guts invert
when a stronger one parts
the camouflage, peers through
as they climb a tree.

Don't think you're different.
The world's full of runts,
stutterers like yourself
who'd save all they have
not to lose it.
They lose it.   30

Leave trails, be separate,
dress warm, travel light.
Eat fear to grow muscle,
even Olympic champs fall.
Store advice
in a cool, dry place.

Robert Pack

---

*Born in New York City in 1929 and educated at Dartmouth and Co-
lumbia, Robert Pack teaches at Middlebury College and directs the annual
Bread Loaf Writers' Conference. He has received a National Institute of Arts
and Letters Award and is the author of nine books of poems, including*
Waking to My Name: New and Selected Poems *(1975),* Keeping
Watch *(1976), and* Faces in a Single Tree: A Cycle of Monologues
(1984). He lives in Cornwall, Vermont.

THE BOAT

I dressed my father in his little clothes,
Blue sailor suit, brass buttons on his coat.
He asked me where the running water goes.

"Down to the sea," I said; "Set it afloat!"
Beside the stream he bent and raised the sail,
Uncurled the string and launched the painted boat.

White birds, circling the mast, wrenched his eyes pale.
He leaped on the tight deck and took the wind.
I watched the ship foam lurching in the gale,

And cried, "Come back, you don't know what you'll find!"   10
He steered. The ship grew, reddening the sky
As waves throbbed back, blind stumbling after blind.

The storm receded in his darkened eyes,
And down he looked at me. A harbor rose.
I asked, "What happens, father, when you die?"

He told where all the running water goes,
And dressed me gently in my little clothes.

CLEANING THE FISH

Mom says she won't; we'll have to clean them, though
she used to do it when I fished with dad.
Dad's illness wore her down; I think she felt
relief after he died, and didn't mourn
him long enough before she married Sam.
I know there is an art to cleaning fish.
In ancient times, prophets could look into
the future by examining the entrails
of an animal; they'd burn it then
to satisfy their chosen deity.   10
Hold down the tail, and use a scraping knife,
stroking the scales to get right to the skin.
Slice through the vent and open up the fish,
just like a box. Then pluck the organs out:
liver, bladder, stomach, and gills; cut off
the head and tail, and wash away the blood.
This tissue here—this irridescent film
that runs along the whole back-bone—must be
removed with care. How smooth the small heart is!
It will continue beating for a while.   20
Fish don't feel pain as people do; they go
right into shock without the fear of death,
like other animals, because they have
no thought of time extending after them.
They don't know what loss is; you mustn't feel
sorry for them. Don't be upset with mom.
It was because of us that she remarried
so soon following dad's death. She knew
we needed money and a healthy father
in the house after those draining years.   30
When Sam bought you that dress with yellow birds
you've wanted for a year, you hardly said
a word of thanks. But I predict that he'll
be kind to you and mom. I've told him how
dad sang to you before you went to bed,
even when he had lost the melody,
until the very end. Sam understands
the way the dead still live within our minds.
The clearest memory I have of dad—
he's pasting in his stamps, studying them   40

with his magnifying glass, looking for
the special marks that make them valuable.
The ones he loved the most were animals,
bright red and blue, I think from Africa.
He told me that he never traded those.
I saved his whole collection for a while,
but then I had to sell it to a friend.
Enough of that! Today we concentrate
on fish! First, rinse it in cold water, dry,
then lightly rub with salt, inside and out.   50
A shallow dish is what we use, and top
with sherry, soy, and peanut oil. Later,
I'll give you all the measurements. Sprinkle
with parsley, garnish with some shredded scallions,
and, behold, a two pound fish should steam
for twenty minutes and be done! Take out
mom's crystal glasses, grandma's silverware,
the yellow tablecloth, and light the candles
when the sun goes down; they shine with orange
merging into purple blue, almost like   60
the inside of the fish. When you grow up
and marry someone whom you really love,
you'll teach your daughter how to clean a fish.
If dad were still with us, he'd show approval
with his eyes: "Life must serve life," they'd say,
"here's to good food!" And Sam, well we'll find out
whether he has an appetite for fish!

Molly Peacock

---

*Molly Peacock was born in Buffalo, New York, in 1947. A graduate of the
State University of New York at Binghamton and Johns Hopkins, she is the
author of* And Live Apart *(1980) and* Raw Heaven *(1984). She makes
her home in New York City, where she teaches at Friends Seminary.*

JUST ABOUT ASLEEP TOGETHER

Just about asleep together, tenderness
of monkey-like swells of grooming ourselves
just about stilled, the duet nonetheless
whispers on, unshelving everything shelved
by the day. A head shifted by nude arms
into its right place soothes the crooked habits
of the body. In lips that talk out of harm's
way is a softness known only to rabbits
and sleepers. It shifts them from the almost to
the genuine: sleep, heavy, black, and blank,   10
the void before the dream. At some cost to
this ankle, that hip, one head, one armpit, a shank
slowly curves, a back turns, an ass is fit
to a belly and two bodies lie frankly
foetal, knees drawn, crook into crook, wing by tit
in the orbit of sleeping. And blankly
shifting and waking without waking
is that much touch that is our sleep making.

John Peck

John Peck was born in Pittsburgh in 1941, grew up in northwest Pennsylvania, and studied at Allegheny College and Stanford. His Shagbark *was published in 1972 and* The Broken Blockhouse Wall *in 1978. His awards include the Prix de Rome and a Guggenheim Fellowship. He has taught at Princeton, Mt. Holyoke, and in Rome, and is currently a free-lance editor and teacher in Europe.*

ROWING EARLY

The mold-brown, moss-green, broad trunk of my wake
Spreads through trees mirrored on the morning lake,

And, through a wafer mist between the shores,
Grows bubble branches, budding from the oars—

Till it hangs wide and tremulous, and I
Stop rowing, watching it as slowly die,

Winking in rhythm—but the trees remain,
Imperfectly reflected, subtle stain

Deep as the sunken trees no one can see
That ride beneath us, like the green ash tree   10

At the lost roots of the world, in morning air—
Air quiet as this lake, trees everywhere.

The boat drifts on its image into theirs,
And they part to receive it, unawares.

IN FRONT OF A JAPANESE PHOTOGRAPH

A sentry and a ladder mark the wall,
But shadows only, on the open wood.
Its paint was burnt away, though not quite all:
It stands yet where the man and ladder stood.

Sun making second morning at ground zero
Had photographed them, silhouettes on white—
Matchstick rungs and the flat outline, no hero,
Of the single human shape, erect and slight.

He might have looked into the glare, or not.
We make out only, once again, the wood,   10
And shadows cast by nothing at that spot.
And looking, that we stand where he had stood.

Robert Pinsky

---

*A poet who wants to "resist the general prejudice against abstract statement"
without abandoning imagery, Robert Pinsky was born in Long Branch, New
Jersey, in 1940 and educated at Rutgers and Stanford. His books include*
Sadness and Happiness *(1975),* An Explanation of America *(1980),
and* History of My Heart *(1984). He has also published* The Situation
of Poetry *(1976), a critical work, and* The Separate Notebooks
(1984), a collection of poems by Czeslaw Milosz which he co-translated.

MEMORIAL

(J.E. and N.M.S.)

Here lies a man. And here, a girl. They live
In the kind of artificial life we give

To birds or statues: imagining what they feel,
Or that like birds the dead each had one call,

Repeated, or a gesture that suspends
Their being in a forehead or the hands.

A man comes whistling from a house. The screen
Snaps shut behind him. Though there is no man

And no house, memory sends him to get tools
From a familiar shed, and so he strolls   10

Through summer shade to work on the family car.
He is my uncle, and fresh home from the war,

With little for me to remember him doing yet.
The clock of the cancer ticks in his body, or not,

Depending if it is there, or waits. The search
Of memory gains and fails like surf: the porch

And trim are painted cream, the shakes are stained.
The shadows could be painted (so little wind

Is blowing there) or stains on the crazy-paving
Of the front walk. . . . Or now, the shadows are moving: 20

Another house, unrelated; a woman says,
Is this your special boy, and the girl says, yes,

Moving her hand in mine. The clock in her, too—
As someone told me a month or two ago,

Months after it finally took her. A public building
Is where the house was: though a surf, unyielding

And sickly, seethes and eddies at the stones
Of the foundation. The dead are made of bronze,

But dying they were like birds with clocklike hearts—
Unthinkable, how much pain the tiny parts   30

Of even the smallest bird might yet contain.
We become larger than life in how much pain

Our bodies may encompass . . . all Titans in that,
Or heroic statues. Although there is no heat

Brimming in the fixed, memorial summer, the brows
Of lucid metal sweat a faint warm haze

As I try to think the pain I never saw.
Though there is no pain there, the small birds draw

Together in crowds above the houses—and cry
Over the surf: as if there were a day,   40

Memorial, marked on the calendar for dread
And pain and loss—although among the dead

Are no hurts, but only emblematic things;
No hospital beds, but a lifting of metal wings.

ICICLES

A brilliant beard of ice
Hangs from the edge of the roof
Harsh and heavy as glass.
The spikes a child breaks off

Taste of wool and the sun.
In the house, some straw for a bed,
Circled by a little train,
Is the tiny image of God.

The sky is fiery blue,
And a fiery morning light   10
Burns on the fresh deep snow:
Not one track in the street.

Just as the carols tell
Everything is calm and bright:
The town lying still
Frozen silver and white.

Is only one child awake,
Breaking the crystal chimes?—
Knocking them down with a stick,
Leaving the broken stems.   20

Sylvia Plath

One of the leading Confessional Poets, Sylvia Plath was born in Boston in 1932. After graduating from Smith College, she received a Fulbright Fellowship to study at Cambridge, where she met and married the British poet Ted Hughes. Her 1965 collection, Ariel, *is one of the most influential books of the contemporary period. According to George Steiner, "no group of poems since Dylan Thomas's* Deaths and Entrances *has had as vivid and disturbing an impact on English critics and readers." Her other books include* The Collected Poems *(1981) and* The Bell Jar *(1963), the best-selling autobiographical novel originally published under the pseudonym of Victoria Lucas. She committed suicide in London in 1963.*

WATERCOLOR OF GRANTCHESTER MEADOWS

There, spring lambs jam the sheepfold. In air
Stilled, silvered as water in a glass
Nothing is big or far.
The small shrew chitters from its wilderness
Of grassheads and is heard.
Each thumb-size bird
Flits nimble-winged in thickets, and of good color.

Cloudrack and owl-hollowed willows slanting over
The bland Granta double their white and green
World under the sheer water   10
And ride that flux at anchor, upside down.
The punter sinks his pole.
In Byron's pool
Cattails part where the tame cygnets steer.

It is a country on a nursery plate.
Spotted cows revolve their jaws and crop
Red clover or gnaw beetroot
Bellied on a nimbus of sun-glazed buttercup.
Hedging meadows of benign
Arcadian green   20
The blood-berried hawthorn hides its spines with white.

Droll, vegetarian, the water rat
Saws down a reed and swims from his limber grove,
While the students stroll or sit,
Hands laced, in a moony indolence of love—
Black-gowned, but unaware
How in such mild air
The owl shall stoop from his turret, the rat cry out.

MEDALLION

By the gate with star and moon
Worked into the peeled orange wood
The bronze snake lay in the sun

Inert as a shoelace; dead
But pliable still, his jaw
Unhinged and his grin crooked,

Tongue a rose-colored arrow.
Over my hand I hung him.
His little vermilion eye

Ignited with a glassed flame   10
As I turned him in the light;
When I split a rock one time

The garnet bits burned like that.
Dust dulled his back to ochre
The way sun ruins a trout.

Yet his belly kept its fire
Going under the chainmail,
The old jewels smoldering there

In each opaque belly-scale:
Sunset looked at through milk glass.   20
And I saw white maggots coil

Thin as pins in the dark bruise
Where his innards bulged as if
He were digesting a mouse.

Knifelike, he was chaste enough,
Pure death's-metal. The yardman's
Flung brick perfected his laugh.

THE STONES

This is the city where men are mended.
I lie on a great anvil.
The flat blue sky-circle

Flew off like the hat of a doll
When I fell out of the light. I entered
The stomach of indifference, the wordless cupboard.

The mother of pestles diminished me.
I became a still pebble.
The stones of the belly were peaceable,

The head-stone quiet, jostled by nothing.   10
Only the mouth-hole piped out,
Importunate cricket

In a quarry of silences.
The people of the city heard it.
They hunted the stones, taciturn and separate,

The mouth-hole crying their locations.
Drunk as a foetus
I suck at the paps of darkness.

The food tubes embrace me. Sponges kiss my lichens away.
The jewelmaster drives his chisel to pry   20
Open one stone eye.

This is the after-hell: I see the light.
A wind unstoppers the chamber
Of the ear, old worrier.

Water mollifies the flint lip,
And daylight lays its sameness on the wall.
The grafters are cheerful,

Heating the pincers, hoisting the delicate hammers.
A current agitates the wires
Volt upon volt. Catgut stitches my fissures.   30

A workman walks by carrying a pink torso.
The storerooms are full of hearts.
This is the city of spare parts.

My swaddled legs and arms smell sweet as rubber.
Here they can doctor heads, or any limb.
On Fridays the little children come

To trade their hooks for hands.
Dead men leave eyes for others.
Love is the uniform of my bald nurse.

Love is the bone and sinew of my curse.   40
The vase, reconstructed, houses
The elusive rose.

Ten fingers shape a bowl for shadows.
My mendings itch. There is nothing to do.
I shall be good as new.

BLACK ROOK IN RAINY WEATHER

On the stiff twig up there
Hunches a wet black rook
Arranging and rearranging its feathers in the rain.
I do not expect a miracle
Or an accident

To set the sight on fire
In my eye, nor seek
Any more in the desultory weather some design,
But let spotted leaves fall as they fall,
Without ceremony, or portent.   10

Although, I admit, I desire,
Occasionally, some backtalk
From the mute sky, I can't honestly complain:
A certain minor light may still
Lean incandescent

Out of kitchen table or chair
As if a celestial burning took
Possession of the most obtuse objects now and then—
Thus hallowing an interval
Otherwise inconsequent   20

By bestowing largesse, honor,
One might say love. At any rate, I now walk
Wary (for it could happen
Even in this dull, ruinous landscape); skeptical,
Yet politic; ignorant

Of whatever angel may choose to flare
Suddenly at my elbow. I only know that a rook
Ordering its black feathers can so shine
As to seize my senses, haul
My eyelids up, and grant   30

A brief respite from fear
Of total neutrality. With luck,
Trekking stubborn through this season
Of fatigue, I shall
Patch together a content

Of sorts. Miracles occur,
If you care to call those spasmodic
Tricks of radiance miracles. The wait's begun again,
The long wait for the angel,
For that rare, random descent.   40

Stanley Plumly

Stanley Plumly was born in Barnsville, Ohio, in 1939 and educated at Wilmington College and Ohio University. He has been awarded a Guggenheim Fellowship, two National Endowment for the Arts Fellowships, and the Delmore Schwartz Memorial Award. His books include In the Outer Dark *(1970),* Out-of-the-Body Travel *(1977), and* Summer Celestial

(1983). He currently lives in Baltimore, where he teaches at the University of Maryland.

TREE FERNS

They were the local Ohio palm, tropic in the heat of trains.
They could grow in anything—pitch, whole grain,
cinders, ash and rust, the dirt
dumped back of the foundry, what

the men wore home. Little willows,
they were made to be brushed back by the traffic of boxcars
the way wind will dust the shade
of the small part of a river.—They'd

go from almost green to almost gray with each long
        passing,
each leaf, each branch a stain   10
on the winded air. They were too thin
for rain—nothing could touch them.

So we'd start with pocketknives, cutting and whittling them
        down
from willow, palm, or any other name.
They were what they looked like. Horsewhip, whipweed.
They could lay on a fine welt if you wanted.

And on a hot, dry day, July, they could all but burn.
At a certain age you try to pull all kinds of things
out of the ground, out of the loose gravel thrown by trains.

Or break off what you can and cut it clean.   20

Katha Pollitt

*Born in New York City in 1949 and educated at Radcliffe and Columbia,
Katha Pollitt is the author of* Antarctic Traveller *(1982), which won the
National Book Critics Circle Award. Among the other honors she's received
for her work are the Discovery/*The Nation *Award, the Robert Frost
Award, and grants from the Ingram Merrill Foundation and the National
Endowment for the Arts. She is currently teaching at Princeton as a fellow
of the Council of the Humanities.*

BALLET BLANC

Baryshnikov leaps higher than your heart
in the moonlit forest, center stage, and pleads
with the ghostly corps, who pirouette, gauzed white
and powdered blue, like pearls, the star Sylphides

of Paris, 1841. You swoon
back in red plush. Oboes, adagio,
sing *love is death*—but death's this lustrous queen
who twirls forever on one famous toe

while hushed in shadows, tier on golden tier
swirls to apotheosis in the ceiling.   10
Miles away, through clouds, one chandelier
swings dizzily. What feeling

sweeps you? Dinner's roses and tall candles,
a certain wine-flushed face, your new blue dress
merge with the scented crush of silks and sables—
through which, you're more and more aware, two eyes

stroke, meltingly, your neck. You glow, you sway,
it's as though the audience were dancing too
and with a last, stupendous tour jeté
turned for a solo suddenly to *you*   20

and you become the Duke, the Queen, Giselle,
and waltz in a whirl of white through the painted grove,
your gestures as extravagant as tulle,
as wild as nineteenth-century hopeless love,

as grand as bravo! and brava! On wings,
you splurge and take a taxi home instead.
The park looms rich and magical. It's spring,
almost. You float upstairs and into bed

and into dreams so deep you never hear
how all night long that witch, your evil fairy,   30
crows her knowing cackle in your ear:
Tomorrow you will wake up ordinary.

OF THE SCYTHIANS

who came whirling out of the North
like a locust swarm, storm-darkening the sky,
their long hair whipping in the wind like the manes of
        horses,
no one remembers anything now but I:

how they screamed to the slaughter, as the skirl of a
        thousand flutes
fashioned from enemies' thighbones shrilled them on.
Naked they rode. We stood by our huts, stunned mute:
gold flashed from each spear, gold glittered on each arm.

I was a child in the temple. The old priest
hid me in a secret cellar with the images.   10
Above my head I heard him chant a last
prayer to the god. Since then

I scorn to mix with those who have come after.
Fat farmers, milky scribblers! What do they know
who have never heard the Scythians' terrible laughter
or seen in the wind their glittering wild hair flow?

Dudley Randall

*Born in Washington, D.C., in 1914, Dudley Randall worked for Ford
Motor Company in Detroit, served in the U.S. Army in the South Pacific,
and earned degrees from Wayne State University and the University of
Michigan. He is the publisher of the influential Broadside Press, which
prints broadsides and books by Black American poets. The poet laureate of
Detroit, he is the author of* Cities Burning *(1968),* After the Killing
(1974), A Litany of Friends *(1981), and other books. He has also edited*
Black Poetry *(1969). Until his recent retirement, he was a reference
librarian and poet-in-residence at the University of Detroit.*

THE SOUTHERN ROAD

There the black river, boundary to hell,
And here the iron bridge, the ancient car,
And grim conductor, who with surly yell
Forbids white soldiers where the black ones are.
And I re-live the enforced avatar
Of desperate journey to a dark abode
Made by my sires before another war;
And I set forth upon the southern road.

To a land where shadowed songs like flowers swell
And where the earth is scarlet as a scar   10
Friezed by the bleeding lash that fell (O fell!)
Upon my father's flesh. O far, far, far
And deep my blood has drenched it. None can bar
My birthright to the loveliness bestowed
Upon this country haughty as a star.
And I set forth upon the southern road.

This darkness and these mountains loom a spell
Of peak-roofed town where yearning steeples soar
And the holy holy chanting of a bell
Shakes human incense on the throbbing air   20
Where bonfires blaze and quivering bodies char.
Whose is the hair that crisped, and fiercely glowed?
I know it; and my entrails melt like tar
And I set forth upon the southern road.

O fertile hillsides where my fathers are,
And whence my woes like troubled streams have flowed,
Love you I must, though they may sweep me far.
And I set forth upon the southern road.

David Ray

David Ray was born in Sapulpa, Oklahoma, in 1932 and holds two degrees from the University of Chicago. With Robert Bly, he founded the organization American Writers Against the Vietnam War. He has published several books of poetry, most recently The Touched Life: New and Selected Poems *(1982) and* On Wednesday I Cleaned Out My Wallet *(1984). In 1984 he and his wife Judy spent three months in France as fellows at the Karolyi Foundation. He teaches at the University of Missouri-Kansas*

City, where he is founding editor of New Letters *and executive producer of* New Letters on the Air, *a weekly national radio program devoted to poetry.*

GREENS

A boy stoops, picking greens with his mother—
This is the scene in the great elm-shadows.
A pail stands by her feet, her dress conceals
Her chill knees, made bitter by the tall man
Who now lifts a glass, she thinks, with his friends,
Or worse, seeks a younger love in the town
While she with her fading muslin aprons
And her dented tin pail seeks greens, always
Greens, and wins, with her intermittent sighs,
Sympathy, love forever from the boy.   10
He does not know, this sharp-boned boy who bends
To his mother, that he has been seduced
Already, that he has known anguish, bliss
Of sex—as much as he will ever know.
He does not know, here in the bees' shadow,
He has become the tall and angry man,
The husband wounding the woman who bends,
Sighs and is ecstatic in her clutching
Of sons—bending, dark of brow, by her pail,
Stooped, brushing back the long, complaining strands   20
Of her hair. She is now too proud to weep,
But not to read the law, to reap greens, greens
Forever in her small, pathetic pail.

THROWING THE RACETRACK CATS
AT SARATOGA

Such cats are useful to calm the horses,
to purr and move among their horny hooves.
In fact a cat will fit precisely there
under the fetlock, bandaged half the time.
Thus they're gathered up in arms, from alleys

of cities, and brought to Saratoga.
When some horse named Herod or Whiskers wins
some low and humble cat has done his share.
But then great vans are backed against the stalls:
It's time to wend down South, to Long Island   10

or Kentucky. In long trailers for nine
horses we find no feline room at all.
Hence this ritual called the throwing of cats.
Both black and white men stand and toss them high,
cats of every color, every lineage.

Over the fence of steel they sail, claws spread.
They brush the pines and land beneath a bough.
Each looks about then like old Balboa,
finding himself quite lost, with dark coming.
His way is blocked back to his friend the horse   20

who at times had nudged him like a true friend.
Neighing, he too seems to be dissolving
into the greenish air. The oat smell's gone
and the boys with buckets and whistling men
who sang of loves lost in dark river towns.

These exiled cats do not confer, but start
in silence padding through the rustling leaves.
Behind them, sailing in parabolas,
their brothers fly like mewling cannonballs
or Roman candles spewing on the Fourth.   30

To die because you are of use no more
may also happen to a groom who throws.
But now he does not choose to think of that.
He merely finds a choice one, throws him high,
lofting toward a pine or the moon he spots

emerging like a silver dollar bright
and clean. First the cats and then the hosing
of stalls, the boarding up of all the doors,
that long dull trip to town, to one Skid Row
or another, where next year's alley cats,   40

pale kittens, stalk the legs of drunks for love.
As for these stumblers through the shadowed trees,
I've chosen one who lifts his paw just like
a horse he looks about to find, as I
absurdly seek and trust to find you still.

Donald Revell

Donald Revell was born in the Bronx in 1954. He holds degrees from Harpur College and the State University of New York at Buffalo, where he earned his Ph.D. in 1980. His From the Abandoned Cities *was a 1983 National Poetry Series selection. He teaches at the University of Denver.*

BELFAST

Go north any way and sadness clings to the ground
like fog. The sound of voices goes wrong and can't
be followed. You hear, you breathe cries with a damp
        wind.

Go north to the ruined counties where girls chant
over a piece of wood called "Doll-Who's-Dead"
and where the streets that you walk are a dead giant

who won't rise. Here, History is the unfed
beast past scaring who comes down from the hills
in daylight. It kills anything, in broad

daylight, then is itself stalked until   10
the men corner it in some back street. They save
the town for the next beast the granite hills

won't hold. And here, Journey's End is the grey
wall, bled white in patches, that divides
bare yard from bare yard, the unsaved from the unsaved.

In the forlorn business of taking sides,
the rain and the rituals of grief have no
part. Each renews the other as each abides

into the next day's routine, into the slow
recessionals of grief and steady rain.   20
Here, one death's as just as its counterpart as both

right nothing and are only as wrong as the changes
they were meant but failed to bring about.
Here, suffering betrays itself in exchange

for a dead march, too wise to ever doubt
that life has no grander end than a parade
into the next street. The bold dead are borne out

of trouble, brought closer to the sea and laid
down. The living are marched back by pipes to their
reprisals in the bare yards. From either side   30

of walls that bleed, voices you can't trace rise and tear
the wind into mad gusts. Tomorrow, History
returns. Tonight, the ruined counties prepare.

IN LOMBARDY

She mocks the bones in you, as if it had
been Lombardy you met in, and around
the time of da Vinci, the man who painted her,
an unboxed body at the center of a sad
procession, womanly, in the veil of a drowned
innocent, and in control. The myrrh,
the acolytes attending, these conjoin

with the figure into an adequate conceit
for what is meant by fear of dying. Her
relationship to the thing is not the point   10
however, nor is that humiliating street

through which she is attended by the boys
the course of it. Germane to all who swing
the censer, chant, or carry candles are
those inamoratas, those comic angels poised
as if in mockery or blackface, wing
to wing in jibing constellations, stars
in rows. Perfection, the maestro's real intent
is laughter, alive as its direction toward
the living drowned, the lucky ones. Effect,   20
a countereffect, and the seduction were all meant
to mock us, to seduce our hearts and record
us, aching in ourselves that way. What was intact

was deformed. There was also that fear's result, and what
love means, considering. It means the blank
regard of one's own feet as they progress
along the assigned paths, recalling those facts,
this dread. It means a failing brain at the brink
of hypnosis, permanently. Being less
and more than that, the woman died to be   30
an object in the mind's expansion, to appear
expansively, as what we desire: a pale
seductress robed in gauze, a fantasy
in black or red or anything as near
a privacy like Ruth's, when alien. Regale

the visual and be recorded, that
is what the body was to have required
of us. Yet if laughter failed, if what took place
did not amuse the angels nor permit
the minds attending to be so inspired   40
as to collapse upon themselves, her face
alone might have done it. Having been close
enough, there is, in the death, a single thought
whose mystery can be almost comic. In
that, only those accompanying her or those
particular amours that she had brought
to Lombardy for the occasion, loves

born of another hand's intention, could
take part. The face is beautiful. These men
she mocks, the redundant, particular ones, perform   50
for her, are the desperately in need and would,
without a doubt, be no impediment
to her complete possession of their more
aesthetic realities, their minds as well
as of their senses. Love, for our
enchanting lady, is an abstracted grove
of familiar symbols where a mind can swell
like music, overcome by its own power
to invent, without compassion and above

regalia. As an event, the woman continues,   60
is in our eyes, by moments indiscrete
or present, then and now depending on
the mind or eyes of imaging. The tense
deformity, the actual defeat
of time through her specific love, is bond
and compact, then, and more than likely years
from then, as well as now in Lombardy
or there in Leonardo's picture. Made
by thoughts of death into a living fear
of bodies, we define a landscape. She   70
records us in it, weeping, nearly mad.

Adrienne Rich

Born in Baltimore in 1929, Adrienne Rich published her first book, A
Change of World, *the 1951 Yale Younger Poets selection, when she was
still an undergraduate at Radcliffe. She has since received numerous other
awards for her work, including the 1974 National Book Award for* Diving

Into the Wreck. *Her other books include* The Dream of a Common Language *(1978),* A Wild Patience Has Taken Me This Far *(1981), and* The Fact of a Doorframe: Poems Selected and New *(1985). An intensely political poet, she has written that "The moment when a feeling enters the body / is political." She lives in western Massachusetts, where she co-edits* Sinister Wisdom, *a feminist journal.*

AT A BACH CONCERT

Coming by evening through the wintry city
We said that art is out of love with life.
Here we approach a love that is not pity.

This antique discipline, tenderly severe,
Renews belief in love yet masters feeling,
Asking of us a grace in what we bear.

Form is the ultimate gift that love can offer—
The vital union of necessity
With all that we desire, all that we suffer.

A too-compassionate art is half an art.   10
Only such proud restraining purity
Restores the else-betrayed, too-human heart.

THE INSUSCEPTIBLES

Then the long sunlight lying on the sea
Fell, folded gold on gold; and slowly we
Took up our decks of cards, our parasols,
The picnic hamper and the sandblown shawls
And climbed the dunes in silence. There were two
Who lagged behind as lovers sometimes do,
And took a different road. For us the night
Was final, and by artificial light
We came indoors to sleep. No envy there
Of those who might be watching anywhere   10

The lustres of the summer dark, to trace
Some vagrant splinter blazing out of space.
No thought of them, save in a lower room
To leave a light for them when they should come.

AUNT JENNIFER'S TIGERS

Aunt Jennifer's tigers stride across a screen,
Bright topaz denizens of a world of green.
They do not fear the men beneath the tree;
They pace in sleek chivalric certainty.

Aunt Jennifer's fingers fluttering through her wool
Find even the ivory needle hard to pull.
The massive weight of Uncle's wedding band
Sits heavily upon Aunt Jennifer's hand.

When Aunt is dead, her terrified hands will lie
Still ringed with ordeals she was mastered by.   10
The tigers in the panel that she made
Will go on striding, proud and unafraid.

John Ridland

John Ridland was born in London, England, in 1933 and grew up in southern California. He studied at Swarthmore, Berkeley, and Claremont Graduate School. He is the author of Fires of Home *(1961),* Ode on Violence *(1969),* Elegy for My Aunt *(1981), and other books. Since 1961 he has taught at the University of California at Santa Barbara.*

ANOTHER EASTER

I

Digging a compost hole
Out behind the garage,
I sifted from the soil

A small bright plastic wreath,
A rusted squarehead nail
In a wood post underneath,

A fractured square-cut stone,
And two curved sliding teeth
In tanned, sandpapered bone—

Half of a gopher's laugh.   10
My spade's long handle groaned.
In fact it broke in half.

*

My sleep was half unclear.
Each hour or two I woke,
My dreams half-brushed with fear.

Like a new unfolded map
In the front seat of a car,
My life spread in my lap.

I traced those empty roads,
Guessing a step or leap   20
At a time, and moved *towards,*

Till suddenly I was here.
Give me your hand, I muttered.
My voice was brushed with fear.

*

It was my son's I held.
All he would say was *da*—
Whatever sense it spelled—

Pure as that *spiritus*
Which breathlessly exhaled
Its thundering Easter news.   30

Do not stop there, I pled,
As hollow as a house
From which the heart has fled.

And then, at syllable's close,
Out of its hopeful bed
Another Easter rose.

II

Six hawks above tall trees
Were circling something big.
They made the mind freeze.

Once on a Georgia bank   40
I saw three vultures ease
Their beaks in a cow's flank.

A bronze New Zealand buzzard
Beside a winter paddock
Lifted from a hare's heart

When I drove up. It wheeled,
Untroubled, turned apart,
Then settled back in the field.

*

Now my old friend Despair,
I greet you as before,   50
At weekend's end. O rare

Late Sunday afternoon
Companion and confrère!—
I lick my ice cream spoon.

Come down, old friend, come in,
And I'll lob you this spiked bomb
From the wild chilicothe vine*—

It's autumn in April for them,
Their lips peel back in a grin
And the big seed beans carom.   60

*

The night winds drop and bunch.
Dragging the open slope,
They grapple all they clench.

A lonesome turkey vulture
Cruised by my grove at lunch.
Its taut, dihedral tilt there

Shadowed the breadth of my lot.
All that my hopes had built there
And failed, sailed under it.

Its harrow turned no prey.   70
The wind hooks little, but
Drags it home, hard, all the way.

III

I rest an infant brain
In wheaten hair, along
My padded shoulder. Drained,

Of muscle and of heat,
Almost of plan, and pain,
I counter in the street

---

*Echinocystis macrocarpa, the Old-Man-in-the-Ground.

Smooth faces, marked with no
Deep woe or weakness—*meat*
For buzzard or for crow,   80

I brood, holding him snug
("How do you *do?*" "Hel*lo!*")
To my shoulder like a jug.

                    *

The body is a hill—
Or so I could believe—
In which the mortal soul

Buries its hopefulness,
Inhabiting its hole
Half in despair of less: 90

In life, in half-despair,
Half-joy, crossing to death's,
Whose harsh mouth brushes yours,

Faint child, whenever you breathe.
Whatever we choose, we are?
Fate has its own neat teeth.

                    *

Again I cannot sleep
But not for dread or fear,
Rather that hope might keep

Its course against despair   100
And partial measures sweep
Their littered meanings bare—

A single light bulb's able
To clear the dusty air
Above a wooden table

At which some needy sage
Taps out his needed fable
Across a trackless page.

Alberto Ríos

*Born in Nogales, Arizona, in 1952, Alberto Ríos is a graduate of the
University of Arizona's M.F.A. program. His books of poetry include*
Whispering to Fool the Wind, *which won the 1981 Walt Whitman
Award, and* Five Indiscretions *(1985). His collection of short stories,* The
Iguana Killer, *won the 1984 Western States Book Award for fiction. He
lives in Chandler, Arizona, and teaches at Arizona State University.*

NANI

Sitting at her table, she serves
the sopa de arroz to me
instinctively, and I watch her,
the absolute mamá, and eat words
I might have had to say more
out of embarrassment. To speak,
now-foreign words I used to speak,
too, dribble down her mouth as she serves
me albóndigas. No more
than a third are easy to me.   10
By the stove she does something with words
and looks at me only with her
back. I am full. I tell her
I taste the mint, and watch her speak
smiles at the stove. All my words
make her smile. Nani never serves
herself, she only watches me
with her skin, her hair. I ask for more.

I watch the mamá warming more
tortillas for me. I watch her   20

fingers in the flame for me.
Near her mouth, I see a wrinkle speak
of a man whose body serves
the ants like she serves me, then more words
from more wrinkles about children, words
about this and that, flowing more
easily from these other mouths. Each serves
as a tremendous string around her,
holding her together. They speak
nani was this and that to me   30
and I wonder just how much of me
will die with her, what were the words
I could have been, was. Her insides speak
through a hundred wrinkles, now, more
than she can bear, steel around her,
shouting, then, What is this thing she serves?

She asks me if I want more.
I own no words to stop her.
Even before I speak, she serves.

Theodore Roethke

*Theodore Roethke was born in 1908 in Saginaw, Michigan, where his
father ran a nursery and floral business. Roethke's childhood experiences in
his father's greenhouses are so integral to his poetic vision that he once called
the greenhouse "my symbol for the whole of life." After earning bachelor's
and master's degrees from the University of Michigan, he taught at several
universities, including Pennsylvania State University (where he was also a
tennis coach) and the University of Washington. One of America's most
honored poets, he received the Pulitzer Prize, two National Book Awards,
the Bollingen Prize, and many other awards. His* Collected Poems *ap-*

peared in 1966. His other books include Straw for the Fire *(1972),
excerpts from his notebooks, and* On the Poet and His Craft *(1965),
selections from his prose. He died in 1963.*

THE WAKING

I wake to sleep, and take my waking slow.
I feel my fate in what I cannot fear.
I learn by going where I have to go.

We think by feeling. What is there to know?
I hear my being dance from ear to ear.
I wake to sleep, and take my waking slow.

Of those so close beside me, which are you?
God bless the Ground! I shall walk softly there,
And learn by going where I have to go.

Light takes the Tree; but who can tell us how?   10
The lowly worm climbs up a winding stair;
I wake to sleep, and take my waking slow.

Great Nature has another thing to do
To you and me; so take the lively air,
And, lovely, learn by going where to go.

This shaking keeps me steady. I should know.
What falls away is always. And is near.
I wake to sleep, and take my waking slow.
I learn by going where I have to go.

MY PAPA'S WALTZ

The whiskey on your breath
Could make a small boy dizzy;
But I hung on like death:
Such waltzing was not easy.

We romped until the pans
Slid from the kitchen shelf;
My mother's countenance
Could not unfrown itself.

The hand that held my wrist
Was battered on one knuckle;   10
At every step you missed
My right ear scraped a buckle.

You beat time on my head
With a palm caked hard by dirt,
Then waltzed me off to bed
Still clinging to your shirt.

I KNEW A WOMAN

I knew a woman, lovely in her bones,
When small birds sighed, she would sigh back at them;
Ah, when she moved, she moved more ways than one:
The shapes a bright container can contain!
Of her choice virtues only gods should speak,
Or English poets who grew up on Greek
(I'd have them sing in chorus, cheek to cheek).

How well her wishes went! She stroked my chin,
She taught me Turn, and Counter-turn, and Stand;
She taught me Touch, that undulant white skin;   10
I nibbled meekly from her proffered hand;
She was the sickle; I, poor I, the rake,
Coming behind her for her pretty sake
(But what prodigious mowing we did make).

Love likes a gander, and adores a goose:
Her full lips pursed, the errant note to seize;
She played it quick, she played it light and loose;
My eyes, they dazzled at her flowing knees;

Her several parts could keep a pure repose,
Or one hip quiver with a mobile nose 20
(She moved in circles, and those circles moved).

Let seed be grass, and grass turn into hay:
I'm martyr to a motion not my own;
What's freedom for? To know eternity.
I swear she cast a shadow white as stone.
But who would count eternity in days?
These old bones live to learn her wanton ways:
(I measure time by how a body sways).

DINKY

O what's the weather in a Beard?
It's windy there, and rather weird,
And when you think the sky has cleared
    —Why, there is Dirty Dinky.

Suppose you walk out in a Storm,
With nothing on to keep you warm,
And then step barefoot on a Worm
    —Of course, it's Dirty Dinky.

As I was crossing a hot hot Plain,
I saw a sight that caused me pain,
You asked me before, I'll tell you again: 10
    —It *looked* like Dirty Dinky.

Last night you lay a-sleeping? No!
The room was thirty-five below;
The sheets and blankets turned to snow.
    —He'd got in: Dirty Dinky.

You'd better watch the things you do.
You'd better watch the things you do.
You're part of him; he's part of you
    —*You* may be Dirty Dinky. 20

William Pitt Root

Born in Austin, Minnesota, in 1941, William Pitt Root grew up near the Everglades and in the West. He was educated at the University of Washington, the University of North Carolina, and Stanford, and he currently teaches at the University of Montana. Among his awards are grants from the Rockefeller and Guggenheim foundations, a National Endowment for the Arts Fellowship, and three Pushcart Prizes. During 1978 and 1979 he was a fellow of the United States/United Kingdom Exchange Artist program. His books include Reasons for Going It on Foot *(1981),* In the World's Common Grasses *(1981), and* Invisible Guests *(1984). He has said that "Heart is the horse, head is the rider, and ideally poets must be centaurs."*

A NATURAL HISTORY OF UNICORNS AND DRAGONS MY DAUGHTER AND I HAVE KNOWN

(Written for her 12th birthday)

Already we are both fans of the green and golden dragon
   who tumbles gloriously out of the terrible heavens
      not only in books and dreams

for us—He cascades also down the side of the seagreen '61
   Valiant we painted once together by the ocean,
      trying to outrace the setting Mendocino sun

four years ago with mist rolling in, and he tumbles
   as well down the side of that van which resembles
      nothing so much as a forest dwarf's hutch on wheels

where he silently roars a great bouquet of flowers   10
   while his green and scaley winding tail anchors
      round the side window. Rose-white, a Unicorn

edged in icy blue rears opposite our flowerbreathing
   fire-eater now, its jewelous horn shining
      by moonlight and headlight, glowing

with a proud shy promise of goodness pure as silver.
   We cannot always be together,
      you and I, and I would have you remember

our fabulous creatures always—the bold Dragon
   as terrible as the horned horse is wonderful, twins of a
      wisdom   20
      older by far than we are in our kingdom

of daily things. Here, then, as a reminder, is the image
   of our Unicorn seen silver as he wades into waters
      ageless
      as the blue sky they reflect, hooves half tangled

in the world's common grasses. Keep him with you
   where you go and try from time to time gazing through
      your eyes as he gazes through his: *a sky beating slowly*
      blue

as the heart of all the air, grass burning green as an emerald's
      cooly imperial
   and incessant stare, the inner brilliance of all that is natural
   held in that eye of his, which is every bit as real as he is
      invisible.   30

KRAA

For Jim Heynen

From the high blue sunspoked wheel of pure dispassion
   an eagle tumbles
as one fish through the deep green shadow rises, bright-
   ening,

and where these arcs concur
    claws seize
    and silver skin erupts
a sudden jewelry of shuddering.

Wind from the great wingbeats flattens the water.

The salmon arches and sips through delicate gills
    the first deep shock of   10
air, locks, its fixed gaze clouding in the thinning waters,
blind to the steadily
    rowing
    figure of their shadow.
Above curve the dark glittering twin suns.

Raymond Roseliep

Raymond Roseliep was born in Farley, Iowa, in 1917. He attended Loras College, Catholic University of America, and Notre Dame, and was ordained a Roman Catholic priest in 1943. He taught English at Loras College from 1946 to 1966, then served as resident chaplain at Holy Family Hall in Dubuque, Iowa, until his death in 1983. Among his eighteen books are Love Makes the Air Light *(1965),* Listen to Light *(1980), and* A Roseliep Retrospective *(1980).*

"CAMPFIRE EXTINGUISHED"

campfire extinguished,
the woman washing dishes
in a pan of stars

Gibbons Ruark

Gibbons Ruark was born in Raleigh, North Carolina, in 1941. He holds degrees from the University of North Carolina at Chapel Hill and the University of Massachusetts. He is the author of A Program for Survival *(1971),* Reeds *(1978), and* Keeping Company *(1983), and he is currently teaching at the University of Delaware.*

TO THE SWALLOWS OF VITERBO

You plummeting shards of the darkness,
You rising stars in the light still
Fumbling for the rickety trellis
Of morning, your suddenness fills

The whole unsteady air with whirring
Where we awaken quiet together,
Breathing soundlessly, no least stirring
While your wingbeats alter the weather

Of daylight arriving beyond
The window, quick-feathered rushing   10
And calling becoming a kind
Of rainfall in Viterbo, brushing

Us over with a mist so fine
The flawed hinges of our shoulders shine.

WATCHING YOU SLEEP UNDER MONET'S WATER LILIES

Beloved, you are sleeping still,
Your light gown rumpled where it fell,

You are sleeping under the dark
Of a down comforter. The heart

Of dawn light blooming on the wall
Has not yet touched you where you still

Lie breathing, though it has wakened
The faint lilies, strewn and broken

Cloud-lights littering the water.
That you breathe is all that matters,   10

That you keep on breathing, lily,
While I wake to write this folly

Down, this breath of song that has your
Beauty lying among the pure

Lilies of the morning water,
Even though a light wind shatter

Them forever, and the too deep
Pool of desiring fill with sleep.

Muriel Rukeyser

---

*Born in New York City in 1913 and educated at Vassar, Harvard, and
Columbia, Muriel Rukeyser was a political activist in the 1930s and was
arrested in Alabama during the second Scottsboro trial. Her numerous books
include* Theory of Flight, *the 1935 winner of the Yale Younger Poets
Prize, and* Collected Poems *(1978). She died in 1980.*

ON THE DEATH OF HER MOTHER

A seacoast late at night and a wheel of wind.
All those years, Mother, your arms were full of absence
And all the running of arrows could never not once find
Anything but your panic among all that substance,
Until your wide eyes opened forever. Until it all was true.
The fears were true. In that cold country, winter,
The wordless king, went isolate and cruel,
And he alone real. His armies all that entered.

But here is peacock daybreak; thought-yoked and warm,
    the light,
The cloud-companions and the greenest star.   10
Starflash on water; the embryo in the foam.
Dives through my body in the waking bright,
Watchmen of birth; I see. You are here, Mother, and you
    are
Dead, and here is your gift: my life which is my home.

RUNE

The word in the bread feeds me,
The word in the moon leads me,
The word in the seed breeds me,
The word in the child needs me.

The word in the sand builds me,
The word in the fruit fills me,
The word in the body mills me,
The word in the war kills me.

The word in the man takes me,
The word in the storm shakes me,   10
The word in the work makes me,
The word in the woman rakes me,
The word in the word wakes me.

Michael Ryan

Michael Ryan was born in St. Louis in 1946 and grew up in Pennsylvania. He earned an A.B. at Notre Dame, an M.A. at Claremont Graduate School, and an M.F.A. and Ph.D. at the University of Iowa. The recipient of National Endowment for the Arts and Guggenheim Fellowships, he lives in North Garden, Virginia, and teaches at Warren Wilson College. His books are Threats Instead of Trees, *which won the 1973 Yale Younger Poets Prize, and* In Winter *(1981).*

CONSIDER A MOVE

The steady time of being unknown,
in solitude, without friends,
is not a steadiness which sustains.
I hear your voice waver on the phone:

Haven't talked to anyone for days.
I drive around. I sit in parking lots.
The voice zeroes through my ear, and waits.
What should I say? There are ways

to meet people you will want to love?
I know of none. You come out stronger   10
having gone through this? I no longer
believe that, if I once did. Consider a move,

a change, a job, a new place to live,
someplace you'd like to be. *That's not it,*
you say. Now time curves back. We almost touch.
Then what is? I ask. What is?

WHERE I'LL BE GOOD

Wanting leads to worse than oddity.
The bones creak like bamboo in wind,
and strain toward a better life outside the body,
the life everything has that isn't human.

Feel the chair under you? What does it want?
Does lust bend it silly like a rubber crutch?
Tell a tree about the silky clasp of cunt.
It won't shift an inch. It won't ache to touch.

Let me not cruise for teens in a red sports car,
or glare too long at what bubbles their clothes.   10
Let me never hustle file clerks in a bar.
Keep me from the beach when the hot wind blows.

If I must go mad, let it be dignified.
Lock me up where I'll feel like wood,
where wanting can't send me flopping outside,
where my bones will shut up, where I'll be good.

David St. John

---

*Born in Fresno, California, in 1949, David St. John took degrees at
California State University at Fresno and the University of Iowa. He is the
author of five books:* Hush *(1976),* The Shore *(1980),* The Olive
Grove *(1980),* No Heaven *(1985), and* The Orange Piano *(1985).
He has received grants and awards from the National Endowment for the
Arts, the Ingram Merrill Foundation, and the Guggenheim Foundation,
and in 1984 he was awarded the Rome Fellowship in Literature by the*

American Academy and Institute of Arts and Letters. He teaches in the writing seminars at Johns Hopkins.

ACADIAN LANE

Indigo against ocher, Atlantic
Blue abutting shore cliffs, bluffs, and sand,
All of the earth on Prince Edward Island
The red of dry blood, of weather-worn brick,
Of this rutted, twisting road leading down
Through the fishing village to the harbor
Where lobster boats rock, scarlet as lobster;
The bay's depth, smoked glass, reflecting the town.
A few dogs rustle in the heat of the noon;
The gulls, the bitterns lift, circling again.   10
A man is walking this Acadian
Lane, the fine red dust rising off his clothes;
He begins to sing a slow French tune—
La mer, la terre, le monde est seulement ces choses!

for Mark

Sherod Santos

Born in 1948, Sherod Santos earned his Ph.D. at the University of Utah, and now teaches at the University of Missouri. The recipient of a Discovery/ The Nation Award, the Delmore Schwartz Memorial Award, and a Guggenheim Fellowship, he is the author of Accidental Weather, *a 1982 National Poetry Series selection.*

THE BREAKDOWN

I

The sun scanned the river with its lidless
eye; before the heat had choked the saffron
fields, already the fishing-boats spotted
the calms, already our table was laid

for a homecoming. Mother's blue bedroom
window steamed behind the light-chinked blind: there,
awhile, her heart was still quiet enough,
a small boat bobbing on the horizon.

II

I dug in wet sedge for a woodchuck's hole:
the murky, rank, underwater smell when   10
I pulled my hands out with a sucking sound,
like a sob, and the imprints filled with mud.

There were puffy white clouds when she stepped out
from the shade. Or was it the heaviness
of the stock-still air that made the shadows
grow increasingly larger around her?

III

By evening the boats had crossed, without sail,
the glassy waters of the Sound. The gulls
intensified their treble calls—passing
masts were blunted now on the shallow sky.   20

On the other bank, the pulp-mill had just
shut down: water rats returned to the weeds
by the open sluices; a hip-booted
worker dragged his rake through the sawdust piles.

IV

She stood too long beside the riverbank.
The fronting fishermen's huts had gone blank
in the moonlight; and when the wind lifted
a few leaves fell, and the water's surface

shuddered, as if from emotion . . . Perhaps
she only grew more distant then, staring   30
downriver as if staring down a road
when there is nothing on it but the night.

                            V

The moon floated through the overhanging
willow, as if nosing through shoals; the bed-
spread swam with splotches of light, yellow-white
on pale-blue; and each wind-shift shook the tree

so the air would fill with those silvery
leaves, like scales scraped down the length of an eel.
I pulled the window-blind shut, but the hand
did not loosen, in the darkness, its grip.   40

May Sarton

---

*May Sarton was born in Wondelgem, Belgium, in 1912, came to the United
States in 1916, and became a citizen in 1924. A prolific author, she has
published forty-two books of poetry, fiction, journals, and memoirs. Her poetry
collections include* Collected Poems, 1930–1973 *(1974),* Selected
Poems *(1978),* A Shower of Summer Days *(1979),* Halfway to
Silence *(1980), and* Letters from Maine *(1984). Among her many
honors are awards from the Guggenheim Foundation, the American Acad-
emy of Arts and Sciences, and the National Foundation for the Arts and
Humanities. She also holds more than ten honorary doctorates. She lives in
York, Maine.*

DUTCH INTERIOR

Pieter de Hooch (1629–1682)

I recognize the quiet and the charm,
This safe enclosed room where a woman sews
And life is tempered, orderly, and calm.

Through the Dutch door, half-open, sunlight streams
And throws a pale square down on the red tiles.
The cosy black dog suns himself and dreams.

Even the bed is sheltered, it encloses,
A cupboard to keep people safe from harm,
Where copper glows with the warm flush of roses.

The atmosphere is all domestic, human,   10
Chaos subdued by the sheer power of need.
This is a room where I have lived as woman,

Lived too what the Dutch painter does not tell—
The wild skies overhead, dissolving, breaking,
And how that broken light is never still,

And how the roar of waves is always near,
What bitter tumult, treacherous and cold,
Attacks the solemn charm year after year!

It must be felt as peace won and maintained
Against those terrible antagonists—   20
How many from this quiet room have drowned?

How many left to go, drunk on the wind,
And take their ships into heartbreaking seas;
How many whom no woman's peace could bind?

Bent to her sewing, she looks drenched in calm.
Raw grief is disciplined to the fine thread.
But in her heart this woman is the storm;

Alive, deep in herself, holds wind and rain,
Remaking chaos into an intimate order
Where sometimes light flows through a windowpane.   30

Roy Scheele

Roy Scheele was born in Houston in 1942. He holds degrees in classical Greek and English from the University of Nebraska. His books include Accompanied *(1974),* Noticing *(1979),* The Sea-Ocean *(1981), and* A Far Allegiance *(1984). At present he lives in Crete, Nebraska, where he teaches English as a second language at Doane College's Midwest Institute for International Studies.*

THE GAP IN THE CEDAR

In memory of my father

I saw this much from the window:
the branch spring lightened into place
with a lithe shudder of snow.

Whatever bird had been there,
chickadee or sparrow,
had so vanished into air,

resilient, beyond recall,
it had to be taken on faith
to be taken at all.

In the moment it took the tree   10
to recover that trembling
something went wide in me—

there was a rush of wings,
the air beaten dim with snow,
and then I saw through the swirling.

Gjertrud Schnackenberg

Gjertrud Schnackenberg was born in Tacoma, Washington, in 1953 and educated at Mt. Holyoke College. She is the author of Portraits and Elegies *(1982) and* The Lamplit Answer *(1985). In 1983 she won the Rome Fellowship in Literature from the American Academy and Institute of Arts and Letters.*

HOW DID IT SEEM TO SYLVIA?

Just like an hour with neighbors, I would think,
Where one, invited by a pallid host,
Disliked the guests and felt too sick to drink.
Yet who, in obligation, mouthed a toast
And took a sip, shook hands, ignored the wink
Of bored and interested alike; at most
The only one who understood the joke,
Who slipped out well before the first glass broke.

THE PAPERWEIGHT

The scene within the paperweight is calm,
A small white house, a laughing man and wife,
Deep snow. I turn it over in my palm
And watch it snowing in another life,

Another world, and from this scene learn what
It is to stand apart: she serves him tea
Once and forever, dressed from head to foot
As she is always dressed. In this toy, history

Comes down in the dark like snow, and we
Wonder if her single deed tells much   10
Or little of the way she loves, and whether he
Sees shadows in the sky. Beyond our touch,

Beyond our lives, they laugh, and drink their tea.
We look at them just as the winter night
With its vast empty spaces bends to see
Our isolated little world of light,

Covered with snow, and snow in clouds above it,
And drifts and swirls too deep to understand.
Still, I must try to think a little of it,
With so much winter in my head and hand.   20

DARWIN IN 1881

Sleepless as Prospero back in his bedroom
In Milan, with all his miracles
Reduced to sailors' tales,
He sits up in the dark. The islands loom.
His seasickness upwells.
Silence creeps by in memory as it crept
By him on water, while the sailors slept,
From broken eggs and vacant tortoiseshells.
His voyage around the cape of middle age
Comes, with a feat of insight, to a close,   10

The same way Prospero's
Ended before he left the stage
To be led home across the blue-white sea,
When he had spoken of the clouds and globe,
Breaking his wand, and taking off his robe:
Knowledge increases unreality.

He quickly dresses.
Form wavers like his shadow on the stair
As he descends, in need of air
To cure his dizziness,   20
Down past the shipsunk emptiness
Of grownup children's rooms and hallways where
The family portraits blindly stare,
All haunted by each other's likenesses.

Outside, the orchard and a piece of moon
Are islands, he an island as he walks,
Brushing against weed stalks.
By hook and plume
The seeds gathering on his trouser legs
Are archipelagoes, like nests he sees   30
Shadowed in branching, ramifying trees,
Each with unique expressions in its eggs.
Different islands conjure
Different beings; different beings call
From different isles. And after all
His scrutiny of Nature
All he can see
Is how it will grow small, fade, disappear,
A coastline fading from a traveler
Aboard a survey ship. Slowly,   40
As coasts depart,
Nature had left behind a naturalist
Bound for a place where species don't exist,
Where no emergence has a counterpart.

He's heard from friends
About the other night, the banquet hall
Ringing with bravos—like a curtain call,
He thinks, when the performance ends,

Failing to summon from the wings
An actor who had lost his taste for verse,   50
Having beheld, in larger theaters,
Much greater banquet-vanishings
Without the quaint device and thunderclap
Required in Act 3.
He wrote, Let your indulgence set me free,
To the Academy, and took a nap
Beneath a London Daily tent,
Then puttered on his hothouse walk
Watching his orchids beautifully stalk
Their unreturning paths, where each descendant   60
Is the last—
Their inner staircases
Haunted by vanished insect faces
So tiny, so intolerably vast.
And, while they gave his proxy the award,
He dined in Downe and stayed up rather late
For backgammon with his beloved mate
Who reads his books and is, quite frankly, bored.

Now, done with beetle jaws and beaks of gulls
And bivalve hinges, now, utterly done,   70
One miracle remains, and only one.
An ocean swell of sickness rushes, pulls,
He leans against the fence
And lights a cigarette and deeply draws,
Done with fixed laws,
Done with experiments
Within his greenhouse heaven where
His offspring, Frank, for half the afternoon
Played, like an awkward angel, his bassoon
Into the humid air   80
So he could tell
If sound would make a Venus's-Flytrap close.
And, done for good with scientific prose,
That raging hell
Of tortured grammars writhing on their stakes,

He'd turned to his memoirs, chuckling to write
About his boyhood in an upright

Home: a boy preferring gartersnakes
To schoolwork, a lazy, strutting liar
Who quite provoked her aggravated look,   90
Shushed in the drawingroom behind her book,
His bossy sister itching with desire
To tattletale—yes, that was good.
But even then, much like the conjurer
Grown cranky with impatience to abjure
All his gigantic works and livelihood
In order to immerse
Himself in tales where he could be the man
In Once upon a time there was a man,

He'd quite by chance beheld the universe: 100
A disregarded game of chess
Between two love-dazed heirs
Who fiddle with the tiny pairs
Of statues in their hands, while numberless
Abstract unseen
Combinings on the silent board remain
Unplayed forever when they leave the game
To turn, themselves, into a king and queen.
Now, like the coming day,
Inhaled smoke illuminates his nerves.   110
He turns, taking the sandwalk as it curves
Back to the yard, the house, the entrance way
Where, not to waken her,

He softly shuts the door,
And leans against it for a spell before
He climbs the stairs, holding the banister,
Up to their room: there
Emma sleeps, moored
In illusion, blown past the storm he conjured
With his book, into a harbor   120
Where it all comes clear,
Where island beings leap from shape to shape
As to escape
Their terrifying turns to disappear.
He lies down on the quilt,
He lies down like a fabulous-headed

Fossil in a vanished riverbed,
In ocean-drifts, in canyon floors, in silt,
In lime, in deepening blue ice,
In cliffs obscured as clouds gather and float;   130
He lies down in his boots and overcoat,
And shuts his eyes.

Anne Sexton

Perhaps the best-known of the Confessional Poets, Anne Sexton was born in Newton, Massachusetts, in 1928 and grew up in Wellesley. She attended Radcliffe and studied writing under Robert Lowell at Boston University and under W. D. Snodgrass at Antioch College. She believed that "Poetry should be a shock to the senses. It should almost hurt." In addition to her many volumes of poetry, she published three children's books with Maxine Kumin. In 1967 she won the Pulitzer Prize for Live or Die, *and in 1968 she was elected a fellow of the Royal Society of Literature in London. Her* Complete Poems *was published in 1981. She committed suicide in the fall of 1974.*

THE MOSS OF HIS SKIN

Young girls in old Arabia were often buried alive next to their dead fathers, apparently as sacrifice to the goddesses of the tribes . . .
        —Harold Feldman, "Children of the Desert"
        Psychoanalysis and Psychoanalytic Review, *Fall 1958*

It was only important
to smile and hold still,
to lie down beside him
and to rest awhile,

to be folded up together
as if we were silk,
to sink from the eyes of mother
and not to talk.
The black room took us
like a cave or a mouth   10
or an indoor belly.
I held my breath
and daddy was there,
his thumbs, his fat skull,
his teeth, his hair growing
like a field or a shawl.
I lay by the moss
of his skin until
it grew strange. My sisters
will never know that I fall   20
out of myself and pretend
that Allah will not see
how I hold my daddy
like an old stone tree.

THE ABORTION

Somebody who should have been born
is gone.

Just as the earth puckered its mouth,
each bud puffing out from its knot,
I changed my shoes, and then drove south.

Up past the Blue Mountains, where
Pennsylvania humps on endlessly,
wearing, like a crayoned cat, its green hair,

its roads sunken in like a gray washboard;
where, in truth, the ground cracks evilly,   10
a dark socket from which the coal has poured,

Somebody who should have been born
is gone.

the grass as bristly and stout as chives,
and me wondering when the ground would break,
and me wondering how anything fragile survives;

up in Pennsylvania, I met a little man,
not Rumpelstiltskin, at all, at all . . .
he took the fullness that love began.

Returning north, even the sky grew thin   20
like a high window looking nowhere.
The road was as flat as a sheet of tin.

Somebody who should have been born
is gone.

Yes, woman, such logic will lead
to loss without death. Or say what you meant,
you coward . . . this baby that I bleed.

Karl Shapiro

Karl Shapiro was born in Baltimore in 1913 and educated at the University of Virginia and Johns Hopkins. A past editor of Poetry *and* Prairie Schooner, *he currently teaches at the University of California at Davis. Among his many books are* V-Letter and Other Poems *(1945), which was awarded the Pulitzer Prize,* Selected Poems *(1968), which won the Bollingen Prize, and* Collected Poems, 1940–1978 *(1978). He has also published several works on traditional forms and prosody, including, with Robert Beum,* A Prosody Handbook *(1965).*

THE FIRST TIME

Behind shut doors, in shadowy quarantine,
There shines the lamp of iodine and rose
That stains all love with its medicinal bloom.
This boy, who is no more than seventeen,
Not knowing what to do, takes off his clothes
As one might in a doctor's anteroom.

Then in a cross-draft of fear and shame
Feels love hysterically burn away,
A candle swimming down to nothingness
Put out by its own wetter gusts of flame,   10
And he stands smooth as uncarved ivory
Heavily curved for some expert caress.

And finally sees the always open door
That is invisible till the time has come,
And half falls through as through a rotten wall
To where chairs twist with dragons from the floor
And the great bed drugged with its own perfume
Spreads its carnivorous flower-mouth for all.

The girl is sitting with her back to him;
She wears a black thing and she rakes her hair,   20
Hauling her round face upward like moonrise;
She is younger than he, her angled arms are slim
And like a country girl her feet are bare.
She watches him behind her with old eyes,

Transfixing him in space like some grotesque,
Far, far from her where he is still alone
And being here is more and more untrue.
Then she turns round, as one turns at a desk,
And looks at him, too naked and too soon,
And almost gently asks: *Are you a Jew?*   30

Judith Johnson Sherwin

Born in New York City in 1936, Judith Johnson Sherwin attended the Juilliard School of Music as a child and at eleven was a finalist in the New York Philharmonic Young Composers Contest. She received her adult education at Barnard and Columbia. A composer and performance artist as well as a poet, she teaches in the women's studies program and in the doctor of arts program in creative writing at the State University of New York at Albany. She is the author of Uranium Poems *(1969), which won the Yale Younger Poets Prize,* Impossible Buildings *(1973),* How the Dead Count *(1978), and other works.*

THE SPOILERS AND THE SPOILS

the night too struggled to escape this pitted field.
the whole night long night waited for us to fail,
while all night's forces muttered in their retreat
as the fires poured over us, melting our shield wall.

the glue of our sinews melted, our joints rained
little meteors down, a hail of melting stones,
knucklebone, ankle and thigh, though the field had been
　　　gained,
it gained nothing from us, and the marrow of our bones

ran clear in the turning currents of suns. when we woke,
the sound of the mortars gone, and the mortars of stars　　10
melted, that joined those weightless blocks of black
eternal zero home to us, we fixed on, as hard,

neither our wills nor our fates. what we had taken
for our world was death without grief and all holds broken.

BALLADE OF THE GRINDSTONES

In the dark all cats are grey.
—Old proverb

when you and i draw close at night and play
those individual tricks all love keeps by,
do you believe i see you or can say
which hand beats mine, or by what bones i lie?
thrown down by dark, who separates the high
from the low card? what flow of skill can claim
to tell by taste the mouth that drinks it dry
that night which makes us all lie down the same?

you ride the dark, but can you choose the bay
from the dark horse, or by your wits descry   10
which cat howled, at that hour when all are grey,
or what bitch held and wrung you, by her cry?
lift up our bodies and like hawks we fly,
circle and soar and, held each one by name,
drop, but all holds are equal when we pry
that night which makes us all lie down the same.

a tremor and a flash cry holiday
and these husks leap. now tell me can we try
by touch which millstones grind our grain away
or whether in that press we love or die?   20
when the fine fever twists our straight awry,
rakes off our soft particulars, how blame,
each one, the other's harsh, unseeing eye,
that night which makes us all lie down the same?

after those teeth have gripped me by the thigh
and made my flesh and yours shake with one flame
shall either know which fire is you, which i,
that night which makes us all lie down the same?

Louis Simpson

Louis Simpson, who believes that "writing well is like meditation, it requires rising above the merely personal," was born in Jamaica, British West Indies, in 1923 and educated there at Murro College. He came to the United States in 1940 to study at Columbia, where he earned his doctorate. His books include At the End of the Open Road, *which won the 1964 Pulitzer Prize,* People Live Here: Selected Poems 1949–1983 *(1983), and* The Best Hour of the Night *(1983). He has also published three important works of criticism,* Three on the Tower *(1975),* A Revolution in Taste *(1978), and* A Company of Poets *(1981). Since 1967 he has been on the faculty at the State University of New York at Stony Brook.*

MY FATHER IN THE NIGHT COMMANDING NO

My father in the night commanding No
Has work to do. Smoke issues from his lips;
    He reads in silence.
The frogs are croaking and the streetlamps glow.

And then my mother winds the gramophone;
The Bride of Lammermoor begins to shriek—
    Or reads a story
About a prince, a castle, and a dragon.

The moon is glittering above the hill.
I stand before the gateposts of the King—   10
    So runs the story—
Of Thule, at midnight when the mice are still.

And I have been in Thule! It has come true—
The journey and the danger of the world,
    All that there is
To bear and to enjoy, endure and do.

Landscapes, seascapes . . . where have I been led?
The names of cities—Paris, Venice, Rome—
    Held out their arms.
A feathered god, seductive, went ahead.   20

Here is my house. Under a red rose tree
A child is swinging; another gravely plays.
    They are not surprised
That I am here; they were expecting me.

And yet my father sits and reads in silence,
My mother sheds a tear, the moon is still,
    And the dark wind
Is murmuring that nothing ever happens.

Beyond his jurisdiction as I move
Do I not prove him wrong? And yet, it's true   30
    They will not change
There, on the stage of terror and of love.

The actors in that playhouse always sit
In fixed positions—father, mother, child
    With painted eyes.
How sad it is to be a little puppet!

Their heads are wooden. And you once pretended
To understand them! Shake them as you will,
    They cannot speak.
Do what you will, the comedy is ended.   40

Father, why did you work? Why did you weep,
Mother? Was the story so important?
    "Listen!" the wind
Said to the children, and they fell asleep.

THE MAN WHO MARRIED MAGDALENE

The man who married Magdalene
Had not forgiven her.
God might pardon every sin . . .
Love is no pardoner.

Her hands were hollow, pale and blue,
Her mouth like watered wine.
He watched to see if she were true
And waited for a sign.

It was old harlotry, he guessed,
That drained her strength away,   10
So gladly for the dark she dressed,
So sadly for the day.

Their quarrels made her dull and weak
And soon a man might fit
A penny in the hollow cheek
And never notice it.

At last, as they exhausted slept,
Death granted the divorce,
And nakedly the woman leapt
Upon that narrow horse.   20

But when he woke and woke alone
He wept and would deny
The loose behavior of the bone
And the immodest thigh.

THE BOARDER

The time is after dinner. Cigarettes
        Glow on the lawn;
Glasses begin to tinkle; TV sets
        Have been turned on.

The moon is brimming like a glass of beer
        Above the town,

And love keeps her appointments—"Harry's here!"
    "I'll be right down."

But the pale stranger in the furnished room
    Lies on his back   10
Looking at paper roses, how they bloom,
    And ceilings crack.

TO THE WESTERN WORLD

A siren sang, and Europe turned away
From the high castle and the shepherd's crook.
Three caravels went sailing to Cathay
On the strange ocean, and the captains shook
Their banners out across the Mexique Bay.

And in our early days we did the same.
Remembering our fathers in their wreck
We crossed the sea from Palos where they came
And saw, enormous to the little deck,
A shore in silence waiting for a name.   10

The treasures of Cathay were never found.
In this America, this wilderness
Where the axe echoes with a lonely sound,
The generations labor to possess
And grave by grave we civilize the ground.

L. E. Sissman

L. E. Sissman was born in Detroit in 1928. As a child, he was a National Spelling Bee champion and a panelist on the old radio program "The Quiz Kids." He studied at Harvard, where he was elected Class Poet, and served as a campaign aide to John F. Kennedy. His first book, **Dying: An Intro-**

duction, *won the 1968 Lamont Prize, and his last, the posthumous* Hello,
Darkness: The Collected Poems of L. E. Sissman, *won the 1979
National Book Critics Circle Award. He was Creative Vice-President of
Quinn and Johnson Advertising Company in Boston and a contributing
editor of* The Atlantic *until his death in 1976.*

DECEMBER 27, 1966

Night sweat: my temperature spikes to 102
At 5 A.M.—a classic symptom—and,
Awake and shaken by an ague, I
Peep out a western window at the worn
Half-dollar of the moon, couched in the rose
And purple medium of air above
The little, distant mountains, a black line
Of gentle ox humps, flanked by greeny lights
Where a still empty highway goes. In Christmas week,
The stars flash ornamentally with the   10
Pure come-on of a possibility
Of peace beyond all reason, of the spheres
Engaged in an adagio saraband
Of perfect mathematic to set an
Example for the earthly, who abide
In vales of breakdown out of warranty,
The unrepairable complaint that rattles us
To death. Tonight, though, it is almost worth the price—
High stakes, and the veiled dealer vends bad cards—
To see the moon so silver going west,   20
So ladily serene because so dead,
So closely tailed by her consort of stars,
So far above the feverish, shivering
Nightwatchman pressed against the falling glass.

Knute Skinner

Born in St. Louis in 1929, Knute Skinner studied at Colorado State College and the University of Iowa. He is co-editor of The Bellingham Review *and author of* A Close Sky Over Killaspuglonane *(1968),* In Dinosaur Country *(1969),* Hearing of the Hard Times *(1981), and other books. He divides his time between homes in Bellingham, Washington, where he teaches at Western Washington State University, and Liscannon Bay, Ireland.*

IMAGINE GRASS

The planet that we plant upon
rolls through its orbit of the sun,
bending our grass upon the breeze.
While far away the galaxies
in a decelerating pace
reach for the outer edge of space.

Imagine in that final sky
("Give me deceleration; I
will give you mass and curvature.")
at journey's end a far-flung star
of an unnumbered magnitude
Mount Palomar has never viewed.   10

In that expanded universe
the furthest star will be the first,
poised at the end of everywhere,
on the edge of nothing, like a prayer,
to turn from nothing and retrace,
pulsating through the curve of space.

So many billion light years since
the particle horizon densed,
conceive the universe defined
within the orbit of the mind,
and somewhere in the measured mass
of everything, imagine grass.   20

Floyd Skloot

Floyd Skloot was born in Brooklyn in 1947 and educated at Franklin and Marshall College and Southern Illinois University. The author of **Rough Edges** *(1979), he has received a writing grant from the Illinois Arts Council and the Emily Dickinson Award from the Poetry Society of America. He resides in Portland, Oregon, where he works as a public policy and management consultant.*

MY DAUGHTER CONSIDERS HER BODY

She examines her hand, fingers spread wide.
Seated, she bends over her crossed legs
to search for specks or scars and cannot hide
her awe when any mark is found. She begs
me to look, twisting before her mirror,
at some tiny bruise on her hucklebone.
Barely awake, she studies creases her
arm developed as she slept. She has grown
entranced with blemish, begun to know
her body's facility for being   10
flawed. She does not trust its will to grow

whole again, but may learn that too, freeing
herself to accept the body's deep thirst
for risk. Learning to touch her wounds comes first.

David R. Slavitt

David R. Slavitt was born in White Plains, New York, in 1935 and educated at Andover, Yale, and Columbia. A former editor and movie critic for Newsweek, *he has written many novels (both under his own name and that of Henry Sutton), translated Virgil, and published several collections of poetry, including* Vital Signs: New and Selected Poems *(1975),* Rounding the Horn *(1978), and* Big Nose & Other Poems *(1983).*

IN MEMORY OF W. H. AUDEN

Not drunk but with a buzz on maybe, he
would have looked odd with carpet slippers (his feet
were bad, his dances mental), come to see
James's grave. He walked up my street.

He wrote that pools of melting snow reflected
clouds, birds, mourners, but he did not
complain that his feet got wet as he inspected
in mud and muddle the Master's simple plot.

He was always good at these poems about the dead—
James, Yeats, his doctor. Now we are left   10
to say to ourselves for him such words as he said.
But which of us is sufficiently wise or deft?

I have downstairs his photograph a friend
took two years ago. Auden was drunk.
No spirits will raise his spirit now, or mend
the sober afternoon into which we have sunk.

Facility, felicity—his tricks
bested the times, were the little rainbows one
sometimes sees around wrecks in the road's oil slicks . . .
sludge now without his light for sun.   20

On the opposite page in another obit, I've read
that Mantan Moreland is dead, the Birmingham Brown
chauffeur for Charlie Chan, the man who said,
"Feets, do your stuff," and made his eyes go round.

That fear is what we all feel now, diminished,
unprotected, bereft. Thick in the tongue,
say Auden's dead but the rest of us are finished,
humming in the dark the songs he'd have sung.

ANOTHER LETTER TO LORD BYRON

Everyone gets junk mail, a bill, a notice
        of a private sale, an alumni fund appeal,
letters from strangers . . . The one that Auden wrote is
        one of these, though clever enough. Did you feel
the eight-krona stamp redeemed it? That's ten zlotys,
        or about a hundred lire—not a great deal,
but the names of the coins are diverting. Or possibly you
collect postage stamps? It's something to do.

It must be dull to be dead. You can't write,
        or, if you do, you can't send it off to the printer   10
the way you used to. So a letter might
        have been fun to get. Did you spend the winter
feeling the envelope, holding it up to the light,
        and wondering whom you knew in such a hinter-
land as Iceland? I know it would pique
my interest to get mail from Reykjavik.

Harwich is less impressive, surely, than is
    Reykjavik. But when I go to post
my letter, I may do so from Hyannis,
    which is more amusing. Or there are a host   20
of towns named after you. The one in Maine is
    closest, but you have a wandering ghost—
which is fitting. There's a Byron or Byronville
in Okla., Wyo., Calif., Minn., and Ill.

But never mind. The postmark's hardly crucial.
    The main thing is that after thirty years
another letter that's addressed to you shall
    seem, I trust, no great intrusion. There's
lots that's happened, though I hope the news shall
    not depress you. Three decades of wars,   30
and the prospect of a future about which it's said
that those who are left alive will envy the dead.

But politics is not at all my métier.
    You took it up at the end, I know, but I
find it vicious enough, if rather petty (a
    moral hedging), to deal with the canaille
of publishers, editors, agents. Those *diavoletti!* (Eh?
    That's nearly impossible to justify.
But then I've just been to Venice, and saw your palazzo.
Is that enough excuse to polyglot so?)   30

I've changed the subject sooner than I'd intended,
    but as long as I'm on the new one, literature
is just as much a mess as ever—splendid
    livings for lousy authors, and good books fewer
and farther than ever between . . . But then, when did
    it ever appear to be better or different? You are
a perfect example of what can happen when
a poet is taken up by other men,

to be praised or damned. The public is mostly jerks.
    The common reader is common, and to hell   40
with him and with critics, trading in smiles and smirks,
    and making careers for themselves with their swell

Collected Essays more in mind than the works
        in hand. Even you're not doing too well.
I mention the disrepair of your reputation
only to demonstrate that of our situation.

No one reads poetry anyway now, except
        other poets—which is quite distressing.
They cannot be much as readers, being inept
        as rhymers (those that can rhyme), while confessing   50
to mental illness, or listing girls they've slept
        with (those that like girls) . . . But I am digressing.
In a time of tastelessness and epic slaughter,
we need some of your hock and soda water.

Not that it's all that bad. There is some verse
        well wrought. One can get in an age of iron
good iron work sometimes. A pigskin purse
        can be made of a sow's ear. One may not expire on
the beauty of it, but one could do worse.
        The manipulation of language . . . But, Lord Byron,   60
I scarcely need tell you. Your magnificent feminine
rhymes are more than fun for apothegming in.

They show contempt for the worst kind of good taste,
        and for readers—most of the few—who save up
            snatches
to make a mental sampler of, the paste
        pot minds of crackpots. And the catch is
that by the way you sneer at the whey-faced
        intellectuals who can't tell dispatches
of the AP from poems, look for meanings,
and of course miss all the point in their dull gleanings.   70

I hadn't meant to go on so. Do excuse
        my grumbling. I know it's rather foolish,
but I've been depressed lately. All the news
        is bad; the weather's damp and has turned coolish;
my mood's dark, the color of a bruise.
        And I've been bothered by the very ghoulish
notion that the books around me may
come to life and attack me any day.

Or not the books, but their authors, all the dead
    giants of letters whom time has not quite hushed.   80
It'd be delightful except that they have shed
    their skins, their flesh, their bones, and are all crushed
to disembodied voices, dull as lead.
    I have the feeling that I am ambushed
by the naked ones who have shown up to haunt
me. But I can't imagine what they want.

I shouldn't like to think it's vampirism,
    nor envy, nor contempt. Perhaps they warn
that poetry is light spread through a prism,
    and suddenly, on some innocuous morn   90
the prism breaks, and the recidivism
    is to the whiteness from which it was born—
no rhetoric, no images, no sound,
just volumes of blank pages, buckram-bound.

Or they sing, hey-diddle, the cat and the fiddle—but
    even its nine lives prove to be finite,
and after performing on lengths of its own gut,
    it dies and the music dies. There's a moral in it.
I'm sure there is. I can't tell you just what,
    but I'm sure I'll think of something. Give me a
       minute.   100
Art is odd. Consider the dog and how
he laughed to see the hell scared out of the cow.

Well, here I am, half-dog, half-cow, half-cat
    (that's too many halves by half). All right, half-wit,
fooling around as you did once. But that
    is greatly comforting: in the little skit
from the Nightmare Follies—now in its fifth week at
    my local, mental theater—you're a big hit.
Among those shades, you shine, and my attention all
focuses on you, who are three-dimensional.   110

You come through whole, and live, and are not merely
    a name on the spine of your book and its index card.
The gestures you make in your poems, the jokes, are
      clearly
    those of a man who's trying very hard

—and willing to pay the price, even pay dearly—
    not only not to be boring, but not to be bored
himself. Yourself. Myself. I know how it is.
It's always tough in the Quality Lit. Biz.

Therefore, my letter. Partly to let you know
    that you're still alive and well, which pleases me   120
as much as it pleases you, and to say hello.
    With any luck, in two thousand and three,
somebody else will drop you a line, and so
    keep the game going. Auden, I, he
thank you for teaching how to play it coolly.
It is, as I am, sir, yours, very truly.

Dave Smith

*Born in Portsmouth, Virginia, in 1942, Dave Smith holds degrees from the
University of Virginia, Southern Illinois University, and Ohio University.
The recipient of two National Endowment for the Arts Fellowships and a
Guggenheim Fellowship, he has published several volumes of poetry, includ-*
ing Homage to Edgar Allan Poe *(1981),* In the House of the Judge
(1983), and The Roundhouse Voices: Poems 1970–1985 *(1985).
Since he has said he cares "little for poems that do not create a narrative,"
it is not surprising that he is also the author of a novel,* Onliness *(1981).
He teaches at Virginia Commonwealth University.*

THE OLD WHORE SPEAKS TO
A YOUNG POET

This is the way we do it dear,
    from post office to pier.
First you learn the age's terminology,
    tone and proper vocables,

the time to speak, the time to leer,
    the weakness of constables,
and then how one applies technology.

The bottom is the last lesson of course,
    the one that fills your purse.
Now when you speak never name the act;   10
    don't curse or mumble,
don't get drunk, don't get sick, worse,
    don't pick tumbles
who can't pay a whole night's contract.

Be elegant, but plainly dress, paint lips,
    keep little breasts, walk hip.
Steel yourself to do what must be done,
    avoid the freaks and simple
minded bastards who have to be whipped
    into shape. Be quick, nimble   20
of wit, have a good ear, and work alone.

Remember the equipment, take care, study
    it, keep it hot and ready.
Don't waste time on the frothy loves
    of children or senile
aristocrats: practice working slow, steady,
    groom your own style.
Success will come as sure as the man above.

Finally, take notes, observe your colleagues,   30
    both the living and the grieved.
Keep always something back against the time
    you're called a symbol,
which means they mean you're overdue for relief.
    But fight back, gambol
while you can, then go with grace in your prime.

CHOPPING WOOD

Strange how the mind will stand outside
the body's snapping torque and sweat
to observe bone and sinew that finds
almost never the perfect throw it wants

to split each round limb where the true
grain must expose itself, empurpled,
satiny as meat inside a beauty's thigh
stroked once in the permanent world

of love the mind summons only as smoke
or the wisps of breath in an iron air.   10
My body heat fogs my glasses, stroke
after stroke. The blade falls unaware

it might do anything else. Wood splits.
Most of it's knotted, and a worm hole,
hidden, is ubiquitous as tall innocence
the mind wants to bend to like a girl

impossibly gorgeous in a doctor's office.
And those hacking, impotent after-chops
at the hanging-on slivers—they exhaust
caveats in the head. The fury of chips   20

flying up like prayers? Only the mind's
sad attempt to love what it must fear,
loose ground, bad aim, faithless hands.
So the mind heats itself with an hour

making fuel for heat: as if all consists
in the nerves hurling the mind out.
The blunt blade dives through the flesh
long dead, soon stacked, used up, mute.

THE ANCESTOR

How well I know him, old soldier in blue
Union suit that might have been fireman's show
duds on the day they burned the whorehouse down.
Captain of the hosing team, he sprayed crowds,
the settees, the porch, but let others scorch
handlebars and muttonchops. Not his torch.
He'd be damned, maybe, but he'd sin enough,
death, fire, and fear, too, at Antietam's bluffs.
Under him, I lie in grandfather's house,

bird-fat for holidays, deepsick of grouse, 10
television news, lies, repeated rapes
by puffing gents with new rights, knowing ropes
bounce the way they always did, but more, worse.
Framed over faces that mumble news, the day's dirt,
his face, distant as a moon, scarred, boot-scuffed,
but oddly close, a man who still spits, gruffs,
sits ram-straight, though brittle with bad back pain,
gutshot by the past, present, and future. Flames
braze each brass button. His whores have names.
Brothers, fathers, we gaze on him for signals, 20
but cold Buck's merciless, locked to the Eagles.

*In Memoriam, Asham Buckner, Captain, Army of Northern
Virginia*

THE COLLECTOR OF THE SUN

Through the small door of a hut
he stares at us, our movements,
the thousands of faces we are,
the booming world's roar

that, later, for a drifting instant,
he will enter. His extra shirt
tied by its arms for a sack,
he will be lost in his luck.

By the freeway, whipped as a weed,
he stalks the malignant ground 10
for bottles, and we wear on.
He doesn't imagine anyone

weeping in anger as he looms up.
And when he comes to the truck
parked, the woman asleep inside,
he thinks of his nights, wide

as the blue glare on the concrete,
full of glass and the clink-clink
of his business. For him sunset
is the good hour, the shapeless 20

beams of headlights always thick,
blending with sun to flick
off what he hunts. He is alone,
himself, dreaming of the blown

treasures of the world, the bottles
like loaves of gold. The rubble
of everything falls about him
like snow. He bends, reaches, grins,

and ignores whatever we scream.
His tarpaper walls are the dream   30
he has given himself. At night
a wind plays over the pipes

he has fashioned from glassy mouths.
The world seems right, as he lies out
in bed, but fingers itch, and a face,
oh whose is it, leans, leans like grace

and he can't remember whose or why.
At dawn, aching, he watches the sky,
sees dark birds pass, then us,
and is himself again, staring, blessed.   40

W. D. Snodgrass

*W. D. Snodgrass was born in Wilkinsburg, Pennsylvania, in 1926, raised
in Beaver Falls, Pennsylvania, and educated at Geneva College and the
University of Iowa. His first book,* Heart's Needle, *won the 1960 Pulitzer
Prize and helped establish the Confessional mode of poetry. However, his more*

recent collections, particularly The Führer Bunker *(1977), a sequence of dramatic monologues spoken by leading figures of the Third Reich, reveal a movement away from personality and confession toward personae and history. Besides poetry, he has published two works of translation,* Six Troubadour Songs *(1977) and* Six Minnesinger Songs *(1980), and a collection of critical essays,* In Radical Pursuit *(1975). He teaches at the University of Delaware.*

SONG

Sweet beast, I have gone prowling,
   a proud rejected man
who lived along the edges
   catch as catch can;
in darkness and in hedges
   I sang my sour tone
and all my love was howling
   conspicuously alone.

I curled and slept all day
   or nursed my bloodless wounds   10
until the squares were silent
   where I could make my tunes
singular and violent.
   Then, sure as hearers came
I crept and flinched away.
   And, girl, you've done the same.

A stray from my own type,
   led along by blindness,
my love was near to spoiled
   and curdled all my kindness.   20
I find no kin, no child;
   only the weasel's ilk.
Sweet beast, cat of my own stripe,
   come and take my milk.

From HEART'S NEEDLE

10

The vicious winter finally yields
   the green winter wheat;
the farmer, tired in the tired fields
   he dare not leave will eat.

Once more the runs come fresh; prevailing
   piglets, stout as jugs,
harry their old sow to the railing
   to ease her swollen dugs

and game colts trail the herded mares
   that circle the pasture courses;   10
our seasons bring us back once more
   like merry-go-round horses.

With crocus mouths, perennial hungers,
   into the park Spring comes;
we roast hot dogs on old coat hangers
   and feed the swan bread crumbs,

pay our respects to the peacocks, rabbits,
   and leathery Canada goose
who took, last Fall, our tame white habits
   and now will not turn loose.   20

In full regalia, the pheasant cocks
   march past their dubious hens;
the porcupine and the lean, red fox
   trot around bachelor pens

and the miniature painted train
   wails on its oval track:
you said, I'm going to Pennsylvania!
   and waved. And you've come back.

If I loved you, they said, I'd leave
    and find my own affairs.   30
Well, once again this April, we've
    come around to the bears;

punished and cared for, behind bars,
    the coons on bread and water
stretch thin black fingers after ours.
    And you are still my daughter.

A VISITATION

*Just as you carried out a policy of not wanting to share the earth with
the Jewish people . . . (as though you and your superiors had any right
to determine who should and who should not inhabit the world), we find
that no member of the human race can be expected to want to share the
earth with you.*
                        —Hannah Arendt on Eichmann

At my window, I pull the curtains wide
On the Detroit night. So; it's you, again,
Old ghost? Not left once since the day you died?

    I am faithful, shivering still and pale,
    Streaked yet by traffic lights, waiting outside
    Like the poor dead soldier in some folktale

The Jews, your jailers, couldn't bear to face
Your dutiful Jewish face, in their jail,
On TV, postered, every public place,

    Come to his true love's window, wanting in   10
    To ask, now their love's final, love's embrace.
    I am true to you; I have always been.

Each usual nightmare. Taking that excuse
You gave to wipe out their (and your own) kin,
They hanged you. So; they've turned you loose.

     My truth enraged them. *You,* perhaps, don't need
     Someone to outcast, loathe, some way to lose
     Track of man's deceit, man's violence, greed—

When were you half so slippery, so alive
As now you're dead? You prowl the world's face, freed   20
To trace your own types, threaten them, connive . . .

     Take me in. Secure me. Once, your own hand
     Held a nightstick, .45 and sheath knife;
     You've chained men to a steel beam on command.

This last, I admit. I can scarcely claim
To be my brother's keeper on so grand
A scale as yours. In a full lifetime's shame

     Luck, friend, not character. We took the parts
     Our time and place allowed. You played the game;
     There's something beats the same in opposed hearts.   30

Philosophy's still your crime: the abstract
Gray lie, the sweet cliché that still imparts
Its drugged glow through the brain. The unsung fact

     Who called his weakness, love? His long rage, lust?
     Who called his worst lusts, honesty? Our days exact
     From you, as from me, the deep faults they must.

Proves all the more cause I should keep you there—
How subtle all that chokes us with disgust
Moves in implacably to rule us, unaware.

     My own love, you're all I could wish to be.   40
     Close your eyes—I'll just wander off somewhere.

Or watch the way your world moves—you can look
    through me.

A FLAT ONE

Old Fritz, on this rotating bed
For seven wasted months you lay
Unfit to move, shrunken, gray,
No good to yourself or anyone
But to be babied—changed and bathed and fed.
      At long last, that's all done.

Before each meal, twice every night,
We set pads on your bedsores, shut
Your catheter tube off, then brought
The second canvas-and-black-iron   10
Bedframe and clamped you in between them, tight,
      Scared, so we could turn

You over. We washed you, covered you,
Cut up each bite of meat you ate;
We watched your lean jaws masticate
As ravenously your useless food
As thieves at hard labor in their chains chew
      Or insects in the wood.

Such pious sacrifice to give
You all you could demand of pain;   20
Receive this haddock's body, slain
For you, old tyrant; take this blood
Of a tomato, shed that you might live.
      You had that costly food.

You seem to be all finished, so
We'll plug your old recalcitrant anus
And tie up your discouraged penis
In a great, snow-white bow of gauze.

We wrap you, pin you, and cart you down below,
    Below, below, because   30

        Your credit has finally run out.
        On our steel table, trussed and carved
        You'll find this world's hardworking, starved
        Teeth working in your precious skin.
The earth turns, in the end, by turn about
            And opens to take you in.

        Seven months gone down the drain; thank God
        That's through. Throw out the four-by-fours,
        Swabsticks, the thick salve for bedsores,
        Throw out the diaper pads and drug   40
Containers, pile the bedclothes in a wad,
            And rinse the cider jug

        Half filled with the last urine. Then
        Empty out the cotton cans,
        Autoclave the bowls and spit pans,
        Unhook the pumps and all the red
Tubes—catheter, suction, oxygen;
            Next, wash the empty bed.

        —All this Dark Age machinery
        On which we had tormented you   50
        To life. Last, gather up the few
        Belongings: snapshots, some odd bills,
Your mail, and half a pack of Luckies we
            Won't light you after meals.

        Old man, these seven months you've lain
        Determined—not that you would live—
        Just to not die. No one would give
        You one chance you could ever wake
From that first night, much less go well again,
            Much less go home and make   60

Your living; how could you hope to find
A place for yourself in all creation?—
Pain was your only occupation.
And pain that should content and will
A man to give it up, nerved you to grind
          Your clenched teeth, breathing, till

Your skin broke down, your calves went flat,
And your legs lost all sensation. Still,
You took enough morphine to kill
A strong man. Finally, nitrogen   70
Mustard: you could last two months after that;
          It would kill you then.

Even then you wouldn't quit.
Old soldier, yet you must have known
Inside the animal had grown
Sick of the world, made up its mind
To stop. Your mind ground on its separate
          Way, merciless and blind,

Into these last weeks when the breath
Would only come in fits and starts   80
That puffed out your sections like the parts
Of some enormous, damaged bug.
You waited, not for life, not for your death,
          Just for the deadening drug

That made your life seem bearable.
You still whispered you would not die.
Yet in the nights I heard you cry
Like a whipped child; in fierce old age
You whimpered, tears stood on your gun-metal
          Blue cheeks shaking with rage   90

And terror. So much pain would fill
Your room that when I left I'd pray
That if I came back the next day
I'd find you gone. You stayed for me—

Nailed to your own rapacious, stiff self-will.
        You've shook loose, finally.

    They'd say this was a worthwhile job
    Unless they tried it. It is mad
    To throw our good lives after bad;
    Waste time, drugs, and our minds, while strong   100
Men starve. How many young men did we rob
        To keep you hanging on?

    I can't think we did *you* much good.
    Well, when you died, none of us wept.
    You killed for us, and so we kept
    You; because we need to earn *our* pay.
No. We'd still have to help you try. We would
        Have killed for you today.

Gary Snyder

The hero of Jack Kerouac's roman à clef The Dharma Bums, *Gary Snyder was born in San Francisco in 1930 and raised in Oregon and Washington. He studied at Reed College, Berkeley, Indiana University, and in a Zen Buddhist monastery in Kyoto, Japan. Among his honors are a Bollingen grant for Buddhist studies and the Pulitzer Prize, in 1975, for* Turtle Island. *He is also the author of* Myths & Texts *(1960),* The Back Country *(1967),* Regarding Wave *(1970),* Axe Handles *(1983), and other books of poetry. In addition, he has published several collections of essays, most recently* The Real Work *(1980).*

From HITCH HAIKU

"THEY DIDN'T HIRE HIM"

They didn't hire him
        so he ate his lunch alone:
the noon whistle

Barry Spacks

Born in Philadelphia in 1931, Barry Spacks studied at the University of Pennsylvania, Indiana University, and Cambridge, where he was a Fulbright Scholar. From 1960 to 1983 he taught at the Massachusetts Institute of Technology. He has published five volumes of poetry, the most recent of which is Spacks Street: New and Selected Poems *(1983), and two novels,* The Sophomore *(1968) and* Orphans *(1972).*

FINDING A YIDDISH PAPER ON THE RIVERSIDE LINE

Again I hold these holy letters,
Never learned. Dark candelabras.

Once they glowed in the yellow light
Through the chicken smell of Friday night,

My father in his peach-stained shirt
Scrubbing off twelve hours' dirt

While I drew my name on misted glass.
Now trim suburban houses pass

And on my lap the headlines loom
Like strangers in the living room.   10

OCTOBER

My wife sits reading in a garden chair
Pope's *Moral Essays* by the failing light,
As leaves turn epileptic in the air
And through the woods come poachers, and the night.

Pope's natural habitat: a bullet rips
The homespun silence and the volume slips,
But catching it she finds her place in time
And never drops the stitches of a rhyme.

Braving the season in the name of wit,
She holds each couplet in such close esteem   10
No maniac can put a hole in it.
The year's in tatters, but she makes a seam;

The house is civil, though the wood's insane,
And man's the missing link who lets the chain-
Of-being shake. It's hanging by a hair.
My wife sits reading in a garden chair.

William Stafford

William Stafford was born in Hutchinson, Kansas, in 1914. He earned B.A. and M.A. degrees from the University of Kansas and a Ph.D. from the University of Iowa. During World War II he served four years in labor camps for conscientious objection, an experience recorded in his memoir Down in My Heart *(1947). He has received a National Book Award, the Shelley Memorial Award, the Melville Cane Award, and the American Academy and Institute of Arts and Letters Award in Literature. His numerous books include* Stories That Could Be True: New and Collected Poems *(1977) and* A Glass Face in the Rain *(1982). He lives in Portland, Oregon, where he taught at Lewis and Clark College from 1956 to 1979.*

TRAVELING THROUGH THE DARK

Traveling through the dark I found a deer
dead on the edge of the Wilson River road.
It is usually best to roll them into the canyon:
that road is narrow; to swerve might make more dead.

By glow of the tail-light I stumbled back of the car
and stood by the heap, a doe, a recent killing;
she had stiffened already, almost cold.
I dragged her off; she was large in the belly.

My fingers touching her side brought me the reason—
her side was warm; her fawn lay there waiting,   10
alive, still, never to be born.
Beside that mountain road I hesitated.

The car aimed ahead its lowered parking lights;
under the hood purred the steady engine.
I stood in the glare of the warm exhaust turning red;
around our group I could hear the wilderness listen.

I thought hard for us all—my only swerving—,
then pushed her over the edge into the river.

THE SWERVE

Halfway across a bridge one night
my father's car went blind. He guided
it on by no star but a light he kept in mind.

Halfway to here, my father died.
He looked at me. He closed his eyes.
The world stayed still. Today I hold in mind

The things he said, my children's lives—
any light. Oh, any light.

FRIEND WHO NEVER CAME

It has not been given me to have a friend
so steady the world becomes an incident
and all else leads us both to that event
when glances cross while two fates depend.
It has not been given. A life will end
somewhere at random, silent of rest, silent
that might have whispered another world and bent
this one around us. Here is my farewell, friend
who never came: There was a morning in June,
when I was young, and a family just from the farm   10
parked by our yard, not knowing what to do.
The daughter trembling lay—"Sunstroke last noon,"
they said. They soothed her, drove slowly on. The harm
had been in her eyes. They rolled, once—"I was for you."

Sometimes in the sun today I glimpse that world in the
    blue.

GLANCES

Two people meet. The sky turns winter,
quells whatever they would say.
Then, a periphery glance into danger—
and an avalanche already on its way.

They have been honest all of their lives;
careful, calm, never in haste;
they didn't know what it is to *meet*.
Now they have met: the world is waste.

They find they are riding an avalanche
feeling at rest, all danger gone.   10
The present looks out of their eyes; they stand
calm and still on a speeding stone.

WINTERWARD

Early in March we pitched our scar,
this fact of a life, in dust;
in summer there was a green alarm,
a foxfire of fear, the distrust
of sighting under a willow tree
a little eggshell, burst.

It was mostly quiet, but threatenings
flared wherever we looked;
in autumn the birds fell to the ground
and crawled away to the rocks;   10
no sleep at night for anyone,
we stared at a moon like chalk.

Now we hear the stars torn upward
out of the sky; the alarm
shadows us as we run away
from this fact of a life, our home.
Oh winter, oh snowy interior,
rocks and hurt birds, we come.

Maura Stanton

Maura Stanton was born in Evanston, Illinois, in 1946 and grew up in Peoria and Minneapolis. A graduate of the University of Minnesota and the University of Iowa, she has received the Yale Younger Poets Prize, two National Endowment for the Arts Fellowships, and the Michigan Quarterly Review *Lawrence Foundation Prize for fiction. Besides her two volumes of poetry,* Snow on Snow *(1975) and* Cries of Swimmers *(1984), she has published a novel,* Molly Companion *(1977). She teaches in the M.F.A. program at Indiana University.*

CHILDHOOD

I used to lie on my back, imagining
A reverse house on the ceiling of my house
Where I could walk around in empty rooms
All by myself. There was no furniture
Up there, only a glass globe in the floor,
And knee-high barriers at every door.
The low silled windows opened on blue air.
Nothing hung in the closet; even the kitchen
Seemed immaculate, a place for thought.
I liked to walk across the swirling plaster   10
Into the parts of the house I couldn't see.
The hum from the other house, now my ceiling,
Reached me only faintly. I'd look up
To find my brothers watching old cartoons,
Or my mother vacuuming the ugly carpet.
I'd stare amazed at unmade beds, the clutter,
Shoes, half-dressed dolls, the telephone,
Then return dizzily to my perfect floorplan
Where I never spoke or listened to anyone.

I must have turned down the wrong hall,   20
Or opened a door that locked shut behind me,
For I live on the ceiling now, not the floor.
This is my house, room after empty room.
How do I ever get back to the real house
Where my sisters spill milk, my father calls,
And I am at the table, eating cereal?
I fill my white rooms with furniture,
Hang curtains over the piercing blue outside.
I lie on my back. I strive to look down.
This ceiling is higher than it used to be,   30
The floor so far away I can't determine
Which room I'm in, which year, which life.

GOOD PEOPLE

The sight of all these people in the street
Heading a dozen directions, in puffy coats,
Icelandic hats, in boots or rubber shoes,

All walking stiffly on the melting ice,
Necks bent against the wind, makes me giddy.
If we could hear each other think, the noise
Would shatter glass, break the best hearts.
A businessman in a camel overcoat
Passes a red-haired girl with a yellow scarf,
And neither will ever see each other again   10

Or see me standing outside the florist's.
I'm buying flowers for my mother, who lies
In the hospital with a blood clot in her vein,
Almost recovered. I saw her yesterday
And through the doors of other rooms I glimpsed
Face after face I didn't recognize,
Twisting on wet pillows, or watching T.V.
How accidental my existence seemed—
I might have sat beside some other bed,
I might have loved that man in blue pajamas   20

Or kissed the silent child in the metal crib
Receiving a transfusion, as I did once,
Thirty years ago to save my life.
Then a car honks. A woman jostles me.
I stare in wonder down the crowded street.
I could be a part of one of these strangers
Breathing hard in the cold, Kentucky air,
That tall man with gnarled, shaky hands
Or that heavy woman, or part of someone dead
Who thought that life was choice, not accident.   30

George Starbuck

*George Starbuck was born in Columbus, Ohio, in 1931 and educated at the
California Institute of Technology, Berkeley, the University of Chicago, and
Harvard. Formerly a fiction editor for Houghton-Mifflin and the director of
the University of Iowa Writers' Workshop, he is now a professor of English*

348

GEORGE STARBUCK

at Boston University. His books include Bone Thoughts *(1960), which won the Yale Younger Poets Prize, and* The Argot Merchant Disaster: New and Selected Poems *(1982), which won the Lenore Marshall Prize. According to Starbuck, writing in forms is "the long way round" that for him is "the only road to truth."*

DOUBLE SEMI-SESTINA

A small foreign car full of farm ladies from Jones County
Iowa is driving around the streets of Iowa City Iowa
asking at every open car window for the St. Patrick's
    Hospital.

You mean Mercy, we say. We know there's a Mercy
    Hospital
along with the Veteran's Hospital, the Johnson County
Home, and the several University of Iowa

Hospitals in the vicinity of Iowa City Iowa
but none of us has heard of a St. Patrick's Hospital.
They drive on. Likely they tried at Mercy. The county

number is on their license plate. Jones County.   10
The Wapsipinicon River. Stone City Iowa.
Slowly we think too late, Psychopathic Hospital.

Somebody must have said Psychopathic Hospital.
Oh Dwayne if it ain't worked out, if they've taken you off
    county
and locked you up somewhere they tell you is Iowa City
    Iowa;

Sharon if all you know in the world is Cascade Iowa
and this isn't Cascade Iowa: Mick if the hospital
two-step keeps overcrowding your saved vacation in County

Clare; patience: the county
womenfolk are in Iowa City Iowa   20
asking for you and for the St. Patrick's Hospital.

Timothy Steele

Timothy Steele was born in Burlington, Vermont, in 1948 and received his B.A. from Stanford and his Ph.D. from Brandeis. He has been awarded Stegner and Guggenheim Fellowships and is the author of one collection of poems, Uncertainties and Rest *(1979), and three chapbooks,* The Prudent Heart *(1982),* Nine Poems *(1984), and* On Harmony *(1984). He lives in Los Angeles, where he is a visiting lecturer at the University of California at Los Angeles.*

SAPPHICS AGAINST ANGER

Angered, may I be near a glass of water;
May my first impulse be to think of Silence,
Its deities (who are they? do in fact they
        Exist? etc.).

May I recall what Aristotle says of
The subject: to give vent to rage is not to
Release it but to be increasingly prone
        To its incursions.

May I imagine being in the *Inferno*,
Hearing it asked: "Vergilio mio, who's   10
That sulking with Achilles there?" and hearing
        Vergil say: "Dante,

That fellow, at the slightest provocation,
Slammed phone receivers down, and waved his arms like
A madman. What Attila did to Europe,
        What Genghis Khan did

To Asia, that poor dope did to his marriage."
May I, that is, put learning to good purpose,
Mindful that melancholy is a sin, though
      Stylish at present.   20

Better than rage is the post-dinner quiet,
The sink's warm turbulence, the streaming platters,
The suds rehearsing down the drain in spirals
      In the last rinsing.

For what is, after all, the good life save that
Conducted thoughtfully, and what is passion
If not the holiest of powers, sustaining
      Only if mastered.

Barry Sternlieb

Born in 1947, Barry Sternlieb was educated at Fairleigh Dickinson University. His poems have appeared in Poetry, Prairie Schooner, Poetry Northwest, Yankee, The Minnesota Review, *and other magazines. He lives in Richmond, Massachusetts, with his wife and two daughters.*

VALLEY BLOOD

With sap running early
and a hundred buckets hung,
Leon can barely keep up. While every
maple on the road is tapped, a long

tale of steam joins the sky
to his swayback shed
where I love to sit in the dead
of night, converse with him, and clear my mind.

He calls childhood a farm
near Middlefield in the Twenties, 10
and fate his father coming home
one day with news: finally

a decent bull for sale
at a fair price, but before
the man could elaborate, his wife turned pale,
then pointing at the door

said, you better think real careful
cause if you buy that beast, I'm gone. Simple
as that. She even twisted her wedding
band off and spent the evening sitting 20

mute as straw. Leon admits he saw
his father walk to the garden, kneel
down and clench the soil.
Next day he bought

that bull and the wife left. Four
children couldn't stop her.
Leon stares at his half-gnarled,
half-nailed fingers while steam purls

vision and syrup-pans hiss.
He feeds the fire and checks the flow 30
from pan to pan, a final gold
the embodiment of sweetness.

Then, with an old tin cup, he skims
a taste for both of us, his eyes
spanned inward over bluest time.
No reason at all, he declares, just a fine
Jersey bull, such a beautiful bull, goddamn!

Pamela Stewart

Pamela Stewart was born in South Hadley, Massachusetts, in 1945 and studied writing at the University of Iowa. The recipient of a Guggenheim Fellowship, she has published several volumes of poetry, including The St. Vlas Elegies *(1977),* Cascades *(1979), and* Silentie Lunae *(1981).*

PUNK PANTOUM

Tonight I'll walk the razor along your throat
You'll wear blood jewels and last week's ochre bruise
There's a new song out just for you and me
There's sawdust on the floor, and one dismembered horse

You'll wear blood jewels and last week's final bruise
I got three shirts from the hokey-man at dawn
There'll be sawdust on the floor and, ha, his dismembered
    horse:
Rust-stained fetlock, gristle, bone and hoof . . .

They'll look good hanging from the shirt I took at dawn.
Bitch, let's be proud to live at Eutaw Place   10
With rats, a severed fetlock, muscle, bone and hooves,
George will bring his snake and the skirt Divine threw out.

For now, I'm glad we live at Eutaw Place
Remember how we met at the Flower Mart last Spring?
George wore his snake and the hose Divine threw out—
Eating Sandoz oranges, we watched the ladies in their spats.

Remember how you burned your hair at the Flower Mart
    last May?
I put it out with Wes Jones' checkered pants,
The pulp of oranges and that old lady's hat—
I knew I loved you then, with your blistered face and
    tracks   20

That I disinfected with Wes Jones' filthy pants.
There's a new song out just for you and me
That says I'll always love you and your face. Let's make
    new tracks
Tonight, dragging the white-hot razor across our throats,
    and back . . .

Leon Stokesbury

Leon Stokesbury was born in 1945 in Oklahoma City and earned degrees from Lamar University, the University of Arkansas, and Florida State University. His books are Often in Different Landscapes *(1976), the winner of the first Associated Writing Programs Poetry Competition,* The Royal Nonesuch *(1984), and* The Drifting Away *(1986). He teaches in the graduate writing program at McNeese State University in Lake Charles, Louisiana.*

EAST TEXAS

The taste in my mouth
Was the taste of blood or rust on backdoor thermometers

Unread for twenty years. With my cheesecloth
Net I waited in the woods. Then the flutters
Of the giant swallowtails could be heard far away. Leaves
Moved. Sweat was acid in my eyes, and my father frowned
In his huge wheelchair. He could not get up the hill. My
    last two loves
But one sat in pine straw, waiting to see what I would do.
    The sound
To my left was the sound of men standing at urinals.
But no. It was only the rain, uncontrollable, and the rain
    took   10
The grey shapes of steam. My father frowned. It was so
    steep.
And those shapes were the shapes of old women with
    shawls
On their heads, of old men sitting down. She shook
Me saying I was talking in my sleep.

THE LOVER REMEMBERETH SUCH AS HE SOMETIMES ENJOYED AND SHOWETH HOW HE WOULD LIKE TO ENJOY HER AGAIN

Luck is something I do not understand:
There were a lot of things I almost did
Last night. I almost went to hear a band
Down at The Swinging Door. I, almost, hid
Out in my room all night and read a book,
The Sot-Weed Factor, that I'd read before;
Almost, I drank a pint of Sunny Brook
I'd bought at the Dickson Street Liquor Store.

Instead I went to the Restaurant-On-The-Corner,
And tried to write, and did drink a beer or two.   10
Then coming back from getting rid of the beer,
I suddenly found I was looking straight at you.
Five months, my love, since I last touched your hand.
Luck is something I do not understand.

TO HIS BOOK

Wafer; thin and hard and bitter pill I
    Take from time to time; pillow I have lain
        Too long on; holding the brief dreams, the styled
Dreams, the nightmares, shadows, red flames high
    High up on mountains; wilted zinnias, rain
        On dust, and great weight, the dead dog, and wild
Onions; mastodonic woman who knows how,—
    I'm tired of you, tired of your insane
        Acid eating in the brain. Sharp stones, piled
Particularly, I let you go. Sink, or float, or fly now,   10
        Bad child.

Mark Strand

Born in Summerside, Prince Edward Island, Canada, in 1934, Mark Strand was educated at Antioch, Yale Art School, and the University of Iowa. Since Strand studied to be a painter, it is not surprising that David Young has compared his poems to paintings, specifically to those of another master of "melancholy beauty," Edward Hopper. The most recent of his five volumes of poetry is Selected Poems *(1980). He has also published translations of Rafael Alberti and Carlos Drummond de Andrade and edited* The Contemporary American Poets *(1969), a popular anthology. He is writer-in-residence at the University of Utah.*

SLEEPING WITH ONE EYE OPEN

Unmoved by what the wind does,
The windows

Are not rattled, nor do the various
Areas
Of the house make their usual racket—
Creak at
The joints, trusses and studs.
Instead,
They are still. And the maples,
Able   10
At times to raise havoc,
Evoke
Not a sound from their branches'
Clutches.
It's my night to be rattled,
Saddled
With spooks. Even the half-moon
(Half man,
Half dark), on the horizon,
Lies on   20
Its side casting a fishy light
Which alights
On my floor, lavishly lording
Its morbid
Look over me. Oh, I feel dead,
Folded
Away in my blankets for good, and
Forgotten.
My room is clammy and cold,
Moonhandled   30
And weird. The shivers
Wash over
Me, shaking my bones, my loose ends
Loosen,
And I lie sleeping with one eye open,
Hoping
That nothing, nothing will happen.

Dabney Stuart

---

*Dabney Stuart was born in Richmond, Virginia, in 1937 and educated at
Davidson College and Harvard. His books include the poetry collections* The
Diving Bell *(1966),* A Particular Place *(1969),* The Other Hand
(1974), Round and Round *(1977), and* Common Ground *(1982),
and the critical study* Nabokov: The Dimensions of Parody *(1978).
He has held two National Endowment for the Arts Fellowships and won the
first Governor's Award for the Arts in Virginia. He teaches at Washington
and Lee University.*

FALL PRACTICE

Some after a night of sex, some hungover,
Some tanned, some fat, all still half asleep,
They'd sit around and give each other lip
Before padding up and cleating the summer clover
The field had grown to cover last season's dust.

"Her? Aw, man, that chick's a highway, I oughtta know,
I've driven it." "You gotta taste
That stuff, grow whiskers on your ass." "The best
I ever had was . . ." and so forth. The old show.
A bunch of scrubs bucking for first team berth.   10

I couldn't believe their talk. They'd cat all night
Yet next day hit the dummies, digging the turf,
Sweating, driving themselves for all they were worth
Into each other like bulls, brute against brute.
Whatever they got, girls, drunk, it wasn't enough.

It went on like that, late August through November.
Though I was the quarterback, the thinker
Who directed that beef, split ends, and set the flanker,
I worked at the center's butt, and I remember
Being primed for the big game, hungering for the cup.   20

DISCOVERING MY DAUGHTER

Most of your life we have kept our separate places:
After I left your mother you knew an island,
Rented rooms, a slow coastal slide Northward
To Boston, and, in summer, another island
Hung at the country's tip. Would you have kept going
All the way off the map, an absolute alien?

Sometimes I shiver, being almost forgetful enough
To have let that happen: it's a longer way,
Under such pressure, from one person to
Another. Our trip proves again the world is   10
Round, a singular island where people may come
Together, as we have, making a singular place.

Barton Sutter

*Barton Sutter was born in Minneapolis in 1949, raised in small towns in
Minnesota and Iowa, and educated at Bemidji State University, Southwest
State University, and Syracuse University. The author of* Cedarhome
(1977), Sequoyah *(1983) and* Pine Creek Parish Hall and Other
Poems *(1985), he has taught, off and on, but has mainly made his living*

as a typesetter. He is married to historian Annette Atkins and lives near St. Cloud, Minnesota.

SWEDISH LESSON

Talk about the mother tongue.
I heard these words when I was young.
I'd gabble gibberish and stutter,
Mimicking my babysitters.
They'd say, "Can you speak svenska?"
I'd answer, "Ya, you betcha."
They'd giggle, slap their laps, and sigh.
Their gossip was my lullabye.
Around the barn their men would grunt
The Esperanto of immigrants.   10

My grandmother risked ridicule
Whenever she opened her mouth at school
But broke the brogue. I speak American,
But, feeling like a bad translation,
I bought the books and paid tuition.
My classmates mock my pronunciation.

Once these words were hawked and spit
By barbarians who meant it
When they swore. They drew swords
And mangled men for what they said.   20
These words are theirs but tamed by time,
Their history a wind chime.
Hearsay now, they sound so gentle
I think of women spinning wool.
Chuckling like a dandling song,
The melodic nonsense passes on
Rumors of the old country. We
Hear the schuss of snow and ski
Past places parents mentioned.
Strange. The teacher's intonation   30
Makes every other word a question.

Blue-collar misfits, dissatisfied
Housewives, we've stood beside
Our ancestors, laid hands on headstones,
Wondering why they ever left home,
Mystified by the rotten spoils
Of the Viking dream of silk and jewels.
We've traced the foreign, familiar names
Chiselled in grim cuneiform.
The rune stones resist interpretation.   40

And so we've begun this reverse migration.
God knows what we hope to learn.
The motives of the arctic tern?
We murmur, uncertain what we're about,
But, counting together, we launch the boat.
I swear by my grandmother's face
And steer to the north, northeast.
I stammer and repeat my faith
In the dead, their hope, their anguish,
Buried alive in this, their language.   50

SHOE SHOP

I shut the door on the racket
Of rush hour traffic,
Inhale the earthy, thick
Perfume of leather and pipe tobacco.

The place might be a barbershop
Where the air gets lathered with gossip.
You can almost hear the whippersnap
Of the straightedge on the razor strop.

It might be a front for agitators,
But there's no back room. A rabble   10
Of boots and shoes lies tumbled
In heaps like a hoard of potatoes.

The cobbler, broad as a blacksmith,
Turns a shoe over his pommel,
Pummels the sole, takes the nail
He's bit between his teeth,

And drives it into the heel. Hunched
At his workbench, he pays the old shoe
More attention than me. "Help you?"
He grunts, as if the man held a grudge   20

Against business. He gives my run-over
Loafer a look. "Plastic," he spits.
"And foreign-made. Doubt I can fix it."
I could be holding a dead gopher.

"The Europeans might make good shoes,
But I never see them. Cut the price.
Advertise! Never mind the merchandise.
You buy yourself a pair, brand new,

"The welt will be cardboard
Where it ought to be leather.   30
There's nothing to hold the shoe together."
He stows my pair in a cupboard.

"And all of them tan with acid.
The Mexicans make fancy boots, but they cure
Their leather in cow manure. Wear
Them out in the rain once. Rancid?

"I had a guy bring me a pair.
Wanted me to get rid of the stink.
Honest to God. I hate to think
My customers are crazy, but I swear."   40

He curses factories, inflation,
And I welcome the glow of conspiracy.
Together we plot, half seriously,
A counter industrial revolution.

His pride's been steeped in bitterness,
His politics tanned with elbow-grease.
To hear him fume and bitch, you'd guess
His guerrilla warfare's hopeless.

But talk about job satisfaction!
To take a tack from a tight-lipped smile,   50
Stick it like a thorn in an unworn sole,
To heft the hammer, and whack it!

When I step back out in the street
The city looks flimsy as a movie set.

May Swenson

Born in 1919 in Logan, Utah, of Swedish parents and educated at Utah State University, May Swenson is a poet who, in Chad Walsh's words, celebrates "the sheer thingness of things." She is the author of six volumes of poetry, including New & Selected Things Taking Place *(1978), and three books of poems for juvenile readers. She has also published translations of Tomas Tranströmer and other Swedish poets. For her work, she has received Guggenheim and Rockefeller Foundation Fellowships and the Shelley Memorial Award, and four times she has been a finalist for the National Book Award. She currently lives in Sea Cliff, New York.*

QUESTION

Body my house
my horse my hound
what will I do
when you are fallen

Where will I sleep
How will I ride
What will I hunt

Where can I go
without my mount
all eager and quick   10
How will I know
in thicket ahead
is danger or treasure
when Body my good
bright dog is dead

How will it be
to lie in the sky
without roof or door
and wind for an eye

With cloud for shift   20
how will I hide?

Joan Swift

*Joan Swift was born in Rochester, New York, and received a B.A. from
Duke and an M.A. from the University of Washington. The recipient of a
National Endowment for the Arts Fellowship, she is the author of* Parts of
Speech *(1978),* The Dark Paths of Our Names *(1985), and other
books of poetry. She has also published a book of prose,* Brackett's Landing
(1975). She makes her home in Edmonds, Washington.

THE LINE-UP

Each prisoner is so sad in the glare
I want to be his mother

tell him the white light will go down
and he will sleep soon.

No need to turn under eyes
to shuffle   poor soldiers   boys

in a play
to wear numbers   obey.

They have hands as limp as wet leaves
the long fingers of their lives   10

hanging. They cannot see
past the sharp edge nor hear me

breathe. O I would tell each one
he will wake small again

in some utterly new place
Trees without bars   sun a sweet juice

a green
field full of pardon.

The walls come in. I am
captured like him   20

locked in this world forever   unable to say   run

be free
I love you

having to accuse
and accuse.

James Tate

James Tate, who has said that poetry is "man's noblest effort because it is utterly useless," was born in Kansas City, Missouri, in 1943 and attended the University of Missouri, Kansas State College, and the University of Iowa. A prolific poet, he is the author of The Lost Pilot *(1967), which won the Yale Younger Poets Prize,* Hints to Pilgrims *(1971; revised 1983),* Viper Jazz *(1976),* Riven Doggeries *(1979),* Constant Defender *(1983), and numerous other books. He teaches at the University of Massachusetts.*

THE BOOK OF LIES

I'd like to have a word
with you. Could we be alone
for a minute? I have been lying
until now. Do you believe

I believe myself? Do you believe
yourself when you believe me? Lying
is natural. Forgive me. Could we be alone
forever? Forgive us all. The word

is my enemy. I have never been alone;
bribes, betrayals. I am lying   10
even now. Can you believe
that? I give you my word.

MISS CHO COMPOSES IN THE CAFETERIA

You are so small, I
am not even sure
that you are at all.

To you, I know I
am not here: you are
rapt in writing a

syllabic poem
about gigantic,
gaudy Christmas trees.

You will send it home   10
to China, and they
will worry about

you alone amid
such strange customs. You
count on your tiny

bamboo fingers; one,
two, three—up to five,
and, oh, you have one

syllable too much.
You shake your head in   20
dismay, look back up

to the tree to see
if, perhaps, there might
exist another

word that would describe
the horror of this
towering, tinselled

symbol. And . . . now
you've got it! You jot
it down, jump up, look   30

at me and giggle.

Lewis Turco

A leading proponent of formalism, Lewis Turco was born in Buffalo, New York, in 1934, grew up in Meriden, Connecticut, and studied at the University of Connecticut and the University of Iowa. Among his books are Awaken, Bells Falling *(1968),* The Inhabitant *(1970),* Pocoangelini: A Fantography *(1971), and* American Still Lifes *(1981). His* The Book of Forms *(1968) is a valuable reference guide to traditional forms. He teaches at the State University of New York at Oswego, where he directs the Program in Writing Arts.*

From BORDELLO

SIMON JUDSON

In this dark place I am still with God.
Here I read the pages of man's lust,
seek the revelation of the sod,
remind the flesh again, "Thou art dust."

I am not of this town. Reverend
Mister Simon Judson is my name,
and my parish is down at the end
of Route 40, miles away. I came
here first just about a year ago—
accidentally, of course. I must   10
be honest; I would not go a rod
for sensual satisfaction. No,
I come to this house because I must
seek the revelation of the sod,

not because my life is cold. I lend
my soul to my flock weekly. The same
is true *in re* my family. To mend
my spirit, I renew it in shame
at the fount of blood, as the saints do.
I drive long distances, for great blame   20
would attend me were I found out. Trust
and good faith are my stock in trade, so
I spare no pains to avoid a nod,
remind the flesh again, "Thou art dust,"

and keep peace. Even my closest friend
might not understand my pilgrim aim.
This sinful hovel is a Godsend,
truly. Here all the worst vices flame
out of the Pit for my study—glow
and glitter like Sodom. That I know   30
man's follies firsthand is fact—disgust
and degradation; the mire, the rust
of will—here I am armored and shod!
Here I read the pages of man's lust. . . .
In this dark place I am still with God.

From BORDELLO

RICK DE TRAVAILLE

Having fallen down the manhole,
I discovered myself to be
in the wrong world. Having no soul
was a problem at first for me,

but I, Rick de Travaille, ignore
the problem now. I split this door
where the women are, and I find
in the flesh a little peace of mind.

THE WIND CAROL

The townspeople peer out of their windows—
The black snow falls, and the wind blows.

From each imprisoning flake that falls
An image looks out at the walls
Of faces, and a thin voice calls
To the townspeople peering out of their windows:

Melisande comes drifting down
Out of the air above the town,
Recalling the lace of her wedding gown,
The years like snow in the wind that blows.   10

The Captain falls, epaulettes gleaming,
Through a pine where the wind's streaming
Rustles, then rises like missiles screaming
Toward some enemy's thin windows.

These are cold voices that comprise
This dark wind touching a storm of eyes—

Mary, trapped in her bit of hoar,
Gazes out of her dim mirror
Thinking of lovers outside her door
Lashing, like limbs, in the wind that blows.   20

Old Tom remembers some fleeting kiss
Which he'd thought lost, but was caught like this
Within his mind's paralysis
Of moments frozen behind windows.

And as it falls or drifts, each face,
Stunned in an attitude of grace
Or of despair, looks for its place
Among its kind in the wind that blows.

These are cold voices that comprise
This dark wind touching a storm of eyes.   30
The townspeople peer out of their windows;
The black snow falls, and the wind blows.

John Updike

John Updike was born in Shillington, Pennsylvania, in 1932 and attended Harvard and the Ruskin School of Drawing and Fine Art in Oxford. From 1955 to 1957 he was a member of the staff of The New Yorker. *The author of such admired novels as* Rabbit, Run *(1960),* The Centaur *(1963), and* Rabbit is Rich *(1981), he has received the Pulitzer Prize, the National Book Award, the American Book Award, and the National Book Critics Circle Award for his fiction. Among his twenty-six books are five collections of poetry:* The Carpentered Hen *(1959),* Telephone Poles and Other Poems *(1963),* Midpoint and Other Poems *(1969),* Tossing and Turning *(1977), and* Facing Nature *(1985).*

EX-BASKETBALL PLAYER

Pearl Avenue runs past the high-school lot,
Bends with the trolley tracks, and stops, cut off
Before it has a chance to go two blocks,
At Colonel McComsky Plaza. Berth's Garage
Is on the corner facing west, and there,
Most days, you'll find Flick Webb, who helps Berth out.

Flick stands tall among the idiot pumps—
Five on a side, the old bubble-head style,

Their rubber elbows hanging loose and low.
One's nostrils are two S's, and his eyes   10
An E and O. And one is squat, without
A head at all—more of a football type.

Once Flick played for the high-school team, the Wizards.
He was good: in fact, the best. In '46
He bucketed three hundred ninety points,
A county record still. The ball loved Flick.
I saw him rack up thirty-eight or forty
In one home game. His hands were like wild birds.

He never learned a trade, he just sells gas,
Checks oil, and changes flats. Once in a while,   20
As a gag, he dribbles an inner tube,
But most of us remember anyway.
His hands are fine and nervous on the lug wrench.
It makes no difference to the lug wrench, though.

Off work, he hangs around Mae's luncheonette.
Grease-grey and kind of coiled, he plays pinball,
Sips lemon cokes, and smokes those thin cigars.
Flick seldom speaks to Mae, just sits and nods
Beyond her face toward bright applauding tiers
Of Necco Wafers, Nibs, and Juju Beads.   30

Mona Van Duyn

Mona Van Duyn was born in 1921 in Waterloo, Iowa, and is a graduate of the University of Iowa. With her husband, Jarvis Thurston, she founded and co-edited Perspective, a Quarterly of Literature. *In 1971 her* To See, To Take *won the National Book Award and the Bollingen Prize. Her*

other collections include Merciful Disguises: Published and Unpub-
lished *(1973) and* Letters from a Father and Other Poems *(1982).
She lives in St. Louis and occasionally teaches at Washington University.*

CAUSES

*"Questioned about why she had beaten her spastic child to death, the mother
told police, 'I hit him because he kept falling off his crutches.' "*—News
item

Because one's husband is different from one's self,
the pilot's last words were "Help, my God, I'm shot!"
Because the tip growth on a pine looks like Christmas tree
        candles,
cracks appear in the plaster of old houses.

And because the man next door likes to play golf,
a war started up in some country where it is hot,
and whenever a maid waits at the bus-stop with her
        bundles,
the fear of death comes over us in vacant places.

It is all foreseen in the glassy eye on the shelf,
woven in the web of notes that sprays from a trumpet,   10
announced by a salvo of crackles when the fire kindles,
printed on the nature of things when a skin bruises.

And there's never enough surprise at the killer in the self,
nor enough difference between the shooter and the shot,
nor enough melting down of stubs to make new candles
as the earth rolls over, inverting billions of houses.

THE BALLAD OF BLOSSOM

The lake is known as West Branch Pond.
It is round as a soapstone griddle.
Ten log cabins nose its sand,
with a dining lodge in the middle.

Across the water Whitecap Mountain
darkens the summer sky,
and loons yodel and moose wade in,
and trout take the feathered fly.

At camp two friendly characters
live out their peaceful days   10
in the flowery clearing edged by firs
and a-buzz with bumblebees:

Alcott the dog, a charming fool
who sniffs out frog and snake
and in clumsy capering will fall
from docks into the lake,

and Blossom the cow, whose yield is vaunted
and who wears the womanly shape
of a yellow carton badly dented
in some shipping mishap,   20

with bulging sack appended below
where a full five gallons stream
to fill puffshells and make berries glow
in lakes of golden cream.

Her face is calm and purged of thought
when mornings she mows down fern
and buttercup and forget-me-not
and panties on the line.

Afternoons she lies in the shade
and chews over circumstance.   30
On Alcott nestled against her side
she bends a benevolent glance.

Vacationers climb Whitecap's side,
pick berries, bird-watch or swim.
Books are read and Brookies fried,
and the days pass like a dream.

But one evening campers collect on the shelf
of beach for a comic sight.
Blossom's been carried out of herself
by beams of pale moonlight.   40

Around the cabins she chases Alcott,
leaping a fallen log,
then through the shallows at awesome gait
she drives the astonished dog.

Her big bag bumps against her legs,
bounces and swings and sways.
Her tail flings into whirligigs
that would keep off flies for days.

Then Alcott collects himself and turns
and chases Blossom back,   50
then walks away as one who has learned
to take a more dignified tack.

Next all by herself she kicks up a melee.
Her udder shakes like a churn.
To watching campers it seems she really
intends to jump over the moon.

Then she chases the cook, who throws a broom
that flies between her horns,
and butts at the kitchen door for a home,
having forgotten barns.   60

Next morning the cow begins to moo.
The volume is astounding.
MOOOAWWW crosses the lake, and MAWWWW
from Whitecap comes rebounding.

Two cow moose in the lake lift heads,
their hides in sun like watered
silk, then scoot back into the woods,
their female nerves shattered.

MOOOAWWW! and in frightened blues and yellows
swallows and finches fly,   70
shaping in flocks like open umbrellas
wildly waved in the sky.

In boats the fishermen lash their poles
and catch themselves with their flies,
their timing spoiled by Blossom's bawls,
and trout refuse to rise.

MAWWOOOO! No one can think or read.
Such agony shakes the heart.
All morning Alcott hides in the woodshed.
At lunch, tempers are short.   80

A distant moo. Then silence. Some said
that boards were fitted in back
to hold her in, and Blossom was led
up a platform into the truck,

where she would bump and dip and soar
over many a rocky mile
to Greenville, which has a grocery store
as well as the nearest bull.

But the camp is worried. How many days
will the bellowing go on?   90
"I hope they leave her there," one says,
"until the heat is gone."

Birds criss-cross the sky with nowhere to go.
Suspense distorts the scene.
Alcott patrols on puzzled tiptoe.
It is late in the afternoon

when back she comes in the bumping truck
and steps down daintily,
a silent cow who refuses to look
anyone in the eye.   100

Nerves settle. A swarm of bumblebees
bends Blue-eyed Grass for slaking.
A clink of pans from the kitchen says
the amorous undertaking

is happily concluded. Porches
hold pairs with books or drinks.
Resident squirrels resume their searches.
Alcott sits and thinks.

Beads of birds re-string themselves
along the telephone wire.   110
A young bull moose in velvet delves
in water near the shore.

Blossom lies like a crumpled sack
in blooms of chamomile.
Her gaze is inward. Her jaw is slack.
She might be said to smile.

At supper, laughter begins and ends,
for the mood is soft and shy.
One couple is seen to be holding hands
over wild raspberry pie.   120

Orange and gold flame Whitecap's peak
as the sun begins to set,
and anglers bend to the darkening lake
and bring up a flopping net.

When lamps go out and the moon lays light
on the lake like a great beachtowel,
Eros wings down to a fir to sit
and hoot like a Long-eared Owl.

ECONOMICS

Out of a government grant to poets, I paid
to be flung through the sky from St. Louis to San Francisco,
and paid for tours and cruises and bars, and paid
for plays and picnics and film and gifts and the ho-

tel for two weeks, and all the niceties
of sea, field and vineyard, and imports potted
and pickled and sugared and dried, and handouts for
      Hippies,
and walking shoes and cable and cab, and, sated

with wild black blare, Brahms, marimba and Musak,
and beaches, and cityscapes, uphill, downhill,   10
and colors of water, oil, neon, acrylic,
and coffees spiced, spiked, blazing, cool,

foamed, thick, clear, on the last night,
two extra suitcases packed to go home again,
with the last of the travellers' checks paid for eight
poets to dine with me in Chinatown:

hour after hour of rich imagery,
waiters and carts, delights of ceremony,
fire of sauce, shaped intricacy
of noodle and dumpling, the chicken cracked from
      clay,   20

its belly crammed with water chestnut and clam,
the shrimp and squid and lobster, the sweet and sour,
beer chill, broth and tea steam,
the great glazed fish coiled on its platter,

the chopped, the chunky, the salty, the meat, the wit,
the custard of almond and mint, the ginger cream,
the eloquent repletion I paid for——And yet,
did I spend enough in that city all that time

of my country's money, my country's right or wrong,
to keep one spoonful of its fire from eating   30
one hangnail, say, of one Viet Cong?

"Don't clear the fish away yet," one poet said.
"The cheek of the fish is a great delicacy."
With a spoon handle he probed away in its head
and brought out a piece of white flesh the size of a
      pea.

"For the hostess," he said, "from all her grateful
    gourmets."
In SAVE THE CHILDREN ads I've seen the babies.
Filled with nothing but gas and sour juice,
their bellies bulge like rotten cabbages.

"One dollar to CARE will pay for ninety meals."   40
They cry. They starve. They're waiting. They are in
    anguish.
How can we bear to imagine how it feels?
Pain. *Pain.* I ate the cheek of the fish.

In an instant of succulence my hideous maw
swallowed, I'd guess, the dinners of fifty children.
What good does it do to really take that in,
and what good does it do to vomit it out again?

Gentle reader, should I economize?
I write poems for fifty cents a line.
This poem is worth what it's worth to the families   50
of two human beings under the age of eighteen

to see them blown to pieces. "Indemnification
for civilian casualties: from eight dollars
and forty cents for a wounded child, on
up to the top sum of thirty-three dollars

and sixty cents for a dead adult." I tipped
the waiter fifteen percent, which came to nine dollars.
The cab drive was a third of a child. I slept
each night for a fourth of his mother. What are dollars?

And what are words, as formed and plump on the page   60
as Chinese dumplings? Or love, that mink stole,
that sweepstakes prize for one in a million? What wage
could I ever earn that would let me afford to feel

how a newborn, somewhere, is learning to focus
on a world that drains its pus in his eyes like an eyesore?
Our right to see the beauties of this world grant us
that we may grant it, or
                    Christ, what are poems for?

Ellen Bryant Voigt

*Ellen Bryant Voigt was born in Danville, Virginia, in 1943 and attended
Converse College and the University of Iowa. She has received fellowships
from the National Endowment for the Arts and the Guggenheim Foundation. The author of two books,* Claiming Kin *(1976) and* The Forces of
Plenty *(1983), she founded the M.F.A. program at Goddard and is currently on the faculty of the M.F.A. program at Warren Wilson College.*

"THE WIFE TAKES A CHILD"

She has come next door to practice our piano.
Fat worms, her fingers hover over the keys,
dolce, dolce, advance to a black note.
I call out answers: she blinks a trusting eye.
From the window I can see the phlox
bank and flower, the violets' broad train
at the yard's edge, and beyond, the bee-boxes,
each one baited for summer with a queen.

Love, how long must we reproduce ourselves
in the neighbors' children, bees in false hives,   10
bright inviting blossoms, mine for a season.
Against the C-scale's awkward lullabye
I carry the offense of my flat belly,
the silent red loss of monthly bleeding.

TROPICS

In the still morning when you move
toward me in sleep for love,
I dream of

an island where long-stemmed cranes,
serious weather vanes,
turn slowly on one

foot. There the dragonfly folds
his mica wings and rides
the tall reed

close as a handle. The hippo yawns,   10
nods to thick pythons,
slack and drowsy, who droop down

like untied sashes
from the trees. The brash
hyenas do not cackle

and run but lie with their paws
on their heads like dogs.
The lazy crow's caw

falls like a sigh. In the field
below, the fat moles build   20
their dull passage with an old

instinct that needs
no light or waking; its slow beat
turns the hand in sleep

as we turn toward each other
in the ripe air of summer
before the change of weather,

before the heavy drop
of the apples.

David Wagoner

Born in Massillon, Ohio, in 1926, David Wagoner grew up in Whiting,
Indiana, and attended Pennsylvania State University and Indiana Univer-
sity. He has published many volumes of poetry, including Collected Poems
1956–1976 *(1976),* In Broken Country *(1979),* Landfall *(1981),*
and First Light *(1983). He has also published several novels and edited*
the notebooks of his former teacher, Theodore Roethke. He lives in Seattle,
where he teaches at the University of Washington and edits Poetry Northwest.

THE SHOOTING OF JOHN DILLINGER OUTSIDE THE BIOGRAPH THEATER, JULY 22, 1934

Chicago ran a fever of a hundred and one that groggy Sunday.
A reporter fried an egg on a sidewalk; the air looked shaky.
And a hundred thousand people were in the lake like shirts
    in a laundry.
Why was Johnny lonely?
Not because two dozen solid citizens, heat-struck, had
    keeled over backward.
Not because those lawful souls had fallen out of their
    sockets and melted.
But because the sun went down like a lump in a furnace or
    a bull in the Stockyards.
Where was Johnny headed?
Under the Biograph Theater sign that said, "Our Air is
    Refrigerated."
Past seventeen FBI men and four policemen who stood in
    doorways and sweated.   10

Johnny sat down in a cold seat to watch Clark Gable get
     electrocuted.
Had Johnny been mistreated?
Yes, but Gable told the D. A. he'd rather fry than be shut
     up forever.
Two women sat by Johnny. One looked sweet, one looked
     like J. Edgar Hoover.
Polly Hamilton made him feel hot, but Anna Sage made
     him shiver.
Was Johnny a good lover?
Yes, but he passed out his share of squeezes and pokes like
     a jittery masher
While Agent Purvis sneaked up and down the aisle like an
     extra usher,
Trying to make sure they wouldn't slip out till the show
     was over.
Was Johnny a fourflusher?   20
No, not if he knew the game. He got it up or got it back.
But he liked to take snapshots of policemen with his own
     Kodak,
And once in a while he liked to take them with an
     automatic.
Why was Johnny frantic?
Because he couldn't take a walk or sit down in a movie
Without being afraid he'd run smack into somebody
Who'd point at his rearranged face and holler, "Johnny!"
Was Johnny ugly?
Yes, because Dr. Wilhelm Loeser had given him a new
     profile
With a baggy jawline and squint eyes and an erased dimple, 30
With kangaroo-tendon cheekbones and a gigolo's mustache
     that should've been illegal.
Did Johnny love a girl?
Yes, a good-looking, hard-headed Indian named Billie
     Frechette.
He wanted to marry her and lie down and try to get over
     it,
But she was locked in jail for giving him first-aid and
     comfort.
Did Johnny feel hurt?
He felt like breaking a bank or jumping over a railing

Into some panicky teller's cage to shout, "Reach for the
    ceiling!"
Or like kicking some vice president in the bum checks and
    smiling.
What was he really doing?   40
Going up the aisle with the crowd and into the lobby
With Polly saying, "Would *you* do what Clark done?" And
    Johnny saying, "Maybe."
And Anna saying, "If he'd been smart, he'd of acted like
    Bing Crosby."
Did Johnny look flashy?
Yes, his white-on-white shirt and tie were luminous.
His trousers were creased like knives to the tops of his
    shoes,
And his yellow straw hat came down to his dark glasses.
Was Johnny suspicious?
Yes, and when Agent Purvis signalled with a trembling
    cigar,
Johnny ducked left and ran out of the theater,   50
And innocent Polly and squealing Anna were left nowhere.
Was Johnny a fast runner?
No, but he crouched and scurried past a friendly liquor
    store
Under the coupled arms of double-daters, under awnings,
    under stars,
To the curb at the mouth of an alley. He hunched there.
Was Johnny a thinker?
No, but he was thinking more or less of Billie Frechette
Who was lost in prison for longer than he could possibly
    wait,
And then it was suddenly too hard to think around a bullet.
Did anyone shoot straight?   60
Yes, but Mrs. Etta Natalsky fell out from under her picture
    hat.
Theresa Paulus sprawled on the sidewalk, clutching her left
    foot.
And both of them groaned loud and long under the
    streetlight.
Did Johnny like that?
No, but he lay down with those strange women, his face in
    the alley,

One shoe off, cinders in his mouth, his eyelids heavy.
When they shouted questions at him, he talked back to
    nobody.
Did Johnny lie easy?
Yes, holding his gun and holding his breath as a last trick,
He waited, but when the Agents came close, his breath
    wouldn't work.   70
Clark Gable walked his last mile; Johnny ran half a block.
Did he run out of luck?
Yes, before he was cool, they had him spread out on
    dished-in marble
In the Cook County Morgue, surrounded by babbling
    people
With a crime reporter presiding over the head of the table.
Did Johnny have a soul?
Yes, and it was climbing his slippery wind-pipe like a
    trapped burglar.
It was beating the inside of his ribcage, hollering, "Let me
    out of here!"
Maybe it got out, and maybe it just stayed there.
Was Johnny a money-maker?   80
Yes, and thousands paid 25¢ to see him, mostly women,
And one said, "I wouldn't have come, except he's a moral
    lesson,"
And another, "I'm disappointed. He feels like a dead
    man."
Did Johnny have a brain?
Yes, and it always worked best through the worst of
    dangers,
Through flat-footed hammerlocks, through guarded doors,
    around corners,
But it got taken out in the morgue and sold to some
    doctors.
Could Johnny take orders?
No, but he stayed in the wicker basket carried by six men
Through the bulging crowd to the hearse and let himself
    be locked in,   90
And he stayed put as it went driving south in a driving
    rain.
And he didn't get stolen?
No, not even after his old hard-nosed dad refused to sell

The quick-drawing corpse for $10,000 to somebody in a
    carnival.
He figured he'd let *Johnny* decide how to get to Hell.
Did anyone wish him well?
Yes, half of Indiana camped in the family pasture,
And the minister said, "With luck, he could have been a
    minister."
And up the sleeve of his oversized gray suit, Johnny
    twitched a finger.
Does anyone remember?   100
Everyone still alive. And some dead ones. It was a new
    kind of holiday
With hot and cold drinks and hot and cold tears. They
    planted him in a cemetery
With three unknown vice presidents, Benjamin Harrison,
    and James Whitcomb Riley,
Who never held up anybody.

STAYING ALIVE

Staying alive in the woods is a matter of calming down
At first and deciding whether to wait for rescue,
Trusting to others,
Or simply to start walking and walking in one direction
Till you come out—or something happens to stop you.
By far the safer choice
Is to settle down where you are, and try to make a living
Off the land, camping near water, away from shadows.
Eat no white berries;
Spit out all bitterness. Shooting at anything   10
Means hiking further and further every day
To hunt survivors;
It may be best to learn what you have to learn without a
    gun,
Not killing but watching birds and animals go
In and out of shelter
At will. Following their example, build for a whole season:
Facing across the wind in your lean-to,
You may feel wilder,
But nothing, not even you, will have to stay in hiding.

If you have no matches, a stick and a fire-bow   20
Will keep you warmer,
Or the crystal of your watch, filled with water, held up to
    the sun
Will do the same in time. In case of snow
Drifting toward winter,
Don't try to stay awake through the night, afraid of
    freezing—
The bottom of your mind knows all about zero;
It will turn you over
And shake you till you waken. If you have trouble sleeping
Even in the best of weather, jumping to follow
With eyes strained to their corners   30
The unidentifiable noises of the night and feeling
Bears and packs of wolves nuzzling your elbow,
Remember the trappers
Who treated them indifferently and were left alone.
If you hurt yourself, no one will comfort you
Or take your temperature,
So stumbling, wading, and climbing are as dangerous as
    flying.
But if you decide, at last, you must break through
In spite of all danger,
Think of yourself by time and not by distance, counting   40
Wherever you're going by how long it takes you;
No other measure
Will bring you safe to nightfall. Follow no streams: they
    run
Under the ground or fall into wilder country.
Remember the stars
And moss when your mind runs into circles. If it should
    rain
Or the fog should roll the horizon in around you,
Hold still for hours
Or days if you must, or weeks, for seeing is believing
In the wilderness. And if you find a pathway,   50
Wheel-rut, or fence-wire,
Retrace it left or right: someone knew where he was going
Once upon a time, and you can follow
Hopefully, somewhere,
Just in case. There may even come, on some uncanny
    evening,

A time when you're warm and dry, well fed, not thirsty,
Uninjured, without fear,
When nothing, either good or bad, is happening.
This is called staying alive. It's temporary.
What occurs after   60
Is doubtful. You must always be ready for something to
        come bursting
Through the far edge of a clearing, running toward you,
Grinning from ear to ear
And hoarse with welcome. Or something crossing and
        hovering
Overhead, as light as air, like a break in the sky,
Wondering what you are.
Here you are face to face with the problem of recognition.
Having no time to make smoke, too much to say,
You should have a mirror
With a tiny hole in the back for better aiming, for
        reflecting   70
Whatever disaster you can think of, to show
The way you suffer.
These body signals have universal meaning: If you are lying
Flat on your back with arms outstretched behind you,
You say you require
Emergency treatment; if you are standing erect and holding
Arms horizontal, you mean you are not ready;
If you hold them over
Your head, you want to be picked up. Three of anything
Is a sign of distress. Afterward, if you see   80
No ropes, no ladders,
No maps or messages falling, no searchlights or trails
        blazing,
Then, chances are, you should be prepared to burrow
Deep for a deep winter.

CANTICLE FOR XMAS EVE

O holy night as it was in the beginning
Under silent stars for the butchering of sheep
And shepherds, is now and ever shall be, night,

How still we see thee lying under the angels
In twisted wreckage, squealing, each empty eye-slit
Brimful of light as it was in the beginning

Of our slumber through the sirens wailing and keening
Over the stained ax and the shallow grave
That was, is now, and ever shall be, night

Of the night-light, chain and deadlatch by the bolt   10
Slammed home, the spell of thy deep and dreamless
Everlasting sleep as it was in the beginning

Of the bursting-forth of bright arterial blossoms
From the pastures of our hearts to the dark streets
Shining what is and shall be for this night

Of bludgeons and hopes, of skulls and fears laid open
To the mercies of our fathers burning in heaven,
O little town of bedlam in the beginning
Of the end as it was, as it is to all, good night.

Diane Wakoski

Diane Wakoski was born in Whittier, California, in 1937 and grew up in southern California. A graduate of Berkeley, she has published fourteen books, including Inside the Blood Factory *(1968),* The Motorcycle Betrayal Poems *(1971),* Virtuoso Literature for Two and Four Hands *(1975),* Cap of Darkness *(1980),* The Magician's Feastletters *(1982), and* The Collected Greeds: Parts I–XIII *(1984). She is writer-in-residence at Michigan State University.*

SESTINA TO THE COMMON GLASS
OF BEER: I DO NOT DRINK BEER

What calendar do you consult for an explosion of the sun?
And how does it affect our poor histories?
The event might be no different to our distant perspective
than a whole hillside of daffodils,
flashing
their own trumpet faces; or a cup of coffee, a glass of
    beer.

A familiar thing to common people: a beer,
when it is hot, and the sun
flashing
into your eyes. Makes you forget history's   10
only meaningful in retrospect. While flowers, like daffodils,
only have their meaning in the fleshy present. Perspective

cannot explain sexual feelings, though. Perspective-
ly, viewing a glass of beer,
we compare the color to daffodils
and perhaps a simple morning view of the sun.
The appetite is history's
fact. Common. Dull. Repetitious. Not flashing.

Suddenly, without explanation. The routine of bowels and
    lips. Flashing
past like a train, they come. No previews or perspective.   20
Sexual feelings are unexplained, as unexpected beauty.
    History's
no good at telling us about love either. Over beer
in a cafe, you might stay up till sun-
rise, but even that's routine for some, as every spring the
    returning daffodils,

waxy, yellow as caged canaries, spring daffodils
make me want to touch them. Is this the flashing
disappearing feeling of love and sex the sun
also brings to my body? With no object, no other body's
    perspective,

only the satisfaction of self wanting completion? I wdn't
   order beer,
I'd order a cognac or wine, instead. History's   30

full of exceptions, and I think I'm one. Yet, what history's
really about is how common, recurring, we all are. The
   daffodils,
once planted, really do come back each spring. And
   drinking beer
is a habit most ordinary men have. The flashing
gold liquid recurs in war, in factories and farms. The sun
has explosions that we do not know, record, or ever keep
   in perspective.

Thus, the sun embodies more of the unknown than most
   human histories.
We get little perspective outside ourselves. Daffodils
lift me above (to the sun), the faces flashing
each springtime when my friends, not I,   40
sit in some bar or outdoor cafe,
drinking beer.

Ronald Wallace

---

*Born in Cedar Rapids, Iowa, in 1945 and raised in St. Louis, Ronald
Wallace studied at the College of Wooster and the University of Michigan,
where he received his Ph.D. in 1971. He is currently director of creative
writing at the University of Wisconsin. His books of poems include* Install-
ing the Bees *(1977),* Plums, Stones, Kisses & Hooks *(1981), and*
Tunes for Bears to Dance To *(1983). He has also published three critical*

studies, most recently God Be with the Clown: Humor in American
Poetry *(1984).*

GRANDMOTHER GRACE

I didn't give her a goodbye kiss
as I went off in the bus for the last time,
away from her house in Williamsburg, Iowa,
away from her empty house with Jesus
on all of the walls, with clawfoot tub and sink,
with the angular rooms that trapped my summers.

I remember going there every summer—
every day beginning with that lavender kiss,
that face sprayed and powdered at the upstairs sink,
then mornings of fragile teacups and old times,   10
afternoons of spit-moistened hankies and Jesus,
keeping me clean in Williamsburg, Iowa.

Cast off, abandoned, in Williamsburg, Iowa,
I sat in that angular house with summer
dragging me onward, hearing how Jesus
loved Judas despite his last kiss,
how he turned his other cheek time after time,
how God wouldn't let the good person sink.

Months later, at Christmas, my heart would sink
when that flowery letter from Williamsburg, Iowa   20
arrived, insistent, always on time,
stiff and perfumed as summer.
She always sealed it with a kiss,
a taped-over dime, and the words of Jesus.

I could have done without the words of Jesus;
the dime was there to make the message sink
in, I thought; and the violet kiss,
quavering and frail, all the way from Williamsburg, Iowa,

sealed some agreement we had for the next summer
as certain and relentless as time.   30

I didn't know this would be the last time.
If I had, I might even have prayed to Jesus
to let me see her once again next summer.
But how could I know she would sink,
her feet fat boats of cancer, in Williamsburg, Iowa,
alone, forsaken, without my last kiss?

I was ten, Jesus, and the idea of a kiss
at that time made my young stomach sink.
Let it be summer. Let it be Williamsburg, Iowa.

Candice Warne

Candice Warne was born in Brainerd, Minnesota, in 1945 and grew up in Coon Rapids, Minnesota. A graduate of Southwest State University in Marshall, Minnesota, she has worked as a bookkeeper, a bartender, and a grain hauler. Her poems have appeared in Southern Poetry Review, The Bellingham Review, Mickle Street Review, Sou'wester, *and elsewhere. She lives in St. Paul, Minnesota.*

BLACKBIRD SESTINA

Below me on the road, the blackbirds
have awaited my descent; the town
is darkened by them, starting like a wind
up the hill to meet me, shaking trees

like dry bones to conjure a new snow.
My road will be trackless, going down.

No one will have seen me going down;
there is only myself, and blackbirds
are the only movement except the snow
falling, like white hair, past to the town. 10
Coming up through the rattling trees,
I hear the quick ascension of a wind.

Some vague expectation of this wind
has veiled my hesitation to go down,
or perhaps it is the hope these trees
will hide me from the crying of blackbirds.
They have left the unfamiliar town
to look for me in their whirling snow.

There is an indifference in this snow;
it moves only in accord with wind, 20
confusing my footsteps toward town,
closing in behind as I move down,
showing my movements to the blackbirds
that are coming closer through the trees.

I have lost sight of all but the trees
nearest me; all else is hid by snow.
Still, I hear the approach of blackbirds
and their confusing talk in the wind
sounds practically human, blowing down
toward me. I can not find the town. 30

It is too dark to look for the town.
Dark sleep falls from the gathering trees.
Cold has numbed to warmth; my falling down
cannot be undone; the weight of snow
blankets me from the rasping of wind,
muffling the sound of the blackbirds.

The lost town is singing in the snow;
The trees run away in the mad wind.
The stars fall down to become blackbirds.

Robert Penn Warren

Described by **Newsweek** *reviewer Annalyn Swan as "America's dean of letters and, in all but name, poet laureate," Robert Penn Warren was born in Guthrie, Kentucky, in 1905 and educated at Vanderbilt, Berkeley, Yale, and Oxford, where he was a Rhodes scholar. The only author to win the Pulitzer Prize for both poetry and fiction, he has also received the National Book Award, the Shelley Memorial Award, the Bollingen Prize, the National Medal for Literature, the Copernicus Award, and a MacArthur Foundation Prize Fellowship. His thirty-odd published books include the poetry collections* Now and Then *(1978),* Being Here *(1980),* Chief Joseph of the Nez Perce *(1983), and* New & Selected Poems, 1923– 1985 *(1985), and the novels* All the King's Men *(1946) and* A Place to Come To *(1977). He lives in Connecticut with his wife, the novelist Eleanor Clark.*

ORIGINAL SIN: A SHORT STORY

Nodding, its great head rattling like a gourd,
And locks like seaweed strung on the stinking stone,
The nightmare stumbles past, and you have heard
It fumble your door before it whimpers and is gone:
It acts like the old hound that used to snuffle your door and
    moan.

You thought you had lost it when you left Omaha,
For it seemed connected then with your grandpa, who
Had a wen on his forehead and sat on the veranda
To finger the precious protuberance, as was his habit to do,
Which glinted in sun like rough garnet or the rich old
    brain bulging through.   10

But you met it in Harvard Yard as the historic steeple
Was confirming the midnight with its hideous racket,
And you wondered how it had come, for it stood so
    imbecile,
With empty hands, humble, and surely nothing in pocket:
Riding the rods, perhaps—or Grandpa's will paid the ticket.

You were almost kindly then, in your first homesickness,
As it tortured its stiff face to speak, but scarcely mewed.
Since then you have outlived all your homesickness,
But have met it in many another distempered latitude:
Oh, nothing is lost, ever lost! at last you understood.   20

It never came in the quantum glare of sun
To shame you before your friends, and had nothing to do
With your public experience or private reformation:
But it thought no bed too narrow—it stood with lips askew
And shook its great head sadly like the abstract Jew.

Never met you in the lyric arsenical meadow
When children call and your heart goes stone in the
    bosom—
At the orchard anguish never, nor ovoid horror,
Which is furred like a peach or avid like the delicious
    plum.
It takes no part in your classic prudence or fondled axiom.   30

Not there when you exclaimed: "Hope is betrayed by
Disastrous glory of sea-capes, sun-torment of whitecaps
—There must be a new innocence for us to be stayed by."
But there it stood, after all the timetables, all the maps,
In the crepuscular clutter of *always, always,* or *perhaps.*

You have moved often and rarely left an address,
And hear of the deaths of friends with a sly pleasure,
A sense of cleansing and hope which blooms from distress;
But it has not died, it comes, its hand childish, unsure,
Clutching the bribe of chocolate or a toy you used to
    treasure.   40

It tries the lock. You hear, but simply drowse:
There is nothing remarkable in that sound at the door.
Later you may hear it wander the dark house
Like a mother who rises at night to seek a childhood
    picture;
Or it goes to the backyard and stands like an old horse cold
    in the pasture.

WHAT VOICE AT MOTH-HOUR

What voice at moth-hour did I hear calling
As I stood in the orchard while the white
Petals of apple blossoms were falling,
Whiter than moth-wing in that twilight?

What voice did I hear as I stood by the stream,
Bemused in the murmurous wisdom there uttered,
While ripples at stone, in their steely gleam,
Caught last light before it was shuttered?

What voice did I hear as I wandered alone
In a premature night of cedar, beech, oak,   10
Each foot set soft, then still as stone
Standing to wait while the first owl spoke?

The voice that I heard once at dew-fall, I now
Can hear by a simple trick. If I close
My eyes, in that dusk I again know
The feel of damp grass between bare toes,

Can see the last zigzag, sky-skittering, high,
Of a bullbat, and even hear, far off, from
Swamp-cover, the whip-o-will, and as I
Once heard, hear the voice: *It's late! Come home.*   20

James Whitehead

James Whitehead, whose poetry reveals a strong sense of place, was born in St. Louis in 1936 and grew up in Mississippi. He took degrees from Vanderbilt, where he played varsity football, and the University of Iowa. The recipient of a Guggenheim Fellowship, he has published several collections of poetry, including Domains *(1966) and* Local Men *(1979), and the novel* Joiner *(1971). The father of seven children, he directs the creative writing program at the University of Arkansas.*

VISIONARY OKLAHOMA SUNDAY BEER

For Clarence Hall and Jane Cooper

The small window opened. I asked for the six-pack
I paid for, then saw the women playing pool
In the loud and common light where ball and stick
Have always met.
            The oldest on a high stool

Was big as a mound but wasn't simply fat.
She glistened and shouted—she was having fun
With all the other Indians—each one great
With child in a way to make that bulb a sun.

All fancy with no men around, they played.
Hey, let me in is what I think I said.   10
I meant of course to ask where are your men
And what of pageantry and life and death?

Her break shook me and a brown arm closed down
A show I would have stayed a season with.

THE FLOOD VIEWED BY THE TOURIST FROM IOWA

They paddled the street as fast as rowboats can,
To fetch back to the Parlor the Negro dead:
Embarrassment . . . that made no sense. A flood—
It was a flood, seven inches of rain
Through a single span of day and night, and all
In trouble just about the same. But still,
When word of the bodies came, the Public Will
Was wonderfully active. It was like Plague Call.

I suppose there was something ancient in it,
Men fearing the dead will walk, or maybe swim . . .   10

You should have seen those white men hurry to it . . .
None of the Negroes seemed nearly so grim
About it. In fact, one black, with a strange wit,
He sang a Freedom Song, hanging from a limb.

Richard Wilbur

A proponent of traditional forms who argues that "limitation makes for power: the strength of the genie comes of his being confined in a bottle," Richard Wilbur was born in New York City in 1921 and educated at Amherst College and Harvard. He has received numerous honors, including the Pulitzer Prize, the National Book Award, the Prix de Rome, and the P.E.N. Translation Award. Among his many collections are The Poems of Richard Wilbur *(1963),* Walking to Sleep *(1969),* The Mind-Reader *(1980), and* The Whale and Other Uncollected Translations

*(1980), as well as much-admired translations of Molière's comedies. He has
taught since 1977 at Smith.*

JUNK

Huru Welandes
                    worc ne geswiceð
monna ænigum
                    ðara ðe Mimming can
heardne gehealdan.
                    WALDERE

An axe angles
                    from my neighbor's ashcan;
It is hell's handiwork,
                    the wood not hickory,
The flow of the grain
                    not faithfully followed.
The shivered shaft
                    rises from a shellheap
Of plastic playthings,
                    paper plates,
And the sheer shards
                    of shattered tumblers
That were not annealed
                    for the time needful.
At the same curbside,
                    a cast-off cabinet
Of wavily-warped
                    unseasoned wood
Waits to be trundled
                    in the trash-man's truck.   10
Haul them off! Hide them!
                    The heart winces
For junk and gimcrack,
                    for jerrybuilt things
And the men who make them
                    for a little money,

Bartering pride
        like the bought boxer
Who pulls his punches,
        or the paid-off jockey
Who in the home stretch
        holds in his horse.
Yet the things themselves
        in thoughtless honor
Have kept composure,
        like captives who would not
Talk under torture.
        Tossed from a tailgate
Where the dump displays
        its random dolmens,   20
Its black barrows
        and blazing valleys,
They shall waste in the weather
        toward what they were.
The sun shall glory
        in the glitter of glass-chips,
Foreseeing the salvage
        of the prisoned sand,
And the blistering paint
        peel off in patches,
That the good grain
        be discovered again.
Then burnt, bulldozed,
        they shall all be buried
To the depth of diamonds,
        in the making dark
Where halt Hephaestus
        keeps his hammer
And Wayland's work
        is worn away.   30

PIAZZA DI SPAGNA, EARLY MORNING

I can't forget
How she stood at the top of that long marble stair
Amazed, and then with a sleepy pirouette
Went dancing slowly down to the fountain-quieted square;

                    Nothing upon her face
But some impersonal loneliness,—not then a girl
   But as it were a reverie of the place,
      A called-for falling glide and whirl;

   As when a leaf, petal, or thin chip
Is drawn to the falls of a pool and, circling a moment
      above it,   10
                    Rides on over the lip—
      Perfectly beautiful, perfectly ignorant of it.

A LATE AUBADE

You could be sitting now in a carrel
Turning some liver-spotted page,
Or rising in an elevator-cage
Toward Ladies' Apparel.

You could be planting a raucous bed
Of salvia, in rubber gloves,
Or lunching through a screed of someone's loves
With pitying head,

Or making some unhappy setter
Heel, or listening to a bleak   10
Lecture on Schoenberg's serial technique.
Isn't this better?

Think of all the time you are not
Wasting, and would not care to waste,
Such things, thank God, not being to your taste.
Think what a lot

Of time, by woman's reckoning,
You've saved, and so may spend on this,
You who had rather lie in bed and kiss
Than anything.   20

It's almost noon, you say? If so,
Time flies, and I need not rehearse
The rosebuds-theme of centuries of verse.
If you *must* go,

Wait for a while, then slip downstairs
And bring us up some chilled white wine,
And some blue cheese, and crackers, and some fine
Ruddy-skinned pears.

YEAR'S END

Now winter downs the dying of the year,
And night is all a settlement of snow;
From the soft street the rooms of houses show
A gathered light, a shapen atmosphere,
Like frozen-over lakes whose ice is thin
And still allows some stirring down within.

I've known the wind by water banks to shake
The late leaves down, which frozen where they fell
And held in ice as dancers in a spell
Fluttered all winter long into a lake;   10
Graved on the dark in gestures of descent,
They seemed their own most perfect monument.

There was perfection in the death of ferns
Which laid their fragile cheeks against the stone
A million years. Great mammoths overthrown
Composedly have made their long sojourns,
Like palaces of patience, in the gray
And changeless lands of ice. And at Pompeii

The little dog lay curled and did not rise
But slept the deeper as the ashes rose   20
And found the people incomplete, and froze
The random hands, the loose unready eyes
Of men expecting yet another sun
To do the shapely thing they had not done.

These sudden ends of time must give us pause.
We fray into the future, rarely wrought
Save in the tapestries of afterthought.

More time, more time. Barrages of applause
Come muffled from a buried radio.
The New-year bells are wrangling with the snow.   30

Miller Williams

A poet who once claimed to "distrust the Romantic vision and dislike the Classical," Miller Williams was born in Hoxie, Arkansas, in 1930 and earned a B.S. in biology from Arkansas State College and an M.S. in zoology from the University of Arkansas. The recipient of the Prix de Rome and other awards, he has published twenty-two books, including Why God Permits Evil *(1978),* Distractions *(1981),* The Boys on Their Bony Mules *(1983), and* Sonnets of Giuseppe Belli *(1981), translations from the Romanesco. He is a professor of English and foreign languages at the University of Arkansas and the director of the University of Arkansas Press.*

WHY GOD PERMITS EVIL: FOR ANSWERS
TO THIS QUESTION OF INTEREST TO
MANY WRITE BIBLE ANSWERS DEPT. E-7
—*Ad on a matchbook cover*

Of interest to John Calvin and Thomas Aquinas
for instance and Job for instance who never got

one straight answer but only his cattle back.
With interest, which is something, but certainly not

any kind of answer unless you ask
God if God can demonstrate God's power

and God's glory, which is not a question.
You should all be living at this hour.

You had Servetus to burn, the elect to count,
bad eyes and the Institutes to write;　　　　　　　　　　　10

you had the exercises and had Latin,
the hard bunk and the solitary night;

you had the neighbors to listen to and your woman
yelling at you to curse God and die.

Some of this to be on the right side;
some of it to ask in passing, Why?

Why badness makes its way in a world He made?
How come he looked for twelve and got eleven?

You had the faith and looked for love, stood pain,
learned patience and little else. We have E–7.　　　　　　20

Churches may be shut down everywhere,
half-written philosophy books be tossed away.

Some place on the south side of Chicago
a lady with wrinkled hose and a small gray

bun of hair sits straight with her knees together
behind a teacher's desk on the third floor

of an old shirt factory, bankrupt and abandoned
except for this just cause, and on the door:

Dept. E–7. She opens the letters
asking why God permits it and sends a brown　　　　　　30

plain envelope to each return address.
But she is not alone. All up and down

the thin and creaking corridors are doors
and desks behind them: E–6, E–5, 4, 3.

A desk for every question, for how we rise
blown up and burned, for how the will is free,

for when is Armageddon, for whether dogs
have souls or not and on and on. On

beyond the alphabet and possible numbers
where cross-legged, naked and alone,   40

there sits a pale, tall and long-haired woman
upon a cushion of fleece and eiderdown

holding in one hand a hand-written answer,
holding in the other hand a brown

plain envelope. On either side, cobwebbed
and empty baskets sitting on the floor

say *in* and *out.* There is no sound in the room.
There is no knob on the door. Or there is no door.

RUBAIYAT FOR SUE ELLA TUCKER

Sue Ella Tucker was barely in her teens.
She often minded her mother. She didn't know beans
About what boys can do. She laughed like air.
Already the word was crawling up her jeans.

Haskell Trahan took her for a ride
Upon his motorbike. The countryside
Was wet and beautiful and so were they.
He didn't think she'd let him but he tried.

They rode along the levee where they hid
To kiss a little while and then he slid   10
His hand inside her panties. Lord lord.
She didn't mean to let him but she did.

And then she thought that she would go to hell
For having let befall her what befell,
More for having thought it rather nice.
And she was sure that everyone could tell.

Sunday morning sitting in the pew
She prayed to know whatever she should do
If Haskell Trahan who she figured would
Should take her out again and ask her to.   20

For though she meant to do as she was told
His hands were warmer than the pew was cold
And she was mindful of him who construed
A new communion sweeter than the old.

Then sure enough, no matter she would try
To turn her head away and start to cry,
He had four times before the week was out
All of her clothes and all his too awry.

By then she'd come to see how she had learned
As women will a lesson often earned: 30
Sweet leads to sweeter. As a matter of fact,
By then she was not overly concerned.

Then in the fullness of time it came to be
That she was full of child and Haskell he
Was not to be found. She took herself away
To Kansas City, Kansas. Fiddle-de-dee.

Fiddle-de-dee, she said. So this is what
My mother meant. So this is what I got
For all my love and whispers. Even now
He's lying on the levee, like as not.   40

She had the baby and then she went to the place
She heard he might be at. She had the grace
To whisper who she was before she blew
The satisfied expression from his face.

The baby's name was Trahan. He learned to tell
How sad his daddy's death was. She cast a spell
Telling how it happened. She left out
A large part of the story but told it well.

FOR VICTOR JARA

Mutilated and Murdered
The Soccer Stadium
Santiago, Chile

This is to say we remember. Not that remembering saves us.
Not that remembering brings anything usable back.

This is to say that we never have understood how to say
    this.
Out of our long unbelief what do we say to belief?

Nobody wants you to be there asking the question you ask
    us.
There had been others before, people who stayed to the
    end:

Utah and Boston and Memphis, Newgate, Geneva,
    Morelos—
Changing the sound of those names, they have embarrassed
    us, too.

What shall we do with the stillness, do with the hate and
    the pity?
What shall we do with the love? What shall we do with the
    grief?   10

Such are the things that we think of, far from the thought
    that you hung there,
Silver inside of our heads, golden inside of our heads:

Would we have stayed to an end or would we have folded
    our faces?
Awful and awful. Good friend. You have embarrassed our
    hearts.

Harold Witt

*Born in Santa Ana, California, in 1923 and educated at Berkeley and the
University of Michigan, Harold Witt is the author of ten books, including*
Beasts in Clothes *(1961),* Now, Swim *(1974),* Winesburg by the Sea
(1979), and The Snow Prince *(1982). In 1972 he won the Poetry
Society of America's Emily Dickinson Award. He lives in Orinda, Califor-
nia, and is co-editor of* Blue Unicorn.

DREAM

Jackie Kennedy Onassis, working at Woolworth's
in my home town in 1939
sold me some of those orange candy corn kernels
and black jellybeans for Halloween

and leaned over the glass counter above cheap chocolates
with cherry centers—friendly as could be—
beautiful almost as one of my female cousins,
her fair face mirrored in the weight machine.

On Fourth Street Packards went by, and Ford V8s
and girls in wool skirts well below the knee   10
and men who are dead now, wearing homburg hats,
and Jackie leaned there whispering to me—

O my God, you don't know how unlucky
you are and I am, standing here in Woolworth's
among the cardboard skeletons and Maybelline
before assassinations and more wars,

the stars in frames—Shirley with her dimples—
all of us dreaming the American dream,
your mother at home baking cinnamon apples,
Jack making a touchdown for the winning team.   20

FIRST PHOTOS OF FLU VIRUS

Viruses, when the lens is right,
change into a bright bouquet.
Are such soft forms of pure delight
viruses? When the lens is right,
instead of swarms of shapeless blight,
we see them in a Renoir way.
Viruses when the lens is right
change into a bright bouquet.

David Wojahn

*David Wojahn was born in St. Paul, Minnesota, in 1953 and is a
graduate of the University of Minnesota and the University of Arizona. His*
Icehouse Lights *(1982) won the Yale Younger Poets Prize and the William Carlos Williams Award. He has twice been a fellow in poetry at the
Fine Arts Work Center in Provincetown, Massachusetts, and currently
teaches creative writing at Indiana University.*

FLOATING HOUSES

The night mist leaves us yearning for a new location
to things impossibly stationary,
the way they'd once float houses
made from dismantled ships, brass and timber,
from Plymouth, Massachusetts, across the sound
to White Horse Beach. You were only a boy.

Years later, gazing out to the red buoys
of the harbor, you sought those houses, each the location
of your childhood's end. Jon, I make this all sound
too complex. Our view of time is stationary,   10
a long prediction of remorse. We're drinking in timber,
camping above Tucson, Arizona. Below, the houses

are vague points of light, describing a grief you've housed
since watching those buildings careen on water, a boy
too sullen for your father. So the aspens creak like timber
in an aging sloop. The others sleep. You locate
the figure of your son, small and stationary,
but tell me he'll die young, body unsound,

a childhood diabetic. The bourbon makes you sound
entranced—to think one day you'll return to the house   20
to find that you've outlived him, maybe the radio station
playing some popular song. Outliving the boy,
you'll outlive yourself. Drunk, we've lost our location.
I shine my flashlight to find the others. The timbre

of your voice grows slack. Leaves and timber
rustle in the promise of rain, in the sound
of distant thunder that, like death, has no location.
Below, relentless clouds will cover houses.
The campfire sputters, then grows, buoyed
by wind, our bodies the only things stationary.   30

Because of death, our small, unstationary
lives become narration—a child is lost in timber
in a fable when night approaches. The boy

can't even see his hands. Only owl-cry, the sound
of his heart. But soon the aspens part, the houses
of his village appear, their location

precise and consoling. He's stationary, not a sound
from below. Beyond the timber, floating houses.
And there his papa's lantern, a light the boy can locate.

Daniel Wolff

*Daniel Wolff was born in New York City in 1951 and now resides in
Upper Nyack, New York. His first collection is* The Real World *(1981).*

"HEAVEN IN ORDINARIE"
—*Prayer,* George Herbert

The sun's going down. Which is nothing new.
    And there's nothing special about the end of this day,
    Even if a lot of the things we thought we knew
Start disappearing with the light. What can you say?

It's a strange feeling, kind of a relief,
    To sit in the dark and try
    Not to believe in any false beliefs—
Not to lie . . .

But it's nothing special. Even when all your ideas are gone,
    The same simple words are left.   10
    You repeat them slowly, as if the world was deaf.
And the lights in the neighboring buildings go on.

What can you say? It's extraordinary.
We live in a time gone black with bravery.

Baron Wormser

Baron Wormser was born in 1948 in Baltimore and attended Johns Hopkins, the University of California at Irvine, and the University of Maine. In 1982 he won the Frederick Bock Prize from Poetry. *The author of two books,* The White Words *(1983) and* Good Trembling *(1985), he writes that his "formal influences include Samuel Johnson and Chuck Berry." He lives in Mercer, Maine, where he works as a librarian.*

PRIVATE

"The pay is good"—that's the sort
Of thing the enlistees commonly say,
Although they tend to look away
When they reply. Being in forts
Was something one thought of doing when one
Was little. Now grown up to a size-
Twelve boot, one holds an actual gun
And salutes each inauspicious sunrise.

If only the sun never rose
And the women didn't figure out   10
That a soldier was a kind of lout
With chipped teeth and broken nose.
Some say it's being told what to do
That befuddles the men the most.

There is an ideology to lacing your shoes.
When they give you a day to go to the coast

In a bus and your civilian clothes
Things rarely ever go quite right.
For one, you've got to be back by night
And the skirts all seem to know   20
You aren't a candidate, that you've sold
Yourself cheap. So you drink beers, throw
The bottles at signs, try out the holds

They've taught you in martial-arts class
On buddies who've had one or two more beers
Than you. To the baseguards it's "Cheers!"
As you rub your groin and roll your ass.
In a cold bed your body throbs.
Your braggart father's in your sleep;
Your mother grabs at you and sobs.   30
A woman laughs; the stalking light leaps.

Charles Wright

Charles Wright was born in 1935 in Pickwick Dam, Tennessee, and grew up in Tennessee and North Carolina. He graduated from Davidson College, spent four years in the U.S. Army Intelligence Service, and earned an M.F.A. at the University of Iowa. Among his books are Country Music: Selected Early Poems *(1982), for which he received the American Book Award, and* The Other Side of the River *(1984). His translation of Eugenio Montale's* The Storm and Other Things *won the 1978 P.E.N. Translation Prize. He currently teaches at the University of Virginia.*

THE DAUGHTERS OF BLUM

The daughters of Blum
Are growing older.
These chill winter days,
Locking their rooms, they
Seem to pause, checking,

Perhaps, for the lights,
The window curtain,
Or something they want
To remember that
Keeps slipping their minds.   10

You have seen them, how
They stand there, perplexed,
—And a little shocked—
As though they had spied,
Unexpectedly,

From one corner of
One eye, the lives they
Must have left somewhere
Once on a dresser—
Gloves waiting for hands.

James Wright

A poet who wrote frequently and compassionately about criminals, derelicts, prostitutes, and other social outcasts, James Wright was born in Martin's Ferry, Ohio, in 1927. He was educated at Kenyon, the University of Washington, and the University of Vienna, where he was a Fulbright scholar. His first book, The Green Wall, *won the Yale Younger Poets Prize in 1954. His subsequent books include* Collected Poems *(1971), which won the Pulitzer Prize,* Two Citizens *(1973),* To a Blossoming Pear Tree *(1977),* This Journey *(1982), and* Collected Prose *(1983). He died in 1980.*

SPEAK

To speak in a flat voice
Is all that I can do.
I have gone every place
Asking for you.
Wondering where to turn
And how the search would end
And the last streetlight spin
Above me blind.

Then I returned rebuffed
And saw under the sun   10
The race not to the swift
Nor the battle won.
Liston dives in the tank,
Lord, in Lewiston, Maine,
And Ernie Doty's drunk
In hell again.

And Jenny, oh my Jenny
Whom I love, rhyme be damned,
Has broken her spare beauty
In a whorehouse old.   20
She left her new baby
In a bus-station can,
And sprightly danced away
Through Jacksontown.

Which is a place I know,
One where I got picked up
A few shrunk years ago

By a good cop.
Believe it, Lord, or not.
Don't ask me who he was.   30
I speak of flat defeat
In a flat voice.

I have gone forward with
Some, a few lonely some.
They have fallen to death.
I die with them.
Lord, I have loved Thy cursed,
The beauty of Thy house:
Come down. Come down. Why dost
Thou hide thy face?   40

A SONG FOR THE MIDDLE OF THE NIGHT

*By way of explaining to my son the following curse by Eustace
Deschamps: "Happy is he who has no children; for babies bring nothing
but crying and stench."*

Now first of all he means the night
      You beat the crib and cried
And brought me spinning out of bed
      To powder your backside.
I rolled your buttocks over
      And I could not complain:
Legs up, la la, legs down, la la,
      Back to sleep again.

Now second of all he means the day
      You dabbled out of doors   10
And dragged a dead cat Billy-be-damned
      Across the kitchen floors.
I rolled your buttocks over
      And made you sing for pain:
Legs up, la la, legs down, la la,
      Back to sleep again.

But third of all my father once
    Laid me across his knee
And solved the trouble when he beat
    The yowling out of me.   20
He rocked me on his shoulder
    When razor straps were vain:
Legs up, la la, legs down, la la,
    Back to sleep again.

So roll upon your belly, boy,
    And bother being cursed.
You turn the household upside down,
    But you are not the first.
Deschamps the poet blubbered too,
    For all his fool disdain: 30
Legs up, la la, legs down, la la,
    Back to sleep again.

SAINT JUDAS

When I went out to kill myself, I caught
A pack of hoodlums beating up a man.
Running to spare his suffering, I forgot
My name, my number, how my day began,
How soldiers milled around the garden stone
And sang amusing songs; how all that day
Their javelins measured crowds; how I alone
Bargained the proper coins, and slipped away.

Banished from heaven, I found this victim beaten,
Stripped, kneed, and left to cry. Dropping my rope   10
Aside, I ran, ignored the uniforms:
Then I remembered bread my flesh had eaten,
The kiss that ate my flesh. Flayed without hope,
I held the man for nothing in my arms.

WITH THE SHELL OF A HERMIT CRAB

Lugete, O Veneres Cupidinesque—Catullus

This lovely little life whose toes
Touched the white sand from side to side,
How delicately no one knows,
Crept from his loneliness, and died.

From deep waters long miles away
He wandered, looking for his name,
And all he found was you and me,
A quick life and a candle flame.

Today, you happen to be gone.
I sit here in the raging hell,   10
The city of the dead, alone,
Holding a little empty shell.

I peer into his tiny face.
It looms too huge for me to bear.
Two blocks away the sea gives place
To river. Both are everywhere.

I reach out and flick out the light.
Darkly I touch his fragile scars,
So far away, so delicate,
Stars in a wilderness of stars.   20

YOUR NAME IN AREZZO

Five years ago I gouged it after dark
Against a little crippled olive's bark.
Somebody there, four, three, two years since then
Scattered the olives back to earth again.
Last summer in the afternoon I took
One tine, and hollowed out your name in rock,
A little one someone had left behind
The Duomo at the mercy of the wind.

The wind, as always sensitive to prayer,
Listed to mine, and left my pebble there,   10
Lifted your glistening name to some great height
And polished it to nothing overnight.
If the old olive wind will not receive
A name from me, even a name I love,
Fragile among Italian silences,
Your name, your pilgrim following cypresses,
I leave it to the sunlight, like the one
Landor the master left his voice upon.

Al Young

Al Young was born in Ocean Springs, Mississippi, in 1939, attended the University of Michigan, Stanford, and Berkeley, and worked as a disc jockey, free-lance musician, actor, and for five years, Jones Lecturer in Creative Writing at Stanford. A former editor of Yardbird, *he now co-edits* Quilt. *His books of poetry include* Geography of the Near Past *(1976) and* The Blues Don't Change: New and Selected Poems *(1982). He has also written screenplays and fiction, including the novels* Who is Angelina? *(1975) and* Sitting Pretty *(1976).*

LESTER LEAPS IN

Nobody but Lester let Lester leap
into a spotlight that got too hot
for him to handle, much less keep
under control like thirst in a drought.

He had his sensitive side, he had
his hat, that glamorous porkpie whose
sweatband soaked up all that bad
leftover energy.

How did he choose
those winning titles he'd lay on favorites
—Sweets Edison, Sir Charles, Lady Day?   10
Oooo and his sound! Once you savor its
flaming smooth aftertaste, what do you say?

Here lived a man so hard and softspoken
he had to be cool enough to hold his horn
at angles as sharp as he was heartbroken
in order to blow what it's like being born.

Lisa Zeidner

*Lisa Zeidner was born in 1955 in Washington, D.C., and educated at
Carnegie-Mellon, Johns Hopkins, and Washington University. Her collection of poems,* **Talking Cure** *(1982), was an Associated Writing Programs
Award Series Selection. She has also published two novels,* **Customs** *(1981)
and* **Alexandra Freed** *(1983). She lives in Philadelphia and teaches at
the Camden College of Arts and Sciences of Rutgers University.*

STILL

We still want to say the one true thing
we almost said by that pond in the beginning.

One of us skipped a rock instead, not well,
and offered something parodoxical:

Then we wanted now. Then, we said, will be best.
Though we know better now, we still miss then.

Later, snowed in—though the only elements
were typographical—we read *Hamlet*

out loud, watching words clink through ice.
How distinct a word was then, how crisp!   10

What is this homesickness?
What do we think we've lost?

Though nothing's wrong, we still suspect
the true thing must be said in verse—so what,

we therefore ask, is verse? The reverse
of how we've spoken all these years?

If so, when did we grow prosaic? Why?
I tell you everything we did was poetry:

our words were stepping stones across
the fairy tale pond, meandering and mossy,   20

yet getting us somewhere—here, perhaps.
Of course it's more complicated than that.

You reminded me—we had a history even then—
how I once said, *You are the perfect sentence.*

I remembered a scarf of yours, bright red.
Was that the true thing needing to be said?

Let's say it to this vulnerable snow, tonight.
This snow, unsaying itself on the pavement.

Paul Zimmer

Born in Canton, Ohio, in 1934 and educated at Kent State University, Paul Zimmer directed presses at the University of Pittsburgh and the University of Georgia before taking a similar position at the University of Iowa. He has also written seven books, the most recent of which is Family Reunion: Selected and New Poems *(1983). "Zimmer" is one of the many personae he has created in his poems.*

A ZIMMERSHIRE LAD

Oh what a lad was Zimmer
  Who would rather swill than think,
Who grew to fat from trimmer,
  While taking ale to drink.

Now his stomach hangs so low,
  And now his belt won't hook,
Now his cheeks go to and fro
  When he leaps across a brook.

Oh lads, ere your flesh decay,
  And your sight grows dimmer,   10
Beware the ale foam in your way
  Or you will end like Zimmer.

APPENDIX A

Meter and Scansion

Although many contemporary American poets have eschewed the conventions of meter in their formal verse, meter remains a vital characteristic of many of today's finest poems. To understand these poems and their art fully, one needs some knowledge of the fundamentals of meter and scansion. In this appendix, we will provide a brief overview of these fundamentals. Readers interested in more detailed examinations of meter and scansion should consult Appendix D, which lists numerous books and articles dealing with both.

The word *meter* is derived from the Greek word *metron,* meaning "measure." To write metrically, then, is to measure. But what does the poet measure? Because there are four different ways to answer this question, there are as many different kinds of meter. The act of analyzing a poem to discover its metrical structure is called "scansion." Throughout our discussion of the four systems of meter, we will use several diacritical marks to indicate our scansions of various lines and poems. These symbols are ´ , the acute accent (or ictus), which represents an accented syllable; x, an unaccented syllable; ¯, the macron, a "long" syllable; ˘, the breve, a "short" syllable; and | , a division between metrical units.

The first type of meter is *accentual.* In accentual poetry, the poet measures the number of accents per line. The number of syllables in each line may vary. Accentual meter is the basis of most Germanic poetry, including Old English. Richard Wilbur's "Junk" is a contemporary example of Old English prosody. As the opening lines indicate, each hemistitch—each half-line—contains two accents and a variable number of unaccented syllables.

x ´ ´ x
An axe angles
x x ´ x ´ x
from my neighbor's ashcan;
x x ´ ´ x x
It is hell's handiwork,
x ´ x ´ x x
the wood not hickory,
x ´ x x ´
The flow of the grain
x ´ x x ´ x
not faithfully followed.

As you can see, the number of unaccented syllables in each line varies from six to eight to seven. Wilbur is measuring his line according to the number of accents, not the number of syllables. Sydney Lea's "The Floating Candles" is more "modern" in appearance than "Junk"—indeed, at first glance it may seem to be free verse—but it too employs the age-old device of accentual meter. As the following passage reveals, each line contains two accents. The number of unaccented syllables, however, ranges from two to four per line.

> The bullfrogs twanged
>
> till you touched a wick
>
> with the stick, still flaming,
>
> then quieted. We heard them
>
> plop in the shallows,
>
> deferring to fire,

The second type of meter is *syllabic*. In syllabic verse, the poet measures only the number of syllables in each line. The number of accents in the lines may vary. Syllabic prosody is the foundation of most poetry written in Japanese and in the Romance languages, but it is relatively rare in English, which is a strongly accentual language. However, many contemporary poets have found it an effective and unobtrusive method to shape and control free verse rhythms. The last two stanzas of Charles Wright's "The Daughters of Blum" will serve as an example.

> You have seen them, how
> They stand there, perplexed,
> —And a little shocked—
> As though they had spied,
> Unexpectedly,
>
> From one corner of
> One eye, the lives they
> Must have left somewhere
> Once on a dresser—
> Gloves waiting for hands.

Each of Wright's lines contains five syllables. The number of accents, however, varies, even in these very short lines, from two to three.

In a syllabic poem containing longer lines, there will be even greater variation in the number of accents per line.

The third type of meter, the *accentual-syllabic,* is the most common in English. In it, both the number of accents and the number of syllables are measured. The basic unit of measurement is the foot. A *foot* may be defined as a rhythmical pattern generally containing one accented syllable and one or more unaccented syllables. Feet consisting of two syllables are called *duple feet;* those consisting of three, *triple.* The following feet predominate in accentual-syllabic prosody:

Iamb (x ´), as in "dᵉˡáy"

Trochee (´ x), as in "súmmᵉʳ"

Anapest (xx ´), as in "intᵉʳfére"

Dactyl (´ xx), as in "fáithfᵘˡˡʸ"

To vary the rhythm of a poem dominated by one of the standard feet, poets will frequently introduce other feet into the lines. Besides the four standard feet listed above, the most common "substitute" feet are the following:

Spondee (´ ´), as in "thᵉ óld | dóg bárks | at níght"

Pyrrhic (xx), as in "a síg | nal of | distréss"

A line of accentual-syllabic verse consists, generally, of one to seven feet. A line composed of one foot is called *monometer;* two feet, *dimeter;* three feet, *trimeter;* four feet, *tetrameter;* five feet, *pentameter;* six feet, *hexameter;* and seven feet, *heptameter.* Following are examples of some of the different kinds of lines possible in accentual-syllabic verse. (Please note that for the purpose of providing examples we have taken these lines out of their metrical contexts; the final determination of meter always depends upon context.)

Iambic monometer: or—yés!
    (Barbara Lefcowitz, "Molly Bloom's Sestina for Emily Dickinson")

Dactylic dimeter: Stillness and moonlight, with
    (Hayden Carruth, "Loneliness: An Outburst of Hexasylla-
    bles")

Anapestic trimeter: With the sun on their faces through sand
    (James Dickey, "The Island")

Trochaic tetrameter: splinters from the window flowers
    (Maxine Kumin, "January 25th")

Iambic pentameter: There sat down, once, a thing on Henry's
heart
    (John Berryman, "Dream Song 29")

Trochaic hexameter: 'course he doesn't have a Buick like the
trooper
    (Edward Hirsch, "At Kresge's Diner in Stonefalls, Arkan-
    sas")

Iambic heptameter: And overtook the Little Fellow on his way to
school.
    (Daniel Hoffman, "In the Days of Rin-Tin-Tin")

Because a metrical pattern can become hypnotically monotonous
if it is too regular, most poets vary the pattern of their lines by
occasionally using different feet as substitutions. James Dickey's
"The Island," for example, is predominantly iambic, but there are
many anapestic substitutions—so many, in fact, that they almost
make the poem anapestic. The opening lines are typical of the poem.

In a wink of the blinding sea
I woke through the eyes, and beheld
No change, but what had been,
And what cannot be seen
Any place but a burnt-out war:
The engines, the wheels, and the gear
That bring good men to their backs

These lines illustrate the difference between "normative" and "actual" meters. The *normative meter* is the one that predominates in the
poem. The normative meter of a line, then, is contextual. (Similarly,

the "meter" of a given word frequently depends upon context—for example, we might consider the first syllable of "interfere" to be accented if the poem in which the word appears is predominantly iambic, but we probably would not if the poem is predominantly anapestic.) The *actual meter* of the line may or may not coincide with the normative meter. The normative meter of "The Island" is iambic trimeter. The actual meter of the third and fourth lines quoted above coincides with this normative meter. The actual meter of the first, second, fifth, sixth, and seventh lines, however, consists of a combination of iambic and anapestic rhythms. In virtually all formal poetry, we find a "tension" between normative and actual meters. One of the purposes of scansion is to discover this tension and its effects. X. J. Kennedy's "Nothing in Heaven Functions as It Ought" provides an excellent example of how the tension between a poem's normative and actual meters can enrich not only its rhythms but also its meaning.

> ´ x x ´ x ´ x ´ x ´
> Nothing in Heaven functions as it ought:
> ´ x   ´ x x   ´   x ´ x ´
> Peter's bifocals, blindly sat on, crack;
> x   ´   ´   x x ´ x ´ x ´
> His gates lurch with the cackle of a cock,
> x   ´   x x ´ x ´ x ´ x x   ´
> Not turn with a hush of gold as Milton had thought;
> ´ x x ´   x ´ x ´ x ´ x
> Gangs of the slaughtered innocents keep huffing
> x ´   x x ´   ´ x x x   ´
> The nimbus off the Venerable Bede
> x ´   x x   ´   ´ x ´ x   ´   x   ´
> Like that of an old dandelion gone to seed;
> x   x ´ x ´ x   ´ x   ´ x ´   ´   x
> And the beatific choir keep breaking up, coughing.

> x   ´   x   ´   x ´ x   ´ x   ´
> But Hell, sleek Hell hath no freewheeling part:
> x   ´   x   ´   x   ´   x   ´ x   ´
> None takes his own sweet time, none quickens pace.
> x   ´ x ´   x   ´   x ´   x   ´
> Ask anyone, How come you here, poor heart?—
> x   ´ x ´ x   ´ x   ´ x   ´
> And he will slot a quarter through his face,
> x   ´ x   ´ x ´ x   ´ x   ´
> You'll hear an instant click, a tear will start
> x ´   x   ´   x ´ x   ´ x   ´
> Imprinted with an abstract of his case.

The normative meter of Kennedy's poem is clearly iambic pentameter. Sixty of its seventy-two and one-half feet are iambs, and eleven of its fourteen lines contain five feet. But the poem contains numerous variations on the normative pattern. The first, second, third, fifth, and eighth lines all contain trochaic substitutions, the fourth and eighth lines contain anapestic substitutions, the sixth and seventh lines contain pyrrhic feet, and the seventh contains a spondee. In addition, the fifth line has an extra syllable, and the seventh and eighth lines each have an extra foot. Some of these variations contribute to the sense of individual lines—for example, the trochaic substitution in line three makes the meter "lurch" like the gates, and the rhythm in line eight keeps "breaking up" like the beatific choir—and all of them help convey, even embody, the poem's meaning. As our scansion should suggest, Kennedy uses metrical substitutions in the first eight lines—the *octave*—to emphasize, formally, the desirable and human "imperfection" of Heaven. Conversely, he rigidly adheres to the normative meter in the last six lines—the *sestet*—in order to suggest the mechanical and inhuman "perfection" of Hell. In this poem, then, the tension between actual and normative meters embodies formally Kennedy's thematic contrast between Heaven and Hell, humanity and mechanization, imperfection and perfection, and freedom and constraint.

Until Gerard Manley Hopkins' experiments with *sprung rhythm* (in which a foot may contain from one to four syllables, only the first of which is accented) and modern poets' experiments with free verse rhythms, virtually all formal verse written in English was accentual-syllabic. The most common meter in accentual-syllabic verse is iambic. Robert Frost once said that there were only two kinds of meter in English-language verse—strict iambic and loose iambic. Although he was obviously exaggerating, he was doing so to make a valid point: the iamb is far and away the predominant foot in our poetry (and, linguists tell us, our speech). It is the basis of such standard English meters as iambic tetrameter and pentameter. Trochaic, anapestic, and dactylic feet are less common and often occur in combination with iambic or other feet. Duple feet are most often employed in serious poetry; triple feet, in light, or comic, verse—though there are important exceptions to this general rule (for example, James Dickey's highly anapestic yet serious poems in this anthology).

The fourth, and final, type of meter is *quantitative* prosody. In quantitative verse, the poet measures "quantity," the length of time required to utter a syllable. In classical Greek and Latin poetry, a syllable was considered long if it contained a long vowel or a short vowel followed by two consonants; otherwise, with a few exceptions, it was considered short. The duration of a long syllable was approximately equal to that of two short syllables. The basic unit of measurement in quantitative verse was a foot composed of two to five syllables arranged in a pattern. Because English is so heavily accentual, quantitative poems are extremely rare (Spenser's "Iambicum Trimetrum" is an example). Nevertheless, quantitative prosody has had considerable influence on poetry written in English, for poets have derived the accentual-syllabic system of alternating accented and unaccented syllables from the quantitative system of alternating long and short syllables. The terms for the standard accentual-syllabic feet—indeed, the term *foot*—are derived from quantitative prosody as well. An iamb, for example, originally was a foot composed of one short syllable and one long syllable. In the accentual-syllabic system, long and short syllables are replaced by accented and unaccented syllables, respectively. Besides the six feet already mentioned above, quantitative prosody employed many others, some of which occasionally appear in accentual-syllabic versions. The most common are listed below.

Amphibrach	˘ – ˘
Amphimacer	– ˘ –
Antibacchius	– – ˘
Bacchius	˘ – –
Choriambus	– ˘ ˘ –
Paeon	– ˘ ˘ ˘ (although the long syllable may occupy any of the four positions)

To this list of four metrical systems, some prosodists would add *free verse,* for it too aims at measuring rhythm into lines. But its principles for organization are generally intuitive, and it tries to avoid patterns. Even though most free verse tends to be what Frost called "loose iambic"—iambic verse with numerous substitutions, chiefly anapestic—it is so largely because the language is basically iambic, not because free verse poets are trying to play variations on a normative meter.

Each of the metrical systems we have discussed provides a method of ordering words into lines. Similarly, traditional forms provide ways to order lines into stanzas and entire poems. Readers who are interested in how poets "measure" stanzas and poems should examine Appendix B, which defines the traditional forms used by contemporary American poets.

APPENDIX B

Definition of Forms and Classification of Poems (Listed by Form)

Note: Since the most salient characteristic of contemporary American formal poetry is experimentation with literary tradition, many of the poems listed below will not conform perfectly to their classical definitions. (See the Introduction for a discussion of contemporary formal experimentation.) Also, some of the poems employ more than one form. In such cases, we have classified each poem according to its predominant form. If no one form predominates, we have classified the poem as "nonce." However, if a poem is *simultaneously* in more than one form, we have listed it under all appropriate categories.

ACCENTUAL VERSE (*See also* Accentual-Alliterative Verse)

Normative Accentual Verse A usually unrhymed poem constructed of lines containing the same number of accented syllables. The number of unaccented syllables may vary from line to line.

Lea, The Floating Candles (p. 189)
Swenson, Question (p. 362)

Quantitative Accentual Verse A usually unrhymed poem in which each line of a stanza or section (which may be of any length) contains the same number of syllables as its corresponding line in subsequent stanzas or sections. The number of unaccented syllables may vary from line to line.

Lea, Issues of the Fall (p. 186)

ACCENTUAL-ALLITERATIVE VERSE

German, Scandinavian, and English in origin. An unrhymed poem constructed of lines containing four accented syllables, two on each side of a *caesura,* or pause. There may be any number of unaccented syllables. The initial sounds of the first three accented syllables, and occasionally the fourth, are identical. Also known as *Anglo-Saxon prosody.*

Chappell, My Grandfather's Church Goes Up (p. 54)
Wilbur, Junk (p. 399)

ACROSTIC

A poem, in any form or meter, in which the first letters of the lines spell a word or words, often a name.

O'Hara, You Are Gorgeous and I'm Coming (p. 254)
Stuart, Discovering My Daughter (p. 358)

ALCAIC STANZA

An unrhymed quatrain stanza of Greek origin. The first two lines consist of an *acephalous iamb* (the last half of an iambic foot), two trochees, and two dactyls, in that order; the third line consists of an acephalous iamb followed by four trochees; and the fourth line is composed of two dactyls followed by two trochees.

Corn, Remembering Mykenai (p. 70)

BALLAD

A narrative verse lyric in any form, though most usually in the ballad stanza, which is identical to common measure except that it may be written in any meter. It frequently employs a refrain.

Creeley, Ballad of the Despairing Husband (p. 74)
Hayden, The Ballad of Nat Turner (p. 121)
Van Duyn, The Ballad of Blossom (p. 372)

BALLADE

A French form. A twenty-eight line syllabic poem divided into three octaves and one quatrain (called the *envoi*). It turns on three rhymes and a refrain, which appears as the last line of each stanza and the envoi. The octaves rhyme *ababbcbC,* and the envoi rhymes *bcbC* (with *C* standing for the refrain). The lines may be of any single length.

Block, Ballade of the Back Road (p. 32)
Randall, Southern Road (p. 273)
Sherwin, Ballade of the Grindstones (p. 315)

BLANK VERSE

Strictly speaking, verse composed of unrhymed lines in any meter.
More commonly, unrhymed iambic pentameter verse.

Davison, The Compound Eye (p. 85)
Hugo, The Church on Comiaken Hill (p. 145)
James, Mummy of a Lady Named Jemutesonekh XXI Dynasty (p. 148)
Kooser, Wild Pigs (p. 176)
Pack, Cleaning the Fish (p. 258)
Ray, Throwing the Racetrack Cats at Saratoga (p. 275)
Sissman, December 27, 1966 (p. 320)
Stanton, Childhood (p. 346)
Stanton, Good People (p. 346)
Updike, Ex-Basketball Player (p. 370)

CANZONE

A Renaissance Provençal and Italian form of varying lengths and
patterns. It often consists of five twelve-line stanzas and a five-line
envoi turning on five repeated words. A common scheme is *abaa-
caaddaee / eaeebeeccedd / deddaddbbdcc / cdcceccaacbb / bcbbdbbeebaa
/ abcde.*

Hacker, Canzone (p. 111)
Lehman, Towards the Vanishing Point (p. 195)

CAROL

French and English. A poem consisting of a *texte* (or refrain) couplet
rhyming *A ¹A ²* and any number of quatrain stanzas rhyming *bbba.*
The last lines of the quatrains rhyme with the refrain or repeat one
or the other of the refrain lines. There is no required meter, but
most carols are written in iambic trimeter or tetrameter.

Turco, The Wind Carol (p. 369)

CHANT ROYAL

French. An expanded form of the ballade consisting of five eleven-
line stanzas and one five-line stanza called the envoi. It turns on
five rhymes and a refrain, which occurs at the end of each stanza
and the envoi. Each stanza rhymes *ababccddedE,* and the envoi
rhymes *ddedE* (with *E* standing for the refrain). The lines may be
of any single length.

Morgan, Chant Royal (p. 243)

COMMON MEASURE *(See also* Ballad, Common Octave, and Hymnal Stanza)

A quatrain stanza rhyming *abcb.* The first and third lines are iambic
tetrameter; the second and fourth, iambic trimeter. Also called
short meter.

Browne, The Wife of Winter's Tale (p. 39)
Hayden, The Ballad of Nat Turner (p. 121)
Kunitz, Three Floors (p. 182)
Wright, J., A Song for the Middle of the Night (p. 416)

COUPLET *(See also* Couplet Quatrain, Couplet Sestet, Couplet Sonnet, Elegiac Verse, and Epigram)

Heroic Couplet A stanza or poem consisting of two rhyming lines
of iambic pentameter.

Carlile, Havana Blues (p. 40)
Cassity, Links (p. 50)
Cunningham, Epitaph for Someone or Other (p. 78)
Engels, The Homer Mitchell Place (p. 96)
Hartman, Double Mock Sonnet (p. 118)
Merwin, Grandfather in the Old Men's Home (p. 224)
Nims, Love and Death (p. 252)
Peck, Rowing Early (p. 261)
Pinsky, Memorial (p. 262)
Rich, Aunt Jennifer's Tigers (p. 282)
Rich, The Insusceptibles (p. 281)
Smith, The Ancestor (p. 330)
Wright, J., Your Name in Arezzo (p. 418)
Zeidner, Still (p. 420)

Short Couplet A stanza or poem formed of two rhyming lines of iambic or trochaic tetrameter.

Creeley, Ballad of the Despairing Husband (p. 74)
Creeley, If You (p. 74)
Dickey, The Island (p. 88)
Justice, First Death (p. 157)
Kumin, Morning Swim (p. 180)
Levertov, Bedtime (p. 199)
Miranda, Horse Chestnut (p. 231)
O'Hara, Poem (p. 253)
Ruark, Watching You Sleep Under Monet's Water Lilies (p. 295)
Skinner, Imagine Grass (p. 321)
Smith, The Collector of the Sun (p. 331)
Spacks, Finding a Yiddish Paper on the Riverside Line (p. 341)
Sutter, Swedish Lesson (p. 359)

Split Couplet A stanza or poem consisting of two rhyming lines, the first of which employs iambic pentameter and the second, iambic dimeter.

Jarrell, A Camp in the Prussian Forest (p. 151)
Strand, Sleeping with One Eye Open (p. 355)

Miscellaneous and Nonce Couplets Two-line rhyming stanzas or poems in any meter.

Ashbery, Some Trees (p. 18)
Bell, From *The Escape into You*
   Obsessive (p. 24)
Brooks, We Real Cool (p. 38)
Corso, Body Fished from the Seine (p. 71)
Creeley, A Wicker Basket (p. 73)
Glück, The Racer's Widow (p. 102)
Goldbarth, The Psychonaut Sonnets: Jones (p. 107)
Hoffman, In the Days of Rin-Tin-Tin (p. 134)
Johnson, Sway (p. 155)
Langland, Conversations from Childhood: The Victrola (p. 185)
Merrill, Mirror (p. 221)
Mezey, My Mother (p. 226)
Oles, A Manifesto for the Faint-Hearted (p. 256)
Plumly, Tree Ferns (p. 270)
Swift, The Line-Up (p. 364)

ELEGIAC VERSE

A Greek couplet form. The first line is a *classical hexameter* (the first four feet are either dactyls or spondees, the fifth foot is a dactyl, and the sixth foot is a spondee) and the second line is a *classical pentameter* (two dactyls, a spondee, and two anapests). It may be rhymed or unrhymed.

Moore, Friends (p. 243)
Williams, For Victor Jara (p. 407)

EPIGRAM

A terse, witty, often satiric poem. Although it is not strictly a "form," it is usually written in rhymed and metered couplets, triplets, or quatrains.

Cunningham, Epitaph for Someone or Other (p. 78)
Feirstein, L'Art (p. 97)
Nims, Love and Death (p. 252)

GLOSE

A Spanish and Portuguese form. Written in any meter and in any line-length, the glose begins with a *texte* (or refrain) quatrain. The remainder of the poem may be any traditional or nonce form of the poet's choosing, provided only that the refrain lines be repeated in a formal order at least once.

Turco, From *Bordello*
    Simon Judson (p. 367)

HAIKU

A Japanese form consisting of three unrhymed lines of five, seven, and five syllables respectively. A classical haiku also must state or imply either a season or a New Year's Month and restrict itself to natural imagery.

Knight, Haiku (p. 174)
Roseliep, "campfire extinguished" (p. 294)
Snyder, From *Hitch Haiku*
    "They didn't hire him" (p. 341)

HYMNAL STANZA (*See also* Alternating Quatrain and Common Measure)

Hymnal Stanza A stanza identical to common measure except that it rhymes *abab*.

Cherry, A Scientific Expedition in Siberia, 1913 (p. 57)
Dugan, Elegy for a Puritan Conscience (p. 93)
Hall, My Son, My Executioner (p. 115)
Kunitz, An Old Cracked Tune (p. 183)
Simpson, The Man Who Married Magdalene (p. 318)
Snodgrass, From *Heart's Needle*
   10 ("The vicious winter finally yields") (p. 334)
Zimmer, A Zimmershire Lad (p. 422)

Long Hymnal Stanza A hymnal stanza in which all four lines are iambic tetrameter.

Kennedy, Nude Descending a Staircase (p. 166)
Levine, For Fran (p. 202)
Wright, J., With the Shell of a Hermit Crab (p. 418)

KYRIELLE

French. An octosyllabic poem composed of any number of quatrain stanzas, usually rhymed. The last line of the first stanza is repeated as the last line of each quatrain.

Roethke, Dinky (p. 291)

MONORHYME

A poem in which all lines have the same end-rhyme. The meter, if any, may vary, as may the number of lines.

Cunningham, Epitaph for Someone or Other (p. 78)
Feirstein, L'Art (p. 97)
Nims, Love and Death (p. 252)
Stafford, The Swerve (p. 343)

OCTAVE (*See also* Ottava Rima and Triolet)

Common Octave A doubled form of common measure rhyming *abcbabcb* or *abcbdefe*.

Wright, J., A Song for the Middle of the Night (p. 416)

Quatrain Octave An eight-line stanza or poem composed of two Sicilian quatrains. It rhymes *ababcdcd*. A variant of the Sicilian octave, which rhymes *abababab*.

Chappell, Rimbaud Fire Letter to Jim Applewhite (p. 51)
Jerome, Eve: Night Thoughts (p. 153)
Wright, J., Speak (p. 415)

Miscellaneous and Nonce Octaves Eight-line stanzas or poems of variable meter and rhyme scheme.

LaBombard, By the Beautiful Ohio (p. 183)
Levine, Night Thoughts over a Sick Child (p. 201)
Snodgrass, Song (p. 333)
Wormser, Private (p. 412)

OTTAVA RIMA

Italian. A stanza or poem consisting of eight iambic pentameter lines rhyming *ababababcc*. Sometimes called the *Ariosto stanza*.

Schnackenberg, How Did It Seem to Sylvia? (p. 305)
Slavitt, Another Letter to Lord Byron (p. 324)

PANTOUM

A Malayan form. It consists of any number of quatrains, lines two and four of which are repeated as lines one and three of the subsequent quatrain. The poem rhymes *abab, bcbc,* and so forth, and it generally ends in one of two ways: in a quatrain whose *repetons* (repeated lines) are lines one and three of the first stanza in reversed order, or in a repeton couplet consisting of lines one and three of the first stanza in reversed order. Also called *pantun*.

Ashbery, Pantoum (p. 19)
Justice, In the Attic (p. 161)
Lux, All the Slaves (p. 211)
Meinke, Atomic Pantoum (p. 217)
Stewart, Punk Pantoum (p. 352)

QUATRAIN (*See also* Alcaic Stanza, Ballad, Carol, Common Measure, Common Octave, Epigram, Hymnal Stanza, Kyrielle, Pantoum, Quatrain Octave, Rispetto, Rubaiyat, and Sapphic Stanza)

Alternating Quatrain A four-line stanza or poem rhyming *abab*. Although this is one of the most common quatrain forms, it has previously been unnamed.

Berryman, He Resigns (p. 26)
Cunningham, For My Contemporaries (p. 77)
Davis, Lost Moments (p. 83)
Garrett, Tiresias (p. 97)
Lea, There Should Have Been (p. 188)
Levine, Night Thoughts over a Sick Child (p. 201)
Merrill, Swimming By Night (p. 222)
Moss, H., Finding Them Lost (p. 245)
Pinsky, Icicles (p. 264)
Roethke, My Papa's Waltz (p. 289)
Ryan, Where I'll Be Good (p. 299)
Simpson, The Boarder (p. 318)
Smith, Chopping Wood (p. 329)
Stafford, Glances (p. 344)
Van Duyn, The Ballad of Blossom (p. 372)
Van Duyn, Economics (p. 376)
Warren, What Voice at Moth-Hour (p. 396)
Wilbur, Piazza di Spagna, Early Morning (p. 400)
Witt, Dream (p. 408)
Wright, J., Speak (p. 415)
Young, Lester Leaps In (p. 419)

Couplet Quatrain (*See also* **Couplet**) A four-line stanza or poem rhyming *aabb*.

Ashbery, Some Trees (p. 18)
Creeley, A Wicker Basket (p. 73)
Creeley, Ballad of the Despairing Husband (p. 74)
Hoffman, In the Days of Rin-Tin-Tin (p. 134)
Plumly, Tree Ferns (p. 270)
Rich, Aunt Jennifer's Tigers (p. 282)
Smith, The Collector of the Sun (p. 331)

Envelope Quatrain A four-line stanza or poem rhyming *abba*.

Dugan, Poem (p. 94)
Heyen, Arrows (p. 130)
Huff, Although I Remember the Sound (p. 143)
Miller, J., Time; or, How the Line About Chagall's *Lovers* Disappears (p. 228)
Ryan, Consider a Move (p. 298)
Schnackenberg, Darwin in 1881 (p. 306)

Sutter, Shoe Shop (p. 360)
Wilbur, A Late Aubade (p. 401)

Italian Quatrain An envelope quatrain written in iambic pentameter measures.

Cooper, The Faithful (p. 67)

Monorhyme Quatrain A four-line stanza or poem rhyming *aaaa.*

Rukeyser, Rune (p. 297)
Wagoner, The Shooting of John Dillinger Outside the Biograph Theater, July 22, 1934 (p. 381)

Sicilian Quatrain (*See also* **Quatrain Octave**) An alternating quatrain written in iambic pentameter measures. Often called the *heroic* or *elegiac quatrain.*

Chappell, Rimbaud Fire Letter to Jim Applewhite (p. 51)
Jerome, Eve: Night Thoughts (p. 153)
Keeler, American Falls (p. 163)
Martin, Signs (p. 216)
Nemerov, Brainstorm (p. 250)
Peck, In Front of a Japanese Photograph (p. 261)
Pollitt, Ballet Blanc (p. 271)
Pollitt, Of the Scythians (p. 272)
Schnackenberg, The Paperweight (p. 306)
Slavitt, In Memory of W. H. Auden (p. 323)
Spacks, October (p. 342)

Miscellaneous and Nonce Quatrains Four-line stanzas or poems of variable meter and rhyme scheme. The most common pattern is *abcb.*

Bishop, The Armadillo (p. 30)
Bricuth, Song of the Darkness (p. 35)
Creeley, Oh No (p. 72)
Davis, The Burial (p. 83)
Dickey, Breath (p. 89)
Halperin, John Clare (p. 116)
Hecht, "More Light! More Light!" (p. 125)
Heyen, Riddle (p. 131)
Lowell, Water (p. 210)
McGrath, The End of the World (p. 213)
Miranda, The Magician (p. 232)
Moffett, Twinings Orange Pekoe (p. 240)
O'Hara, Aubade (p. 255)

Sexton, The Moss of His Skin (p. 310)
Simpson, My Father in the Night Commanding No (p. 316)
Sternlieb, Valley Blood (p. 350)
Swenson, Question (p. 362)
Williams, Why God Permits Evil: For Answers to This Question of Interest
  to Many Write Bible Answers Dept. E–7 (p. 403)

QUINTET

English Quintet A five-line stanza or poem rhyming *ababb.* Although this is the most common quintet in English-language poetry, it has previously been unnamed.

Jarrell, Eighth Air Force (p. 151)
Warren, Original Sin: A Short Story (p. 394)

Sicilian Quintet A stanza or poem composed of five iambic pentameter lines rhyming *ababa.*

Dickey, On the Hill Below the Lighthouse (p. 86)
Simpson, To the Western World (p. 319)

Miscellaneous and Nonce Quintets Five-line stanzas or poems of variable meter and rhyme scheme.

Booth, First Lesson (p. 34)
Kinnell, To Christ Our Lord (p. 169)
Stuart, Fall Practice (p. 357)

RIMAS DISSOLUTAS

A Provençal syllabic form in which each line of a nonrhyming stanza (which may be of any length) rhymes with its corresponding line in subsequent stanzas. For example, a three-stanza poem in four-line stanzas would rhyme *abcd abcd abcd.* The lines may be of any single length.

Anderson, The Blue Animals (p. 17)
Merrill, A Renewal (p. 221)
O'Hara, To the Poem (p. 252)
Plath, Black Rook in Rainy Weather (p. 268)
Van Duyn, Causes (p. 372)
Wagoner, Staying Alive (p. 385)

RIME ROYAL

A Scottish stanza form composed of seven iambic pentameter lines rhyming *ababbcc*. Sometimes called the *Chaucerian* or *Troilus stanza*.

Dacey, Jack, Afterwards (p. 78)
Lee, Beside My Grandmother (p. 192)

RISPETTO

Italian. Generally speaking, any poem consisting of two rhyming quatrains, but usually, a Sicilian quatrain followed by an Italian quatrain, rhyming *abab cddc*. Another version, written in iambic pentameter measures, rhymes *abab ccdd*.

Creeley, Oh No (p. 72)
Turco, From *Bordello*
    Rick de Travaille (p. 368)

RONDEAU

A French syllabic form consisting of a quintet, a quatrain, and a sestet turning on two rhymes and one refrain. The refrain consists of the first few words of the first line. The rhyme scheme (with *R* standing for the refrain) is *aabba aabR aabbaR*. The lines may be of any single length.

Bertram, Is It Well-Lighted, Papa? (p. 28)
Hacker, Rondeau After a Transatlantic Telephone Call (p. 113)
Howes, Death of a Vermont Farm Woman (p. 142)

RONDEL

French. A thirteen-line syllabic poem divided into two quatrains and one quintet. It turns on two rhymes and has a two-line refrain. The rhyme scheme is *ABba abAB abbaA* (with *A* and *B* standing for the refrains). The lines may be of any single length.

Dacey, Rondel (p. 82)
Kennedy, Rondel (p. 167)

RUBAIYAT

Arabic. A poem consisting of any number of *rubai* (quatrains rhyming *aaba*). The lines are usually iambic tetrameter or pentameter.

Gildner, Meeting My Best Friend from the Eighth Grade (p. 98)
Williams, Rubaiyat for Sue Ella Tucker (p. 405)

SAPPHIC STANZA

Greek. An unrhymed stanza composed of three *sapphic* lines, each of which consists of two trochees, a dactyl, and two additional trochees, and a final line, called an *adonic,* which consists of one dactyl followed by one trochee. A spondee may be substituted for a trochee in lines one and two, feet two and five; and in line three, foot five.

Hartman, A Little Song (p. 119)
Meredith, Effort at Speech (p. 219)
Steele, Sapphics Against Anger (p. 349)

SEPTET *(See also* Rime Royal)

A seven-line stanza or poem of variable meter and rhyme scheme.

Howard, R., Personal Values (p. 138)
Hugo, The Way a Ghost Dissolves (p. 144)
Kinnell, The Fundamental Project of Technology (p. 170)
Merwin, The Drunk in the Furnace (p. 224)
Plath, Watercolor of Grantchester Meadows (p. 265)
Roethke, I Knew a Woman (p. 290)
Smith, The Old Whore Speaks to a Young Poet (p. 328)

SESTET *(See also* Sestina and Sextilla)

Couplet Sestet (*See also* Couplet) A six-line stanza or poem rhyming *aabbcc.*

Bell, From *The Escape into You*
   Obsessive (p. 24)
Oles, A Manifesto for the Faint-Hearted (p. 256)
Skinner, Imagine Grass (p. 321)

Heroic Sestet A stanza or poem composed of six iambic pentameter lines rhyming *ababcc.* Often called the *Venus and Adonis stanza.*

Baker, Ice River (p. 22)
Hopes, Lament for Turlough O'Carolan (p. 136)
Kinnell, For William Carlos Williams (p. 168)

Italian Sestet A stanza or poem composed of six iambic pentameter lines rhyming *abcabc.*

Berryman, From *The Dream Songs*
    29 ("There sat down, once, a thing on Henry's heart") (p. 26)
Goedicke, Wise Owl (p. 105)
Revell, In Lombardy (p. 278)
Shapiro, The First Time (p. 313)

Sicilian Sestet A stanza or poem composed of six iambic pentameter lines rhyming *ababab.*

James, Snakebite (p. 149)
Stafford, Winterward (p. 344)

Miscellaneous and Nonce Sestets Six-line stanzas or poems of variable meter and rhyme scheme.

Clampitt, The Kingfisher (p. 62)
Cooper, In the Last Few Moments Came the Old German Cleaning Woman (p. 68)
Hecht, The End of the Weekend (p. 124)
Heffernan, Daffodils (p. 127)
Hemschemeyer, I Remember the Room Was Filled with Light (p. 129)
Leithauser, A Quilled Quilt, a Needle Bed (p. 197)
Snodgrass, A Flat One (p. 337)
Wilbur, Year's End (p. 402)

SESTINA

A French syllabic form consisting of six sestets and a final three-line stanza called the *envoi.* The stanzas turn not on terminal rhymes but on the repetition in an elaborate established order of six terminal words. The standard arrangement of the terminal words in the sestets is: *abcdef faebdc cfdabe ecbfad deacfb bdfeca.* In the envoi, one end-word is buried in each line and one concludes each line; the envoi's pattern is *be dc fa.* The lines may be of any single length.

Ashbery, Farm Implements and Rutabagas in a Landscape (p. 20)
Bishop, Sestina (p. 29)
Cooley, Naked Poetry (p. 65)

Dacey, Jill, Afterwards (p. 80)
Hirsch, At Kresge's Diner in Stonefalls, Arkansas (p. 132)
Justice, Sestina: Here in Katmandu (p. 159)
Kroll, Sestina (p. 178)
Lefcowitz, Emily Dickinson's Sestina for Molly Bloom (p. 193)
Logan, W., Tatiana Kalatschova (p. 206)
Ríos, Nani (p. 287)
Starbuck, Double Semi-Sestina (p. 348)
Wakoski, Sestina to the Common Glass of Beer: I Do Not Drink Beer
   (p. 389)
Wallace, Grandmother Grace (p. 391)
Warne, Blackbird Sestina (p. 392)
Wojahn, Floating Houses (p. 410)

SEXTILLA

A Spanish form. A six-line octosyllabic stanza or poem rhyming
either *aabccb* or *ababcc.*

Moffett, Mezzo Cammin (p. 236)

SONNET

Couplet Sonnet (*See also* Couplet) A fourteen-line stanza or poem
consisting of seven couplets.

Corso, Body Fished from the Seine (p. 71)
Goldbarth, The Psychonaut Sonnets: Jones (p. 107)
Hartman, Double Mock Sonnet (p. 118)
Johnson, Sway (p. 155)
Rich, The Insusceptibles (p. 281)

Curtal Sonnet A ten-and-one-half line poem which rhymes *abcabc
dbcdc.* The last line consists of a spondee. Invented by Gerard
Manley Hopkins, the form is a truncated version of an Italian
sonnet—its "octave" being six lines long, and its "sestet" being
four and one half.

Stokesbury, To His Book (p. 355)

Double Sonnet Usually, a poem which consists of two sonnet "stanzas." Also, a poem composed by doubling the requirements of a
particular sonnet. A double Italian sonnet, for example, would
rhyme *abbaabbaabbaabba cdecdecdecde.*

Hecht, Double Sonnet (p. 126)
Hartman, Double Mock Sonnet (p. 118)

English Sonnet A fourteen-line poem composed of three Sicilian quatrains and one heroic couplet written in iambic pentameter measures. It rhymes *abab cdcd efef gg.* Also called the *Elizabethan* or *Shakespearean sonnet.*

Brock, Lying on a Bridge (p. 36)
Goldbarth, Joe Gillon Hypnotizes His Son (p. 106)
Glück, Bridal Piece (p. 102)
Hollander, From *Sonnets for Roseblush*
   18 ("Why drink, why touch you now? If it will be") (p. 135)
Howard, B., The Diver (p. 137)
Jordan, Sunflower Sonnet Number One (p. 156)
Jordan, Sunflower Sonnet Number Two (p. 156)
Kooser, Anniversary (p. 176)
McPherson, Lament, with Flesh and Blood (p. 214)
Miller, V., Without Ceremony (p. 230)
Moss, H., To the Islands (p. 247)
Nemerov, A Primer of the Daily Round (p. 248)
Ruark, To the Swallows of Viterbo (p. 295)
Sherwin, The Spoilers and the Spoils (p. 314)
Skloot, My Daughter Considers Her Body (p. 322)
Stokesbury, The Lover Remembereth Such as He Sometimes Enjoyed and Showeth How He Would Like to Enjoy Her Again (p. 354)
Wolff, "Heaven In Ordinarie" (p. 411)

Envelope Sonnet A variant of the Italian sonnet consisting of two envelope quatrains and a sestet, usually Italian or Sicilian. It generally rhymes *abbacddc efgefg* or *abbacddc efefef.*

Bennett, The True Story of Snow White (p. 25)
Brooks, The Rites for Cousin Vit (p. 39)
Hummer, The Rural Carrier Stops to Kill a Nine-Foot Cottonmouth (p. 147)
Kennedy, Nothing in Heaven Functions as It Ought (p. 167)
Martin, Sharks at the New York Aquarium (p. 215)
Moffett, From *Now or Never*
   I ("They gave me in my kindergarten year") (p. 233)
   II ("Each morning of my tenth summer *swears Memory*") (p. 234)
   V ("And all that windy, sunny diaper-summer") (p. 235)
   VI ("so late as 65 a man has time") (p. 236)
St. John, Acadian Lane (p. 300)
Whitehead, The Flood Viewed by the Tourist from Iowa (p. 398)

Heroic Sonnet Strictly speaking, an eighteen-line sonnet composed of two *heroic octaves* (iambic pentameter octaves rhyming *abababcc*) and a heroic couplet. Also, an eighteen-line sonnet composed of four heroic (Sicilian) quatrains and a concluding heroic couplet (i.e., an English sonnet with an additional quatrain). It rhymes *abab cdcd efef ghgh ii.*

Ciardi, At My Father's Grave (p. 61)
Peacock, Just About Asleep Together (p. 260)

Hybrid Sonnet A half-English, half-Italian sonnet. One type is composed of two Sicilian quatrains followed by a sestet, usually Italian or Sicilian. It generally rhymes *ababcdcd efgefg* or *ababcdcd efefef.* Another type follows the pattern of the English sonnet but substitutes Italian quatrains for Sicilian ones. It rhymes *abba cddc effe gg.*

Hacker, Sonnet Ending with a Film Subtitle (p. 114)
Hathaway, Why That's Bob Hope (p. 120)
Lowell, In the Cage (p. 209)
Moffett, From *Now or Never*
   III ("Those were the clean ones, but I don't think") (p. 234)
Rukeyser, On the Death of Her Mother (p. 297)
Stokesbury, East Texas (p. 353)
Voigt, "The Wife Takes a Child" (p. 379)
Whitehead, Visionary Oklahoma Sunday Beer (p. 397)
Wright, J., Saint Judas (p. 417)

Italian Sonnet A fourteen-line poem composed of an Italian octave and a sestet, usually Italian or Sicilian, written in iambic pentameter measures. It generally rhymes *abbaabba cdecde* or *abbaabba cdcdcd.* Also called the *Petrarchan sonnet.*

Carruth, Late Sonnet (p. 49)
Cunningham, The Aged Lover Discourses in the Flat Style (p. 77)
Hecht, Double Sonnet (p. 126)
Miranda, Love Poem (p. 231)
Stafford, Friend Who Never Came (p. 344)

Sonnet Sequence A group of sonnets on a single subject.

Goldbarth, The Psychonaut Sonnets: Jones (p. 107)
Moffett, Now or Never (p. 233)

Miscellaneous and Nonce Sonnets Fourteen-line stanzas or poems of variable meter and rhyme scheme.

SYLLABIC VERSE (*See also* Haiku, Pantoum, and Sestina)

Normative Syllabic Verse A usually unrhymed poem in which each line contains the same number of syllables. The number of accented syllables may vary from line to line.

Quantitative Syllabic Verse A usually unrhymed poem in which each line of a stanza or section (which may be of any length) contains the same number of syllables as its corresponding line in subsequent stanzas or sections. The number of accented syllables may vary from line to line.

TERCET (*See also* Terza Rima and Triplet)

Enclosed Tercet A stanza or poem consisting of three lines rhyming *aba*.

Howes, A Rune for C. (p. 140)
Merwin, River Sound Remembered (p. 225)
Scheele, The Gap in the Cedar (p. 304)
Sexton, The Abortion (p. 311)

Sicilian Tercet An enclosed tercet written in iambic pentameter measures.

Rich, At a Bach Concert (p. 281)
Sarton, Dutch Interior (p. 303)

Miscellaneous and Nonce Tercets Three-line stanzas or poems of variable meter rhyming either *abb* or *aab*.

Plath, The Stones (p. 266)

TERZA RIMA

Terza Rima Italian. A poem composed of interlocking enclosed or Sicilian tercets. The first and third lines of a stanza rhyme, and the second line rhymes with the first and third of the following stanza. The poem usually ends with a couplet which rhymes with the second line of the last tercet. A five-stanza example would rhyme *aba bcb cdc ded ee*.

Brock, The Sea Birds (p. 37)
Pack, The Boat (p. 257)
Plath, Medallion (p. 266)
Revell, Belfast (p. 277)

Inverted Terza Rima A poetic form identical to regular terza rima except that the second line of a stanza rhymes with the first and third lines of the previous stanza, rather than with the first and third lines of the following stanza. A five-stanza example would rhyme *aba cac dcd ede fef.*

Ridland, Another Easter (p. 283)
Snodgrass, A Visitation (p. 335)

TRIOLET

French. An eight-line syllabic stanza or poem turning on two rhymes and built on two refrains. It rhymes *ABaAabAB* (with *A* and *B* standing for the refrains). Its lines may be of any single length.

Howes, Early Supper (p. 141)
McPherson, Triolet (p. 215)
Witt, First Photo of Flu Virus (p. 409)

TRIPLET

A three-line stanza or poem rhyming *aaa*.

Feirstein, L'Art (p. 97)
Ginsberg, From *Don't Grow Old*
   Father Death Blues (p. 100)
Greenberg, The Faithful Wife (p. 109)
Root, A Natural History of Dragons and Unicorns My Daughter and I Have
   Known (p. 292)
Voigt, Tropics (p. 379)

VILLANELLE

A French syllabic form. A nineteen-line poem divided into six stanzas—five tercets and one quatrain—turning on two rhymes and two refrains. The refrains consist of lines one and three. The rhyme scheme is $A^1bA^2\ abA^1\ abA^2\ abA^1\ abA^2\ abA^1A^2$ (with A^1 and A^2 standing for the refrains). The lines may be of any single length.

Bishop, One Art (p. 31)
Collins, The Story We Know (p. 64)
Disch, The Rapist's Villanelle (p. 92)
Dunn, Tangier (p. 95)
Hacker, Villanelle (p. 111)
Harkness, The Man in the Recreation Room (p. 117)
Hugo, The Freaks at Spurgin Road Field (p. 146)
Justice, Women in Love (p. 160)
Kees, From *Five Villanelles*
   1 ("The crack is moving down the wall.") (p. 165)
Klappert, Ellie Mae Leaves in a Hurry (p. 172)
Levertov, Obsessions (p. 199)

Roethke, The Waking (p. 289)
Wagoner, Canticle for Xmas Eve (p. 387)

MISCELLANEOUS NONCE FORMS

Stanzas or poems which employ rhyme, meter, or the repetition of
  terminal words in patterns invented "for the nonce" (i.e., for the
  occasion).

Glück, Phenomenal Survivals of Death in Nantucket (p. 103)
Kumin, January 25th (p. 181)
Lowell, Mr. Edwards and the Spider (p. 208)
McBride, A Blessing (p. 212)
Moss, S., Prayer (p. 248)
Nemerov, The Goose Fish (p. 249)
Tate, The Book of Lies (p. 365)

APPENDIX C

Classification of Poems (Listed by Author)

Note: See prefatory note to Appendix B.

Jon Anderson
The Blue Animals—*rimas dissolutas* (p. 17)

John Ashbery
Farm Implements and Rutabagas in a Landscape—*sestina* (p. 20)
Pantoum—*pantoum* (p. 19)
Some Trees—*nonce couplets; couplet quatrains* (p. 18)

David Baker
Ice River—*heroic sestets* (p. 22)

Marvin Bell
From *The Escape into You*
Obsessive—*nonce couplets; couplet sestets* (p. 24)

Bruce Bennett
The True Story of Snow White—*envelope sonnet* (p. 25)

John Berryman
He Resigns—*alternating quatrains* (p. 26)
From *The Dream Songs*
29 ("There sat down, once, a thing on Henry's heart")—*Italian sestets* (p. 26)
The Poet's Final Instructions—*nonce sonnet* (p. 27)

James Bertram
Is It Well-Lighted, Papa?—*rondeau* (p. 28)

Elizabeth Bishop
One Art—*villanelle* (p. 31)
Sestina—*sestina* (p. 29)
The Armadillo—*nonce quatrains* (p. 30)

Ron Block
Ballade of the Back Road—*ballade* (p. 32)

Philip Booth
First Lesson—*nonce quintets* (p. 34)

John Bricuth
Song of the Darkness—*nonce quatrains* (p. 35)

Van K. Brock
Lying on a Bridge—*English sonnet* (p. 36)
The Sea Birds—*terza rima* (p. 37)

Gwendolyn Brooks
The Rites for Cousin Vit—*envelope sonnet* (p. 39)
We Real Cool—*nonce couplets* (p. 38)

Michael Dennis Browne
The Wife of Winter's Tale—*common measure* (p. 39)

Henry Carlile
Havana Blues—*heroic couplets* (p. 40)

Hayden Carruth
Late Sonnet—*Italian sonnet* (p. 49)
Loneliness: An Outburst of Hexa-

APPENDIX D

Selected Bibliography of Books and Articles about Traditional Forms and Prosody

Abbott, Charles David, and S. P. Capen. *Poets at Work*. New York: Harcourt, Brace & World, 1948.

Allen, Gay Wilson. *American Prosody*. New York: American Book Company, 1934.

Attridge, Derek. *The Rhythm of English Poetry*. London and New York: Longman, 1982.

Baum, Paull Franklin. *The Principles of English Versification*. Cambridge, Mass.: Harvard University Press, 1922.

Beum, Robert. "Syllabic Verse in English." *Prairie Schooner*, Vol. 31, No. 3 (Fall 1957), 259–275.

Boomsliter, Paul C., Warren Creel, and George S. Hastings, Jr. "Perception and English Poetic Meter." *Publications of the Modern Language Association of America*, Vol. 88, No. 2 (March 1973), 200–208.

Boulton, Marjorie. *The Anatomy of Poetry*. London: Routledge & Kegan Paul, 1953.

Burke, Kenneth. "On Musicality in Verse." *Poetry*, Vol. 57, No. 1 (October 1940), 31–40.

Chatman, Seymour. *A Theory of Meter*. The Hague: Mouton & Company, 1965.

Costello, Sister Mary Cleophas. *Between Fixity and Flux: A Study of the Concept of Poetry in the Criticism

of T. S. Eliot*. Washington, D.C.: The Catholic University of America Press, 1947.

Cruttwell, Patrick. *The English Sonnet*. London and New York: McKay, 1966.

Cummins, Paul. "The Sestina in the 20th Century." *Concerning Poetry*, Vol. 2, No. 1 (Spring 1978), 15–23.

Cunningham, J. V. "The Problem of Form." *Shenandoah*, Vol. 14, No. 2 (Winter 1963), 3–6.

Fowler, Roger. " 'Prose Rhythm' and Metre," in *Essays on Style and Language: Linguistic and Critical Approaches to Literary Style*, ed. Roger Fowler. New York: Humanities Press, 1966.

Fraser, G. S. *Metre, Rhyme and Free Verse*. New York: Methuen, 1970.

Frye, Northrop, ed. *Sound and Poetry*. New York: Columbia University Press, 1957.

Fussell, Edwin. *Lucifer in Harness: American Meter, Metaphor, and Diction*. Princeton, N.J.: Princeton University Press, 1973.

Fussell, Paul, Jr. *Poetic Meter and Poetic Form*. New York: Random House, 1965 (second revised edition, 1979).

Gross, Harvey. *Sound and Form in Modern Poetry: A Study of Prosody from Thomas Hardy to Robert Low-*

ell. Ann Arbor: University of Michigan Press, 1964.

Gross, Harvey, ed. *The Structure of Verse: Modern Essays on Poetry.* New York: Ecco Press, 1979.

Hall, Donald. "Goatfoot, Milktongue, Twinbird: The Psychic Origins of Poetic Form," in *Goatfoot Milktongue Twinbird: Interviews, Essays, and Notes on Poetry, 1970–1976.* Ann Arbor: University of Michigan Press, 1978.

———."Notes on Free Verse and Fashion." *Ohio Review,* No. 28 (August 1982), 25–30.

Halpern, Martin. "On the Two Chief Metrical Modes in English." *Publications of the Modern Language Association of America,* Vol. 77, No. 3 (June 1962), 177–186.

Hamm, Victor M. "Meter and Meaning." *Publications of the Modern Language Association of America,* Vol. 69, No. 4 (September 1954), 695–710.

Hartman, Charles O. "At the Border." *Ohio Review,* No. 28 (August 1982), 81–92.

———. *Free Verse: An Essay on Prosody.* Princeton, N.J.: Princeton University Press, 1980.

Harvey, Marshall L. "A Reconciliation of Two Current Approaches to Metrics." *Language and Style: An International Journal,* Vol. 13, No. 1 (1980), 64–76.

Hemphill, George, ed. *Discussions of Poetry: Rhythm and Sound.* Boston: Heath, 1961.

Hewitt, Elizabeth Kennedy. "Prosody: A Structuralist Approach." *Style,* Vol. 6, No. 3 (Fall 1972), 229–259.

Hollander, John. *Rhyme's Reason: A Guide to English Verse.* New Haven, Conn.: Yale University Press, 1981.

———. *Vision and Resonance: Two Senses of Poetic Form.* New York: Oxford University Press, 1975.

Hoover, Paul. "Moral Poetry." *American Book Review,* Vol. 7, No. 1 (November–December 1984), 14–15.

Jason, Philip K. "Modern Versions of the Villanelle." *College Literature,* Vol. 7, No. 2 (Spring 1980), 136–145.

Justice, Donald. "Notes of an Outsider." *The Iowa Review,* Vol. 13, Nos. 3 and 4 (1982/83), 43–52.

Kaplan, Bernard, ed. *Mississippi Review* (special issue, "Freedom and Form"), Vol. 6, No. 1 (Winter 1977).

Lapides, Frederick R., and John T. Shawcross. *Poetry and Its Conventions: An Anthology Examining Poetic Forms and Themes.* New York: The Free Press, 1972.

Lawler, Justus George. *Celestial Pantomime.* New Haven, Conn.: Yale University Press, 1979.

McAuley, James. *Versification: A Short Introduction.* East Lansing: Michigan State University Press, 1966.

MacFarland, Ronald. "The Contemporary Villanelle." *Modern Poetry Studies,* Vol. 11, Nos. 1 and 2 (1982), 113–127.

Malof, Joseph. *A Manual of English Meters.* Bloomington: Indiana University Press, 1970.

———. "The Native Rhythm of English Meters." *Texas Studies in*

Literature and Language, Vol. 5, No. 4 (Winter 1964), 580–594.

Nemerov, Howard. "On the Measure of Poetry." *Critical Inquiry,* Vol. 6, No. 2 (Winter 1979), 331–341.

Olson, Elder. *General Prosody.* Chicago: University of Chicago Press, 1938.

Oppenheimer, Paul. "The Origin of the Sonnet." *Comparative Literature,* Vol. 34, No. 4 (Fall 1982), 289–304.

Pound, Ezra. "Treatise on Metre," in *ABC of Reading.* Norfolk, Conn.: New Directions, 1951.

Preminger, Alex, Frank J. Warnke, and O. B. Hardison, Jr., eds. *Princeton Encyclopedia of Poetry and Poetics.* Princeton, N.J.: Princeton University Press, 1965; enlarged edition, 1974.

Richards, I. A. *Principles of Literary Criticism.* New York: Harcourt, Brace & Company, 1924.

Saintsbury, George. *A History of English Prosody from the Twelfth Century to the Present Day.* 3 vols. London: Macmillan & Company, 1906–1910.

———. *Some Recent Studies in English Prosody.* London: Oxford University Press, 1919.

Shapiro, Karl. *A Bibliography of Modern Prosody.* Baltimore: Johns Hopkins University Press, 1948.

———. *English Prosody and Modern Poetry.* Baltimore: Johns Hopkins University Press, 1948.

———. *Essay on Rime.* New York: Reynal & Hitchcock, 1945.

Shapiro, Karl, and Robert Beum. *A Prosody Handbook.* New York: Harper & Row, 1965.

Stauffer, Donald A. *The Nature of Poetry.* New York: Norton, 1946.

Stewart, George R. *The Technique of English Verse.* New York: Holt, Rinehart and Winston, 1930.

Sutherland, Ronald. "Structural Linguistics and English Prosody." *College English,* Vol. 20, No. 1 (October 1958), 12–17.

Swann, Robert, and Frank Sidgwick. *The Making of Verse.* London: Sidgwick & Jackson, 1934.

Thompson, John. *The Founding of English Metre.* New York: Columbia University Press, 1961.

Turco, Lewis. *Poetry: An Introduction Through Writing.* Reston, Va.: Reston Publishing Co., 1973.

———. *The Book of Forms: A Handbook of Poetics.* New York: Dutton, 1968.

Untermeyer, Louis. *The Forms of Poetry.* New York: Harcourt, Brace & Company, 1926.

———. *The Pursuit of Poetry: A Guide to Its Understanding and Appreciation with an Explanation of Its Forms and a Dictionary of Poetic Terms.* New York: Simon & Schuster, 1969.

Viereck, Peter. "Strict Form in Poetry: Would Jacob Wrestle with a Flabby Angel?" *Critical Inquiry,* Vol. 5, No. 2 (Winter 1978), 203–222.

Wesley, Donald. *The Chances of Rhyme: Device and Modernity.* Berkeley and Los Angeles: University of California Press, 1980.

Wimsatt, W. K., Jr. "In Search of Verbal Mimesis," in *The Day of the Leopards.* New Haven, Conn.: Yale University Press, 1976.

————. "One Relation of Rhyme to Reason," in *The Verbal Icon.* Lexington: The University Press of Kentucky, 1954.

Wimsatt, W. K., Jr., ed. *Versification: Major Language Types.* New York: New York University Press for MLA, 1972.

Wimsatt, W.K., Jr., and Monroe C. Beardsley. "The Concept of Meter: An Exercise in Abstraction." *Publications of the Modern Language Association of America,* Vol. 74, No. 5 (December 1959), 585–598.

Winters, Yvor. "The Influence of Meter on Poetic Convention," in *Primitivism and Decadence: A Study in American Experimental Poetry.* New York: Arrow Editions, 1937.

Wright, Rose Elizabeth. *Critique of Teaching Literary Forms.* Philadelphia: Dolphin Press, 1941.

Zillman, Lawrence John. *The Elements of English Verse.* New York: Macmillan, 1935.

Acknowledgments

JON ANDERSON: "The Blue Animals" from *The Milky Way: Poems 1967–1982* (Ecco Press, 1983). Reprinted by permission of the author.

JOHN ASHBERY: "Some Trees" and "Pantoum" from *Some Trees* (Holt, Rinehart and Winston, 1956). Reprinted with the permission of Georges Borchardt, Inc., and the author. Copyright © 1956 by John Ashbery. "Farm Implements and Rutabagas in a Landscape" from *The Double Dream of Spring* (Dutton, 1970). Reprinted with the permission of Georges Borchardt, Inc., and the author. Copyright © 1970 by John Ashbery.

DAVID BAKER: "Ice River" copyright 1981 by David Baker. Reprinted by permission of Ahsahta Press/Boise State University and *Mid-American Review*.

MARVIN BELL: "Obsessive" from *The Escape into You* (Atheneum, 1971). Copyright 1971 by Marvin Bell. Reprinted with the permission of the publisher and author.

BRUCE BENNETT: "The True Story of Snow White" reprinted from *Mosaic* and *The Ardis Anthology of New American Poetry* by permission of the author.

JOHN BERRYMAN: "The Poet's Final Instructions" from *Short Poems* by John Berryman. Copyright © 1958 by John Berryman. "He Resigns" © 1972 by the Estate of John Berryman. From *Delusions, Etc.* by John Berryman. Copyright © 1969, 1971 by John Berryman. "Dream Song #29" from *The Dream Songs* by John Berryman. Copyright © 1959, 1962, 1963, 1964, 1969 by John Berryman. All three reprinted by permission of Farrar, Straus and Giroux, Inc.

JAMES BERTRAM: "Is It Well-lighted, Papa?" from *Mississippi Review* (volume VI, no. 1, 1977). Reprinted by permission of *Mississippi Review*.

ELIZABETH BISHOP: "Sestina," "The Armadillo," and "One Art" from *The Complete Poems 1927–1979* by Elizabeth Bishop. Copyright © 1983 by Alice Helen Methfessel. Copyright © 1951, 1956, 1976 by Elizabeth Bishop. Copyright renewed © 1979 by Elizabeth Bishop. Reprinted by permission of Farrar, Straus and Giroux, Inc.

RON BLOCK: "Ballade of the Back Road" from *The Iowa Review*. Reprinted by permission of the author.

PHILIP BOOTH: "First Lesson" from *Letter from a Distant Land,* reprinted by permission of Viking Penguin Inc. Copyright 1957 by Philip Booth.

JOHN BRICUTH: "Song of the Darkness" from *The Heisenberg Variations* (University of Georgia Press, 1976). Reprinted by permission of the author.

VAN K. BROCK: "The Sea Birds." Copyright 1965 by Van K. Brock. First appeared in *The New Yorker.* Reprinted by permission of author. "Lying on a Bridge." Copyright 1967 by Van K. Brock. First appeared in *Southern Poetry Review.* Reprinted by permission of author.

GWENDOLYN BROOKS: "We Real Cool: The Pool Players. Seven at the Golden Shovel" and "The Womanhood: the Rites for Cousin Vit" from *The World of Gwendolyn Brooks* by Gwendolyn Brooks. Copyright © 1959 and 1949 respectively by Gwendolyn Brooks. Reprinted by permission of Harper & Row, Publishers, Inc.

MICHAEL DENNIS BROWNE: "The Wife of Winter's Tale" from *The Wife of Winter* (Scribner, 1970). Reprinted by permission of author.

HENRY CARLILE: "Havana Blues" from *Running Lights* (Dragon Gate Press, 1981). Reprinted by permission of author. Copyright Henry Carlile.

HAYDEN CARRUTH: "Late Sonnet" from *Brothers, I Loved You All* (Sheep Meadow Press, 1978). Section II of "The Asylum" ("Winds; words of the wind") from *The Crow and the Heart* (Macmillan, 1959). "Loneliness: An Outburst of Hexasyllables" from *If You Call This Cry a Song* (Countryman Press, 1983). All three poems reprinted by permission of the author.

TURNER CASSITY: "Links" first appeared in *Cumberland Poetry Review.* Reprinted by permission of author.

FRED CHAPPELL: "Rimbaud Fire Letter to Jim Applewhite" and "My Grandfather's Church Goes Up" from *Bloodfire.* Reprinted by permission of Louisiana State University Press. Copyright 1978, Fred Chappell.

KELLY CHERRY: "A Scientific Expedition in Siberia, 1913" first appeared in *The Southern Review* (vol. 18, no. 1, January 1982). Reprinted by permission of the author.

JOHN CIARDI: "At My Father's Grave" copyright by John Ciardi 1984. Reprinted by permission of the author.

AMY CLAMPITT: "The Kingfisher," reprinted from *The Kingfisher,* by Amy Clampitt, by permission of Alfred A. Knopf, Inc. Copyright © 1983 by Amy Clampitt. Reprinted also by permission of Faber and Faber Ltd. from *The Kingfisher* by Amy Clampitt.

MARTHA COLLINS: "The Story We Know" first appeared in *Poetry,* copyright 1980, and is reprinted by permission of the Editor of *Poetry.*

PETER COOLEY: "Naked Poetry" reprinted from *The Massachusetts Review,* copyright 1975 by The Massachusetts Review, Inc.

JANE COOPER: "The Faithful" and "In the Last Few Moments Came the

Old German Cleaning Woman" reprinted with permission of Macmillan Publishing Company from *The Weather of Six Mornings.* Copyright 1969 by Jane Cooper. Same poems from *Scaffolding: New and Selected Poems,* reprinted by permission of Anvil Press.

CID CORMAN: "The Tortoise" from *In Good Time* (Origin Press/Kyoto-Japan, 1964). Reprinted by permission of author.

ALFRED CORN: "Remembering Mykenai" from *The Various Light.* Copyright 1980 by Alfred Corn. Reprinted by permission of Viking Penguin Inc.

GREGORY CORSO: "Body Fished from the Seine" from *Elegiac Feelings American* by Gregory Corso. Copyright © by Gregory Corso. Reprinted by permission of New Directions Publishing Corporation.

ROBERT CREELEY: "If You," "Oh No," "A Wicker Basket," and "Ballad of the Despairing Husband" all from *Collected Poems of Robert Creeley, 1945–1975.* Copyright 1982 by The Regents of the University of California. Reprinted by permission of the University of California Press.

J. V. CUNNINGHAM: "The Aged Lover Discourses in the Flat Style," "Epitaph for Someone or Other," and "For My Contemporaries" from *The Collected Poems and Epigrams of J. V. Cunningham,* Swallow Press, 1971. Reprinted with the permission of Ohio University Press.

PHILIP DACEY: "Jack, Afterwards" and "Rondel" from *How I Escaped from the Labyrinth and Other Poems* (Carnegie-Mellon University Press, 1977). Reprinted by permission of author. "Jill, Afterwards" first appeared in *Prairie Schooner.* Reprinted by permission of author.

GLOVER DAVIS: "The Burial" from *August Fires* (University of Nebraska at Omaha: Abattoir Editions, 1978). Reprinted by permission of author. "Lost Moments" first appeared in *The Shenandoah Review.* Reprinted by permission of author.

PETER DAVISON: "The Compound Eye" from *A Voice in the Mountain.* Copyright © 1977 Peter Davison. Reprinted with the permission of Atheneum Publishers.

JAMES DICKEY: "On the Hill Below the Lighthouse" copyright 1960 by James Dickey. Reprinted from *Poems 1957–1967* by permission of Wesleyan University Press. "Breath" copyright 1963 James Dickey. Reprinted from *Helmets* by permission of Wesleyan University Press. "Breath" first appeared in *The New Yorker.* "The Island" copyright 1959 James Dickey. Reprinted from *Drowning with Others* by permission of Wesleyan University Press.

THOMAS M. DISCH: "The Rapist's Villanelle" from *ABCDEFG HIJKLM NPOQRST UVWXYZ* (Anvil Press, 1981). Reprinted by permission of author.

ALAN DUGAN: "Elegy for a Puritan Conscience" and "Poem" ("What's the balm") from *New and Collected Poems, 1961–1983* (Ecco Press, 1983).

Copyright 1983 by Alan Dugan. Reprinted by permission of Ecco Press and author.

STEPHEN DUNN: "Tangier" from *Not Dancing* (Carnegie-Mellon University Press, 1984). Reprinted by permission of author.

JOHN ENGELS: "The Homer Mitchell Place" from *The Homer Mitchell Place* (University of Pittsburgh Press, 1968). Reprinted by permission of author.

FREDERICK FEIRSTEIN: "L'Art" first appeared in *Counter/Measures*. Reprinted by permission of author.

GEORGE GARRETT: "Tiresias" from *The Sleeping Gypsy* (University of Texas Press, 1958). Reprinted by permission of author.

GARY GILDNER: "Meeting My Best Friend from the Eighth Grade" from *Nails* (University of Pittsburgh Press, 1975). Copyright 1975 by Gary Gildner. Reprinted by permission of author. Section XII from "Letters from Vicksburg" ("Dear wife and bosom friend") from *Blue Like the Heavens: New & Selected Poems* (University of Pittsburgh Press, 1984). Copyright 1984 by Gary Gildner. Reprinted by permission of author.

ALLEN GINSBERG: "Father Death Blues" from *Collected Poems 1947–1980*. Copyright 1978 and 1985 by Allen Ginsberg. Reprinted by permission of Harper & Row, Publishers, Inc.

LOUISE GLÜCK: "Bridal Piece," "The Racer's Widow," and "Phenomenal Survivals of Death in Nantucket" from *Firstborn* (Ecco Press, 1983). Copyright 1968 by Louise Glück. Reprinted by permission of Ecco Press and author.

PATRICIA GOEDICKE: "Wise Owl" from *Between Oceans* (Harcourt Brace Jovanovich, 1968). Reprinted by permission of author.

ALBERT GOLDBARTH: "Joe Gillon Hypnotizes His Son" first appeared in *Counter/Measures*. "The Psychonaut Sonnets: Jones" first appeared in *The Little Magazine*. Both poems reprinted by permission of author.

BARBARA GREENBERG: "The Faithful Wife" was first published in *Poetry Northwest*, vol. XIX, no. 2 (Summer 1978). Reprinted by permission of author.

MARILYN HACKER: "Villanelle" from *Presentation Piece* (Viking, 1974). Reprinted by permission of author. "Canzone," "Rondeau After a Transatlantic Telephone Call," and "Sonnet Ending with a Film Subtitle" from *Taking Notice* (Knopf, 1980). Reprinted by permission of author.

DONALD HALL: "My Son, My Executioner." Copyright Donald Hall 1954, 1981. "The Long River." Copyright Donald Hall. Both poems reprinted by permission of author.

MARK HALPERIN: "John Clare" from *Backroads* (University of Pittsburgh Press, 1976). Reprinted by permission of author.

EDWARD HARKNESS: "The Man in the Recreation Room" first appeared in *American Review #18*. Reprinted by permission of author.

CHARLES O. HARTMAN: "Double Mock Sonnet" and "A Little Song" first appeared in *Poetry*. Copyright 1978 and 1974 by the Modern Poetry Association. Reprinted by permission of the Editor of *Poetry*.

WILLIAM HATHAWAY: "Why That's Bob Hope" from *Fish, Flesh & Fowl* (Louisiana State University Press, 1985). Reprinted by permission of author.

ROBERT HAYDEN: "The Ballad of Nat Turner" is reprinted from *Angle of Ascent: New and Selected Poems* by Robert Hayden, by permission of Liveright Publishing Corporation. Copyright © 1975, 1972, 1970, 1966 by Robert Hayden.

ANTHONY HECHT: "The End of the Weekend," " 'More Light! More Light!' " and "Double Sonnet" from *The Hard Hours*. Copyright © 1967 Anthony E. Hecht. Reprinted with the permission of Atheneum Publishers.

MICHAEL HEFFERNAN: "Daffodils" reprinted from *The Cry of Oliver Hardy* by permission of the University of Georgia Press. Copyright 1979 by the University of Georgia Press. "A Colloquy of Silences" reprinted from *To the Wreakers of Havoc* by permission of the University of Georgia Press. Copyright 1984 by Michael Heffernan.

JUDITH HEMSCHEMEYER: "I Remember the Room Was Filled with Light" copyright © 1978 by Judith Hemschemeyer. Reprinted from *I Remember the Room Was Filled with Light* by permission of Wesleyan University Press.

WILLIAM HEYEN: "Riddle" reprinted from *Erika: Poems of the Holocaust* (Vanguard Press, 1984) by permission of the author. Copyright 1984 by William Heyen. "Arrows" first appeared in *Poetry*. Copyright 1981 by the Modern Poetry Association. Reprinted by permission of the Editor of *Poetry*.

EDWARD HIRSCH: "At Kresge's Diner in Stonefalls, Arkansas" copyright © 1976 by Edward Hirsch. Reprinted from *For the Sleepwalkers*, by Edward Hirsch, by permission of Alfred A. Knopf, Inc.

DANIEL HOFFMAN: "In the Days of Rin-Tin-Tin" from *A Little Geste* (New York: Oxford University Press), copyright 1960 by Daniel Hoffman. Reprinted with permission of the author.

JOHN HOLLANDER: "Sonnet 18" ("Why drink, why touch you now?") from *Town and Country Matters* (David R. Godine, 1972). Reprinted by permission of the author.

DAVID BRENDAN HOPES: "Lament for Turlough O'Carolan" reprinted by permission of the University of Massachusetts Press.

BEN HOWARD: "The Diver" from *Father of Waters* (University of Nebraska at Omaha: Abattoir Editions, 1979). Reprinted by permission of the author.

RICHARD HOWARD: "Personal Values" from *Fellow Feelings*. Copyright © 1976 Richard Howard. Reprinted with the permission of Atheneum Publishers.

BARBARA HOWES: "A Rune for C." from *Looking Up at Leaves* (Knopf).

Reprinted by permission of author. "Death of a Vermont Farm Woman" and "Early Supper" reprinted from *Light and Dark* with permission from Wesleyan University Press. Copyright 1956 by Barbara Howes.

ROBERT HUFF: "Although I Remember the Sound" from *Colonel Johnson's Ride* (Wayne State University Press, 1959). Copyright 1959 by Robert Huff. Reprinted with permission of author.

RICHARD HUGO: Selections are reprinted from *Making Certain It Goes On: The Collected Poems* by Richard Hugo, by permission of W. W. Norton & Company, Inc. Copyright © 1984 by The Estate of Richard Hugo.

T. R. HUMMER: "The Rural Carrier Stops to Kill a Nine-Foot Cottonmouth" from *The Angelic Orders* (Louisiana State University Press, 1982). Reprinted by permission of author.

THOMAS JAMES: "Mummy of a Lady Named Jemutesonekh, XXI Dynasty," "Snakebite," from *Letters to a Stranger.* Copyright © 1972 by Thomas James. Reprinted by permission of Houghton Mifflin Company.

RANDALL JARRELL: "A Camp in the Prussian Forest" and "Eighth Air Force" from *The Complete Poems* by Randall Jarrell. Copyright 1946, 1947, 1969 by Mrs. Randall Jarrell. Copyright renewed © 1973 by Mrs. Randall Jarrell. Reprinted by permission of Farrar, Straus and Giroux, Inc.

JUDSON JEROME: "Eve: Night Thoughts" first appeared in *Perspective.* Reprinted by permission of author.

DENIS JOHNSON: "Passengers" and "Sway" copyright © 1980, 1982 by Denis Johnson. Reprinted from *The Incognito Lounge* by permission of Random House, Inc.

JUNE JORDAN: "Sunflower Sonnet Number One" and "Sunflower Sonnet Number Two" from *Things That I Do in the Dark* by June Jordan. Copyright 1977 by June Jordan. Reprinted by permission of the Beacon Press.

DONALD JUSTICE: "First Death" and "In the Attic" from *Selected Poems.* Copyright © 1979 Donald Justice. Reprinted with the permission of Atheneum Publishers, Inc. "Women in Love" copyright 1952 and "Sestina: Here in Katmandu" copyright 1956 by Donald Justice reprinted from *The Summer Anniversaries* by permission of Wesleyan University Press. "Sestina: Here in Katmandu" first appeared in *Poetry.* "The Thin Man" copyright 1967 by Donald Justice. Reprinted from *Night Light* by permission of Wesleyan University Press.

RICHARD KATROVAS: "Elegy for My Mother" copyright © 1983 by Richard Katrovas. Reprinted from *Green Dragons* by permission of Wesleyan University Press.

GREG KEELER: "American Falls" from *Spring Catch* (Confluence Press, 1982). Reprinted by permission of author.

WELDON KEES: "For My Daughter" and "The Crack Is Moving Down the Wall" reprinted from *The Collected Poems of Weldon Kees,* edited by Donald Justice, by permission of University of Nebraska Press. Copyright 1975 by the University of Nebraska Press.

X. J. KENNEDY: "Nothing in Heaven Functions as It Ought" copyright 1969 by X. J. Kennedy. Reprinted by permission of the author. "Rondel" and "Nude Descending a Staircase" reprinted by permission of the author.

GALWAY KINNELL: "For William Carlos Williams" and "To Christ Our Lord" from *What a Kingdom It Was* by Galway Kinnell. Copyright © 1960 by Galway Kinnell. Reprinted by permission of Houghton Mifflin Company. "The Fundamental Project of Technology" copyright by Galway Kinnell, 1984. Reprinted with his permission.

PETER KLAPPERT: "Ellie Mae Leaves in a Hurry" from *Lugging Vegetables to Nantucket.* Reprinted by permission of Yale University Press.

ETHERIDGE KNIGHT: "Haiku" reprinted by permission of the author.

TED KOOSER: "Anniversary" first appeared in *Counter/Measures III,* 1974. "Wild Pigs" from *Grass County* (Windflower Press, 1971). "Beer Bottle" from *Official Entry Blank* (University of Nebraska Press, 1969). Permission from author to reprint all three.

JUDITH KROLL: "Sestina" from *In the Temperate Zone: Poems* (Scribners, 1973). Reprinted by permission of the poet.

MAXINE KUMIN: "Morning Swim" and "January 25th" from *Our Ground Time Here Will Be Brief* by Maxine Kumin. Copyright © 1965 by Maxine Kumin. Reprinted by permission of Viking Penguin Inc.

STANLEY KUNITZ: "Three Floors" from *The Poems of Stanley Kunitz: 1928–1978* by Stanley Kunitz. Copyright © 1962 by Stanley Kunitz. Originally appeared in *Poetry.* By permission of Little, Brown and Company in association with the Atlantic Monthly Press. "An Old Cracked Tune" from *The Poems of Stanley Kunitz: 1928–1978* by Stanley Kunitz. Copyright © 1971 by Stanley Kunitz. Reprinted by permission of Little, Brown and Company in association with the Atlantic Monthly Press. Same poems from *The Terrible Threshold,* reprinted by permission of Martin Secker & Warburg, Limited (London).

JOAN LaBOMBARD: "By the Beautiful Ohio" first appeared in *Poetry Northwest* (Autumn 1968; vol. IX, no. 3). Reprinted by permission of the author.

JOSEPH LANGLAND: "Conversations from Childhood: The Victrola" from *Any Body's Song* (Doubleday, 1980). Reprinted by permission of the author.

SYDNEY LEA: "There Should Have Been," "The Floating Candles," "Issues of the Fall" first appeared in *The Ohio Review, The New Yorker, Abatis,* respectively. Reprinted by permission of the author.

AL LEE: "Beside My Grandmother." Reprinted by permission of the author.

BARBARA LEFCOWITZ: "Emily Dickinson's Sestina for Molly Bloom" from *A Risk of Green* (Gallimaufry Press). Reprinted by permission of author.

DAVID LEHMAN: "Toward the Vanishing Point" first appeared in *Sun & Moon* (Summer 1980). Reprinted by permission of the poet.

BRAD LEITHAUSER: "A Quilled Quilt, a Needle Bed" from *Hundreds of Fireflies* (Knopf). Reprinted by permission of author.

DENISE LEVERTOV: "Obsessions" from *Collected Earlier Poems 1940–1960.* Copyright © 1958 by Denise Levertov Goodman. Reprinted by permission of New Directions Publishing Corporation. "Bedtime" from *Poems 1960–1967.* Reprinted by permission of New Directions Publishing Corporation.

PHILIP LEVINE: "Night Thoughts over a Sick Child" and "For Fran" from *On the Edge* (The Stone Wall Press, 1963). Reprinted by permission of the author. "Animals Are Passing from Our Lives" copyright © 1968 by Philip Levine. Reprinted from *Not This Pig* by permission of Wesleyan University Press.

JOHN LOGAN: "To a Young Poet Who Fled" from *Spring of the Thief* (Knopf, 1963). "Shore Scene" from *Ghosts of the Heart* (University of Chicago Press, 1960). Both poems reprinted by permission of the author.

WILLIAM LOGAN: "Tatiana Kalatschova" from *Sad-faced Men.* Reprinted with permission of David R. Godine, Publisher. Copyright 1982 by William Logan.

ROBERT LOWELL: "Water" from *For the Union Dead* by Robert Lowell. Copyright © 1962, 1964 by Robert Lowell. Reprinted by permission of Farrar, Straus and Giroux, Inc. "Mr. Edwards and the Spider" and "In the Cage" from *Lord Weary's Castle,* copyright 1946, 1974 by Robert Lowell. Reprinted by permission of Harcourt Brace Jovanovich, Inc.

THOMAS LUX: "All the Slaves" reprinted by permission of the author.

MEKEEL McBRIDE: "A Blessing" reprinted by permission of the author. Poem first appeared in *The New Yorker.*

THOMAS McGRATH: "The End of the World" from *Echoes Inside the Labyrinth* (Thunder's Mouth Press, 1983). Reprinted by permission of the author.

SANDRA McPHERSON: "Lament, with Flesh and Blood" first appeared in *The Georgia Review* (Fall 1983). Reprinted by permission of the author. "Triolet" copyright 1978 by Sandra McPherson. From *The Year of Our Birth,* published by The Ecco Press and reprinted by permission.

CHARLES MARTIN: "Signs" reprinted by permission of the author. "Sharks at the New York Aquarium" first appeared in *Poetry.* Copyright 1976 by the Modern Poetry Association. Reprinted by permission of the Editor of *Poetry.*

PETER MEINKE: "Atomic Pantoum" first appeared in *Poetry.* Copyright

1983 by the Modern Poetry Association. Reprinted by permission of the Editor of *Poetry.*

WILLIAM MEREDITH: "Effort at Speech" from *Earth Walk: New and Selected Poems* (Knopf, 1970). Copyright William Meredith 1970. Reprinted by permission of the author.

JAMES MERRILL: "Mirror," "Swimming by Night," and "A Renewal" in *From the First Nine Poems 1946–1976.* Copyright © 1981, 1982 James Merrill. Reprinted with the permission of Atheneum Publishers.

W. S. MERWIN: "River Sound Remembered," "The Drunk in the Furnace," and "Grandfather in the Old Men's Home" from *The First Four Books of Poems.* Copyright © 1975 by W. S. Merwin. Reprinted with the permission of Atheneum Publishers.

ROBERT MEZEY: "My Mother" from *The Door Standing Open* (Houghton Mifflin and Oxford University Press, 1970). Reprinted by permission of the author.

JANE MILLER: "Time; Or, How the Line About Chagall's *Lovers* Disappears" from *The Greater Leisures.* Copyright 1983 by Jane Miller. Reprinted by permission of Doubleday & Company, Inc.

GARY MIRANDA: "Horse Chestnut" first appeared in *The Atlantic Monthly.* "Love Poem" and "The Magician" from *Listeners at the Breathing Place* (Princeton University Press, 1978). Reprinted by permission of author.

JUDITH MOFFETT: "Now or Never" from *Keeping Time* (Louisiana State University Press, 1976). Copyright 1976, Judith Moffett. Reprinted by permission of the author. "Twinings Orange Pekoe" and "Mezzo Cammin" from *Whinny Moor Crossing* (Princeton University Press, 1984). Reprinted by permission of Princeton University Press.

N. SCOTT MOMADAY: "Comparatives" from *The Gourd Dancer* by N. Scott Momaday. Copyright © 1976 by N. Scott Momaday. Reprinted by permission of Harper & Row, Publishers, Inc.

RICHARD MOORE: "Friends" first appeared in *Poetry.* Copyright 1981 by the Modern Poetry Association. Reprinted by permission of the Editor of *Poetry.*

ROBERT MORGAN: "Chant Royal" first appeared in *Poetry.* Copyright 1978 by the Modern Poetry Association. Reprinted by permission of the Editor of *Poetry.*

HOWARD MOSS: "Finding Them Lost" from *Selected Poems.* Copyright © 1971 Howard Moss. Reprinted with the permission of Atheneum Publishers, Inc. "To the Islands" from *Rules of Sleep.* Copyright © 1984 Howard Moss. Reprinted with the permission of Atheneum Publishers, Inc.

STANLEY MOSS: "Prayer" reprinted by permission of the author.

HOWARD NEMEROV: "A Primer of the Daily Round," "The Goose Fish," "Brainstorm" all from *The Collected Poems of Howard Nemerov*

(University of Chicago Press, 1977). Reprinted by permission of the author.

JOHN FREDERICK NIMS: "Love and Death" from *Selected Poems* (University of Chicago Press, 1982). Reprinted by permission of the University of Chicago Press.

FRANK O'HARA: "Poem" ("At night Chinamen jump") from *Meditations in an Emergency* (Grove Press, 1956). Reprinted by permission of Grove Press, Inc. Copyright 1957 by Frank O'Hara. "To the Poem," "Aubade," and "You Are Gorgeous and I'm Coming" copyright 1952, © 1960 by Maureen Granville-Smith, Administratrix of the Estate of Frank O'Hara. Reprinted from *The Collected Poems of Frank O'Hara*, edited by Donald Allen, by permission of Alfred A. Knopf, Inc.

CAROLE OLES: "A Manifesto for the Faint-Hearted" from *The Loneliness Factor* (Texas Tech Press, 1979). Reprinted by permission of the author.

ROBERT PACK: "The Boat" from *Guarded by Women* (Random House, 1963). Reprinted by permission of the author. "Cleaning the Fish" from *Faces in a Single Tree: A Cycle of Monologues* (David R. Godine, 1984). Reprinted by permission of the author.

MOLLY PEACOCK: "Just About Asleep Together" first appeared in *New Letters* (Summer 1981; vol. 47, no. 4). Copyright 1982 by Molly Peacock. Reprinted by permission of the author.

JOHN PECK: "Rowing Early" and "In Front of a Japanese Photograph" from *Shagbark* (Bobbs-Merrill, 1972). Copyright 1972 by John Peck. Reprinted by permission of the author.

ROBERT PINSKY: "Icicles" first appeared in *The New Yorker*. Reprinted by permission of the author. "Memorial" from *Sadness and Happiness: Poems* (Princeton University Press, 1975). Copyright 1975 by Princeton University Press. Reprinted by permission of Princeton University Press.

SYLVIA PLATH: "The Stones" copyright © 1962 by Sylvia Plath. Reprinted from *The Colossus and Other Poems*, by Sylvia Plath, by permission of Alfred A. Knopf, Inc. "Medallion" from *The Collected Poems of Sylvia Plath*, edited by Ted Hughes. Copyright 1981 by Estate of Sylvia Plath. Reprinted by permission of Harper & Row, Publishers, Inc. "Watercolor of Grantchester Meadows" copyright © 1960 by Sylvia Plath. Reprinted from *The Colossus and Other Poems* by permission of Alfred A. Knopf, Inc. Originally appeared in *The New Yorker*. Published in Great Britain by Faber and Faber, London, copyright Ted Hughes 1967. "Black Rook in Rainy Weather" from *The Collected Poems of Sylvia Plath*, edited by Ted Hughes. Poem copyright © 1960 by Ted Hughes. Reprinted by permission of Harper & Row, Publishers, Inc. "Medallion" and "Black Rook in Rainy Weather" from *The Colossus* by Sylvia Plath, published by Faber & Faber, London, copyright Ted Hughes 1967.

STANLEY PLUMLY: "Tree Ferns" first appeared in *The New Yorker*. Reprinted by permission of the author.

KATHA POLLITT: "Ballet Blanc" and "Of the Scythians" copyright ©
1980, 1981 by Katha Pollitt. Reprinted from *Antarctic Traveller,* by Katha
Pollitt, by permission of Alfred A. Knopf, Inc.

DUDLEY RANDALL: "The Southern Road" from *Poem Counterpoem.*
Copyright 1968 by Dudley Randall. Reprinted by permission of the
author.

DAVID RAY: "Throwing the Racetrack Cats at Saratoga" first appeared in
The Iowa Review. Copyright 1984 by David Ray. Reprinted by permission
of author. "Greens" from *X:Rays, A Book of Poems* (Cornell University
Press, 1965). Copyright 1965 by David Ray. Reprinted by permission of
author.

DONALD REVELL: "Belfast" and "In Lombardy" from *From the Abandoned Cities: Poems by Donald Revell.* Copyright 1983 by Donald Revell.
Reprinted by permission of Harper & Row, Publishers, Inc.

ADRIENNE RICH: "At a Bach Concert" and "Aunt Jennifer's Tigers"
are reprinted from *The Fact of a Doorframe: Poems Selected and New, 1950–
1984* by Adrienne Rich, by permission of W. W. Norton & Company,
Inc. Copyright © 1984 by Adrienne Rich. Copyright © 1975, 1978 by
W. W. Norton & Company, Inc. Copyright © 1981 by Adrienne Rich.
"The Insusceptibles" is reprinted from *Poems, Selected and New, 1950–
1974* by Adrienne Rich, by permission of W. W. Norton & Company,
Inc. Copyright © 1975, 1973, 1971, 1969, 1966 by W. W. Norton
& Company, Inc. Copyright © 1967, 1963, 1962, 1961, 1960,
1959, 1958, 1957, 1956, 1955, 1954, 1953, 1952, 1951 by Adrienne
Rich.

JOHN RIDLAND: "Another Easter" first appeared in *Ploughshares* (vol. 9,
no. 1, pp. 193–194, for correction of text first printed in vol. 8, nos. 2
and 3). Copyright 1981 by John Ridland. Reprinted by permission of
author.

ALBERTO RÍOS: "Nani" from *Whispering to Fool the Wind* (Sheep Meadow
Press, 1983). Copyright 1982 by Alberto Ríos. Reprinted by permission
of Sheep Meadow Press.

THEODORE ROETHKE: "Dinky" copyright 1953 by Theodore
Roethke. "My Papa's Waltz," "The Waking," and "I Knew a Woman"
copyright 1942 by Hearst Magazines, Inc., copyright 1953 by Theodore
Roethke, and copyright 1954 by Theodore Roethke. All four poems from
The Collected Poems of Theodore Roethke. Reprinted by permission of Dou-
bleday & Company, Inc.

WILLIAM PITT ROOT: "A Natural History of Dragons and Unicorns My
Daughter and I Have Known" from *In the World's Common Grasses* (Mov-
ing Parts Press, 1981). Copyright 1981 by William Pitt Root. Reprinted
by permission of the author. "KRAA" from *Reasons for Going It on Foot.*
Copyright © 1981 William Pitt Root. Reprinted with the permission of
Atheneum Publishers, Inc.

RAYMOND ROSELIEP: " 'Campfire Extinguished' " reprinted by permission of Alembic Press.

GIBBONS RUARK: "To the Swallows of Viterbo" and "Watching You Sleep Under Monet's Water Lilies" from *Keeping Company* (Johns Hopkins University Press, 1983). Reprinted by permission of The Johns Hopkins University Press and the author.

MURIEL RUKEYSER: "On the Death of Her Mother" from *Collected Poems* (1958). Copyright 1958 by Muriel Rukeyser. Reprinted by permission of International Creative Management, Inc. "Rune" from *The Gates* (1976). Copyright 1976 by Muriel Rukeyser. Reprinted by permission of International Creative Management, Inc.

MICHAEL RYAN: "Consider a Move" and "Where I'll Be Good" from *In Winter* (Holt, Rinehart and Winston, 1981). Copyright 1981 by Michael Ryan. Reprinted by permission of the author.

DAVID ST. JOHN: "Acadian Lane" first published in *Columbia Magazine*. Copyright 1982 by David St. John. Reprinted by permission of the author.

SHEROD SANTOS: "The Breakdown" from *Accidental Weather* (Doubleday, 1982). Reprinted by permission of Doubleday & Company, Inc.

MAY SARTON: "Dutch Interior" from *Collected Poems 1930–1973* (W. W. Norton, 1974). Reprinted by permission of author.

ROY SCHEELE: "The Gap in the Cedar" from *Accompanied* (Best Cellar Press, 1974). Copyright 1974 by Roy Scheele. Reprinted by permission of author.

GJERTRUD SCHNACKENBERG: "How Did It Seem to Sylvia?," "The Paperweight," and "Darwin in 1881" from *Portraits and Elegies* by Gjertrud Schnackenberg. Copyright © 1982 by Gjertrud Schnackenberg. Reprinted by permission of David R. Godine, Publisher, Inc.

ANNE SEXTON: "The Moss of His Skin" from *To Bedlam and Part Way Back* by Anne Sexton. Copyright © 1960 by Anne Sexton. Reprinted by permission of Houghton Mifflin Company. "The Abortion" from *All My Pretty Ones* by Anne Sexton. Copyright © 1962 by Anne Sexton. Reprinted by permission of Houghton Mifflin Company.

KARL SHAPIRO: "The First Time" reprinted by permission of the author.

JUDITH JOHNSON SHERWIN: "The Spoilers and the Spoils" first appeared in *Poetry*. Copyright 1978 by the Modern Poetry Association. Reprinted by permission of the Editor of *Poetry*. "Ballade of the Grindstones" first appeared in *The New Yorker*. Reprinted by permission of the author.

LOUIS SIMPSON: "The Man Who Married Magdalene" copyright 1955 and 1983 by Louis Simpson. Reprinted from *People Live Here: Selected Poems 1949–1983* with the permission of BOA Editions, Ltd. "My Father in the Night Commanding No" copyright © 1963 by Louis Simpson. Reprinted from *At the End of the Open Road* by permission of Wesleyan University Press. First appeared in *The New Yorker*. "To the Western

World" and "The Boarder" copyright 1957 and 1959 respectively. Reprinted from *A Dream of Governors* by permission of Wesleyan University Press.

L. E. SISSMAN: "December 27, 1966" from *Hello, Darkness* (Little, Brown, 1974). Copyright © 1974 by L. E. Sissman. First appeared in *The New Yorker.* Reprinted by permission of Little, Brown and Company in association with the Atlantic Monthly Press, and of Martin Secker & Warburg, Ltd.

KNUTE SKINNER: "Imagine Grass" from *A Close Sky Over Killaspuglonane,* Second Edition (Burton International, 1975). Copyright 1975 by Knute Skinner. Reprinted by permission of author.

FLOYD SKLOOT: "My Daughter Considers Her Body" first appeared in *Southern Poetry Review* (Fall 1979). Reprinted by permission of the author and the Editor of *Southern Poetry Review.*

DAVID R. SLAVITT: "In Memory of W. H. Auden" from *Vital Signs* (Doubleday, 1975). Reprinted by permission of author. "Another Letter to Lord Byron" from *Day Sailing* (University of North Carolina Press, 1969). Reprinted by permission of the author.

DAVE SMITH: "The Ancestor" from *Cumberland Station* (University of Illinois Press, 1977). Reprinted by permission of University of Illinois Press. "An Old Whore Speaks to a Young Poet" from *The Fisherman's Whore* (Ohio University Press, 1974). Reprinted by permission of the author. "Chopping Wood" and "The Collector of the Sun" from *The Roundhouse Voices: Poems 1970–1985* (Harper & Row, 1985). Reprinted by permission of Harper & Row, Publishers, Inc.

W. D. SNODGRASS: "A Visitation" and "A Flat One" from *After Experience.* Copyright 1975 by W. D. Snodgrass. Reprinted by permission of Harper & Row, Publishers, Inc. "Song" ("Sweet beast, I have gone prowling") and Section 10 from *Heart's Needle* copyright © 1957, 1959 by W. D. Snodgrass. Reprinted from *Heart's Needle,* by W. D. Snodgrass, by permission of Alfred A. Knopf, Inc.

GARY SNYDER: " 'They Didn't Hire Him' " copyright 1967 by Gary Snyder. Reprinted by permission of the author.

BARRY SPACKS: "Finding a Yiddish Paper on the Riverside Line" from *Imagining a Unicorn* (University of Georgia Press, 1978). Reprinted by permission of the author. "October" from *The Company of Children* (Doubleday, 1969). Reprinted by permission of the author.

WILLIAM STAFFORD: "Glances," "Traveling Through the Dark," "Winterward," "The Swerve" from *Stories That Could Be True: New and Collected Poems* (Harper & Row, 1977). Copyright © 1960, 1977 by William Stafford. Reprinted by permission of Harper & Row, Publishers, Inc. "Friend Who Never Came" first appeared in *New Letters* (Fall 1975). Reprinted by permission of the author.

MAURA STANTON: "Childhood" reprinted by permission of the University of Utah Press from *Cries of Swimmers,* copyright 1984 Maura Stanton.

"Good People" first appeared in *Crazyhorse* (Spring 1984). Reprinted by permission of the author.

GEORGE STARBUCK: "Double Semi-Sestina" first appeared in *The Atlantic Monthly*. Reprinted by permission of the author.

TIMOTHY STEELE: "Sapphics Against Anger" first appeared in *Threepenny Review*. Reprinted by permission of the author.

BARRY STERNLIEB: "Valley Blood" printed by permission of the author.

PAMELA STEWART: "Punk Pantoum" first appeared in *Crazyhorse* (Spring 1979). Reprinted by permission of the author.

LEON STOKESBURY: "To His Book" and "East Texas" from *Often in Different Landscapes*. Reprinted by permission of University of Texas Press. Copyright 1976, University of Texas Press. "The Lover Remembereth Such as He Sometimes Enjoyed and Showeth How He Would Like to Enjoy Her Again" is reprinted from *The Drifting Away of All We Once Held Essential* by permission of Trilobite Press.

MARK STRAND: "Sleeping with One Eye Open" first appeared in *The New Yorker*. Reprinted by permission of the author.

DABNEY STUART: "Fall Practice" from *The Diving Bell* (Knopf, 1966). Copyright 1966 Dabney Stuart. Reprinted by permission of the author. "Discovering My Daughter" first appeared in *Tar River Poetry* and is reprinted by permission of the author.

BARTON SUTTER: "Shoe Shop" first appeared in *Poetry*. Copyright 1980 by the Modern Poetry Association. Reprinted by permission of the Editor of *Poetry*. "Swedish Lesson" first appeared in *Carolina Quarterly*. Reprinted by permission of the author.

MAY SWENSON: "Question" from *New and Selected Things Taking Place* by May Swenson. Copyright 1954 by May Swenson. Reprinted by permission of Little, Brown and Company in association with the Atlantic Monthly Press.

JOAN SWIFT: "The Line-Up" first appeared in *The Yale Review* (Spring 1971). Copyright Joan Swift 1975. Reprinted by permission of the author.

JAMES TATE: "The Book of Lies" and "Miss Cho Composes in the Cafeteria" from *The Lost Pilot* (Yale University Press, 1967). Reprinted by permission of the author.

LEWIS TURCO: "The Wind Carol" first appeared in *Mississippi Review*. Reprinted by permission of the author. "Rick de Travaille" and "Simon Judson" from *Pocoangelini: A Fantography & Other Poems* (Despa Press, 1971). Copyright 1971 by Lewis Turco. Reprinted by permission of author.

JOHN UPDIKE: "Ex-Basketball Player" copyright © 1957, 1982 by John Updike. Reprinted from *The Carpentered Hen and Other Tame Creatures*, by John Updike, by permission of Alfred A. Knopf, Inc.

MONA VAN DUYN: "The Ballad of Blossom" from *Letters from a Father and Other Poems.* Copyright 1982 Mona Van Duyn. Reprinted with permission of Atheneum Publishers. "Causes" and "Economics" from *Merciful Disguises.* Copyright 1973 Mona Van Duyn. Reprinted with permission of Atheneum Publishers.

ELLEN BRYANT VOIGT: "Tropics" first appeared in *Shenandoah.* Reprinted by permission of the author. " 'The Wife Takes a Child' " from *Claiming Kin* (Wesleyan University Press, 1976). Reprinted by permission of author.

DAVID WAGONER: "Canticle for Xmas Eve" from *First Light* by David Wagoner. Copyright © 1983 by David Wagoner. Reprinted by permission of Little, Brown and Company in association with the Atlantic Monthly Press. "The Shooting of John Dillinger . . ." and "Staying Alive" from *New and Selected Poems* by David Wagoner, © 1969 by Indiana University Press. Reprinted by permission of Indiana University Press.

DIANE WAKOSKI: "Sestina to the Common Glass of Beer: I Do Not Drink Beer" from *Waiting for the King of Spain* (Black Sparrow Press, 1976). Reprinted by permission of the author.

RONALD WALLACE: "Grandmother Grace" first appeared in *New Letters* (Fall 1981). Reprinted by permission of the author.

CANDICE WARNE: "Blackbird Sestina" first appeared in *Perceptions* (volume 12). Reprinted by permission of the author.

ROBERT PENN WARREN: "Original Sin: A Short Story" from *Selected Poems: 1923–1975* (Random House, 1976). "What Voice at Moth-Hour" from *Rumor Verified: Poems 1979–1980* (Random House, 1981). Both poems reprinted by permission of the author.

JAMES WHITEHEAD: "Visionary Oklahoma Sunday Beer" from *Local Men* (University of Illinois Press, 1979). Reprinted by permission of the author. "The Flood Viewed by the Tourist from Iowa" copyright 1966. Reprinted by permission of author.

RICHARD WILBUR: "A Late Aubade" reprinted from *Walking to Sleep* and "Junk" reprinted from *Advice to a Prophet and Other Poems* by permission of Harcourt Brace Jovanovich, Inc. "A Late Aubade" © 1968 by Richard Wilbur. "Junk" © 1961 by Richard Wilbur. "Piazza di Spagna" from *Things of This World,* copyright © by Richard Wilbur 1965. Reprinted by permission of Harcourt Brace Jovanovich, Inc. "Year's End" copyright 1949, 1977 by Richard Wilbur. Reprinted from his *Ceremony and Other Poems* by permission of Harcourt Brace Jovanovich. First published in *The New Yorker.*

MILLER WILLIAMS: "Why God Permits Evil" from *Why God Permits Evil* (Louisiana State University Press, 1977). Reprinted by permission of the author. "Rubaiyat for Sue Ella Tucker" and "For Victor Jara" from *The Boys on Their Bony Mules* (Louisiana State University Press, 1983). Reprinted by permission of the author.

HAROLD WITT: "First Photos of Flu Virus" first appeared in *Shaping: New*

Poems in Traditional Prosodies, edited by Philip K. Jason (Dryad Press, 1978). Reprinted by permission of author. "Dream" first appeared in *New Letters* (vol. 47, no. 4). Reprinted by permission of author.
DAVID WOJAHN: "Floating Houses" from *Icehouse Lights* (Yale University Press, 1982). Reprinted by permission of Yale University Press.
DANIEL WOLFF: "Heaven in Ordinarie" first appeared in *Ploughshares* (vol. 6, no. 2). Reprinted by permission of author.
BARON WORMSER: "Private" from *The White Words* by Baron Wormser. Copyright © 1983 by Baron Wormser. Reprinted by permission of Houghton Mifflin Company.
CHARLES WRIGHT: "The Daughters of Blum" copyright © 1967 by Charles Wright. Reprinted from *The Grave of the Right Hand* by permission of Wesleyan University Press, "The Daughters of Blum" first appeared in *The New Yorker.*
JAMES WRIGHT: "Speak," "A Song for the Middle of the Night," and "Saint Judas" copyright 1968, 1957, and 1967 respectively by James Wright. Reprinted from *Collected Poems* by permission of Wesleyan University Press. "With the Shell of a Hermit Crab" reprinted from *To a Blossoming Pear Tree* by James Wright with permission of Farrar, Straus and Giroux, Inc. Copyright © 1977 by James Wright. "Your Name in Arezzo" copyright © 1979 by Anne Wright, Executrix of the Estate of James Wright. Reprinted from *This Journey,* by James Wright, by permission of Random House, Inc.
AL YOUNG: "Lester Leaps In." Copyright 1982 by Al Young. Reprinted with permission of the author.
LISA ZEIDNER: "Still" from *Selections: University and College Poetry Prizes, 1973–1978* (Academy of American Poets, 1980). Reprinted by permission of the author.
PAUL ZIMMER: "A Zimmershire Lad" from *Family Reunion: Selected and New Poems* (University of Pittsburgh Press, 1983). Reprinted by permission of the author.

The Editors also wish to thank the following people for their advice and assistance: David Baker, Ralph Burns, Zabelle Derounian, Carol Hirmer, Bill Holm, X. J. Kennedy, Michael Kleine, Judith Moffett, Don Olsen, Lewis Turco, Bruce Weigl, Richard Wilbur, Miller Williams, and David Wojahn.

Index